WITHDRAWN

D1131083

# MIXED MARTIAL ARTS

# MIXED MARTIAL ARTS

## *A History from Ancient Fighting Sports to the UFC*

## L. A. Jennings

ROWMAN & LITTLEFIELD
Lanham • Boulder • New York • London

Published by Rowman & Littlefield
An imprint of The Rowman & Littlefield Publishing Group, Inc.
4501 Forbes Boulevard, Suite 200, Lanham, Maryland 20706
www.rowman.com

6 Tinworth Street, London SE11 5AL, United Kingdom

Copyright © 2021 by The Rowman & Littlefield Publishing Group, Inc.

*All rights reserved.* No part of this book may be reproduced in any form or by any electronic or mechanical means, including information storage and retrieval systems, without written permission from the publisher, except by a reviewer who may quote passages in a review.

British Library Cataloguing in Publication Information Available

**Library of Congress Cataloging-in-Publication Data**

Name: Jennings, L. A., author.
Title: Mixed martial arts : a history from ancient fighting sports to the UFC / L. A. Jennings.
Other titles: MMA : a history from ancient fighting sports to the Ultimate Fighting Championship
Description: Lanham : The Rowman & Littlefield Publishing Group, 2021. | Includes bibliographical references and index. | Summary: "This book is a fascinating history of mixed martial arts, from ancient fighting sports to the present day. It examines the growth and development of the different sports and features vignettes of famous moments in fighting history alongside stories of the fighters themselves"—Provided by publisher.
Identifiers: LCCN 2020044087 (print) | LCCN 2020044088 (ebook) | ISBN 9781538141953 (Cloth) | ISBN 9781538141960 (eBook) Subjects: LCSH: Mixed martial arts—History.
Classification: LCC GV1102.7.M59 J46 2021 (print) | LCC GV1102.7.M59 (ebook) | DDC 796.8109—dc23
LC record available at https://lccn.loc.gov/2020044087
LC ebook record available at https://lccn.loc.gov/2020044088

For Mike

# CONTENTS

# ACKNOWLEDGMENTS

This book would not have been possible without my parents, Bill and Priscilla, who always support my writing and read every draft, or without the love of my dear friends, my kindred spirits. May we continue to celebrate our accomplishments, wherever we are, and for years to come.

I could not have written this book without my tribe at Train.Fight.Win., who inspired me to share my love of martial arts in person and on the page. Finally, to my husband, Mike, who is my favorite training partner and my best friend, thank you for encouraging me to write this book.

# INTRODUCTION

## For the Love of Fighting

In 564 BCE, Arrichion of Phigelia stood in a large sand pit the size of a football field, his body covered in oil and nothing else. He was an accomplished wrestler, determined to defeat the man facing him and uphold the Greek ideal of masculine virility and strength. As the men grappled, each looking to execute a throw, the man suddenly leaped on Arrichion's back, sinking a deep choke into Arrichion's neck. Arrichion's lungs burned for air and blood rushed to his face, but Arrichion would not allow himself to admit defeat. He fell onto his back, landing heavily on his opponent, who immediately released the choke and declared himself vanquished. In Arrichion's final attempt to break the hold, he inadvertently dislocated his opponent's ankle, and the man now wailed in agony. Arrichion technically won the match when his opponent surrendered, but it was too late for the intrepid Arrichion, who was already dead from strangulation. He was named champion posthumously.

In 1520 CE, the English king, Henry VIII, challenged his French counterpart, King Francis I, to a friendly wrestling match in front of each man's royal courtiers, knights, soldiers, and servants. It was a risky proposition for both men, one of whom could end up defeated and, perhaps, humiliated. Francis won the day, and Henry took his defeat well, but the match functioned as a symbol of their highly tumultuous relationship. A few hundred years later, in 1976, boxing legend Muhammad Ali left the confines of the boxing world to compete in a mixed-discipline fight against Japanese professional wrestler Antonio Inoki. The fight ended in a draw, and both fighters were censured for engaging in a crude event that dared to mix boxing, kickboxing, and wrestling in one ring. For Ali, whose boxing career was waning, it was an opportunity to challenge himself, but the media saw the event as folly. In 2017, mixed martial arts champion Conor McGregor challenged Floyd Mayweather Jr., the most successful boxer of his generation, to compete in a boxing match. McGregor was at a serious disadvantage, for he was abandoning the vast majority of his fighting tools in order to fight a far more experienced and better prepared Mayweather. McGregor, like Henry before him, lost the match. And like Ali and Inoki, both he and Mayweather were criticized for what was seen as a media ploy and money grab.

From Arrichion to Ali, martial artists have fought for more than just victory, money, fame, and glory. Fighting risks everything a person may hold dear, from his physical well-being to his mental health, to his pride, even to his position in society. Fighting challenges the social imperatives that regulate most communities but also upholds virtues that many cultures value—hard work, loyalty, commitment, and drive. This is because fighting, above all else, is a profoundly human sport. It has been passed down through generations and is deeply rooted in people and cultures across place and throughout history.

When fighters prepare for competition, be it in a boxing ring, on a wrestling mat, or in a mixed martial arts (MMA) cage, they bring with them not only their individual experiences but also the long and varied history of their fighting art. Fighting sports, such as wrestling, boxing, kickboxing, and MMA, are the most universal sports on our planet. Although basketball, baseball, or soccer now might be ubiquitous, that was not the case thousands of years ago, or even one hundred years ago. But thousands of years ago, across every community on earth, people competed in fighting as a sport. Indeed, it has been exceedingly difficult to find any small group of people in history that did not have a martial art.

This book explores the rich history of fighting sports around the world, revealing how these unique fighting arts contributed to the cultural zeitgeist of modern MMA. It is a celebration of both the universality of fighting sports and the many individual arts practiced and contested in cultures and communities across time and place. Nearly every small group, tribe, village, state, country, and community throughout human history has had some type of martial arts as part of their culture, making fighting sports perhaps the most universal activity on Earth. Yet, when many people reflect on the history of MMA, diversity is lacking, and the focus remains solely on certain cultures. This book seeks to expand that view and demonstrate how every fighter, throughout history, has paved the way for the sport of MMA that is both beloved and maligned today. More than anything, this book is a tribute to our fighting ancestors who developed their arts, passed them down through the generations, and shared them around the world.

Before we delve into the fantastic history of MMA, it is necessary to establish a vocabulary. For this book, I define fighting sports as empty-hand fighting (no weapons) between individuals as competition. Although I will briefly discuss weapons training, armed combat, and warfare, the purpose of this book is to explore the history of fighting as sport, which includes boxing, wrestling, kickboxing, submission grappling, and mixed martial arts. Those arts involve numerous iterations, emerging from diverse places and different times, practiced and refined in various and distinct cultures.

For this book, *MMA* typically refers to the modern version of the sport that includes striking, wrestling, submission grappling, and ground striking. These fights end by submission, knockout, technical knockout, referee stoppage, doctor stoppage, and decision by judges based on points.

*Wrestling*, the most universal of all fighting sports, manifests differently in each culture, but it typically does not include any type of striking and has rules based on how one gets an opponent to the ground and what one does on the ground.

*Boxing* includes striking to the head and body with the fist, although before the adaptation of various rule systems, boxers often would kick, scratch, knee, and throw opponents to win a fight.

*Kickboxing*, under which martial arts such as Muay Thai, karate, and tae kwon do might be classified, depending on the rules, adds kicks, knees, and elbow strikes to boxing.

*Submission wrestling* or *grappling* includes joint manipulations and chokes in addition to standard wrestling.

Some martial arts styles are empty hand but do not translate to sport fighting. It is important to note that martial arts training for military purposes and martial arts training for performances were both entirely different from martial arts training for competition or sport. Those arts are fascinating and deserve attention, but they do not fit within the parameters of this book. However, many modern-day MMA fighters started their martial arts training in a traditional art. Over time, those fighters expanded their training, seeking to fulfill all of the technical requirements for a successful MMA fighter. In the end, although their performance in the cage may not look at all like a traditional martial art, they still pay homage to their original training. This is an important aspect of modern-day MMA that is not always apparent to fans not steeped in martial arts. A successful athlete is not just a fighter; he or she is a martial artist.

In many traditional martial arts, even the newer ones developed in the twentieth century, practitioners struggle as to the legitimacy of their art. Factions of one martial arts family tree will argue about who has the correct version of the art, or who holds the proprietary right to share the style. These fights tend to take place in print, in books or articles or social media, where arguments rage over who teaches the most "authentic" martial arts. It is understandable that many instructors might feel threatened, especially in an increasingly digitized world where knowledge can be shared over computers rather than in dojos, or schools. In fighting sports, though, lineage does not matter as much as efficacy, so the definition of legitimacy pertains only to which technique or movement is effective in the cage. Even then, MMA pundits and experts may declare a technique "ineffective" in the cage, but when someone manages to make it work, does that not make it a "legitimate" technique? This book focuses less on specific instructor lineages and instead reveals how those arts morphed over time and with increased globalization.

Athletes from around the world compete against each other, yet few fans and practitioners are aware of the global history that developed the sport of MMA. Martial arts has a vast and diverse history from around the world and more than seven thousand years of human development that contributed to the modern version of MMA contested in cages. The history of MMA is the story of people and places and a consideration of how cultural forces, including imperialization, the rise of capitalism, the increase of global communications technologies, and social movement impacted the trajectory of the sport.

This book is not a taxonomy of every single fighter in the history of sport; to include every athlete in the twenty-first century alone would be an impossible endeavor. Many fighters who made a significant impact on the sport will be omitted, not because their contribution did not matter, but because space is limited. Although this book cannot catalog every moment in the history of MMA, it does offer an overview of fighting sports that will introduce readers to new fighters and unique martial arts traditions from around the world to admire and enjoy.

Chapter 1 examines the ancient martial arts practiced in parts of Egypt, India, China, Mesopotamia, Greece, and Africa, including the history of boxing, wrestling, and pankration (an early form of MMA) competitions in ancient Greece, the development of the ancient Olympic Games, the rise of the Roman Empire and its impact on fighting sports, including the popularity of gladiator events.

Chapter 2 covers the fighting sports practiced from the fall of Rome until approximately 1500 CE. It examines the militarism of the Byzantine Empire, China, and the Ottoman Empire and the scientific combat manuals that the masters of defense published in Europe. This chapter focuses on how indigenous martial arts operated in their places of origin, before the incursion of colonialism in Africa, Asia, South America, and Oceania.

Spanning from the sixteenth through the nineteenth century, chapter 3 reveals the cultural ramifications of imperialism and how martial arts became translated as people migrated, immigrated, or invaded foreign lands, bringing their own cultural traditions and creating new ones. This chapter notes the emergence of fighters competing abroad and the development of boxing, wrestling, and kickboxing variations around the world. It also explores the birth of fighting sports in the new United States and how the African diaspora, through the slave trade, expanded martial arts in the new world.

Chapter 4 concentrates on the twentieth century, a time of exponential growth of media technologies, which fomented the demand for fight-related content. It explains how the development of governing bodies such as athletic commissions in the late nineteenth century standardized sport rules and led to the exclusion and marginalization of many fighters, such as women and minorities in the U.S. and British boxing communities. Chapter 4 studies how MMA developed in the twentieth century as an attempt to pit specific fighting sports against each other, from mixed-match bouts between boxers and wrestlers in Japan to the interdisciplinary fights that the Ultimate Fighting Championship (UFC) first brought to the public in 1993.

Chapter 5 analyzes the globalization of fighting sports and the streamlining of MMA into a specific sport, with its own rules and governance in the twenty-first century. It reflects on how fighters changed their training and competitive approach in order to be more dominant in this new, mixed platform that required technical skills in boxing, kickboxing, wrestling, Brazilian jujitsu, and other fighting styles. This chapter investigates how the process of globalization and the dual powers of media and capitalism continue to impact the growth of MMA. Finally, chapter 5 reveals the stories of numerous fighters from around the world and how each brought his cultural traditions to the creation of this new sport, even though it, too, eventually would become as institutionalized and rule based as any other fighting sports.

As the sport of MMA developed in the late twentieth and early twenty-first centuries, many traditional martial artists and fighting sports fans expressed misgivings about the future of fighting sports. Some people believed that MMA was a mere fad that soon would become an embarrassing moment in the history of boxing and wrestling. Others feared the rise of MMA, afraid that it could overshadow boxing and wrestling, and even, according to some alarmists, manage to kill off these classic sports. Instead, the sport of wrestling has expanded tremendously in the past decade, and boxing remains one of the most popular international sports. Despite the apprehension of some martial artists and sports fans, MMA has not destroyed indigenous fighting arts such as Muay Thai or Senegalese wrestling, nor has it diminished the prominence of professional boxing or Olympic wrestling. In fact, the success of MMA helped bolster many indigenous arts that might otherwise have been homogenized in an increasingly global market.

This book, ultimately, is my love letter to martial arts, which has given me so much. Through martial arts, I discovered myself. I found my passion, met my husband and my best friends, and kept my body, soul, and mind active and healthy. And after my many years of training, teaching, researching, and writing about fighting sports, my passion for martial arts never waned, even when faced with the realities of corporatization and globalization in the twenty-first century, or the systemic injustices that plagued many elements of sport throughout history. Part of appreciating martial arts is understanding the problems that humans engender wherever and whatever we do. When I look at recent UFC cards, with fighters from around the world representing their cultures, and see the way that the majority of the MMA community has embraced social movements such as Black Lives Matter and LGBTQ equality, I have hope for the future.

To anticipate the future of MMA, we must first understand and study the past. In this book, I pay homage to the many teachers and students who contributed to the diverse and beautiful arts that have had such a profound impact on my own life. I hope that you, too, will read this book with the hunger of a student, the wisdom of a teacher, the appreciation of a master, and the spirit of a fighter as together we explore the rich, global history of mixed martial arts.

# 1

# ANCIENT FIGHTING SPORTS

In Homer's epic tale *The Iliad*, a boxing match takes place during the funeral games of Patroclus between Epeus and Euryalus, two men eager to showcase their pugilistic skills in front of hordes of other soldiers. Epeus, a Greek soldier and one of the builders of the Trojan Horse, strutted around the ring, calling for any man to fight him, for he was "the best boxer of all here present."[1] Unwilling to let a challenge go by, and apparently interested in winning the prize mule, Euryalus, a fellow Grecian and part of Jason's Argonauts, agreed to fight Epeus. The men met in the middle of a ring and began striking each other immediately with "punishing" blows. Covered in sweat and blood, the men hit each other repeatedly; the crowd could hear their jaws crunching under the punches. Then, Euryalus made an error; he took his eyes off Epeus, and in that moment, the latter threw a devastating punch to the jaw. Euryalus fell heavily, and despite his attempt moments later to rise and continue, he was vanquished. As Euryalus struggled and failed to stand, it was his opponent, Epeus, who caught him before he could hit the ground again. Epeus stood victorious, his arms around Euryalus, who spat clots of blood, his head hanging and his feet not able to support him. After punching each other relentlessly for the sake of glory, honor, and a mule, Epeus and Euryalus were back to being comrades, standing side by side as blood poured from their faces and the crowd that surrounded them cheered rapturously.

This story is part of ancient Greek myth, but it feels strikingly modern for anyone who has ever faced the rigors of fighting. To an outsider, fighting may seem barbaric and crude, but across the world and throughout history, people have competed for fame, national pride, personal glory, and, ultimately, for survival. Fighting sports have long been considered primitive, and to a certain extent, that belief is true. Fighting may be one of the most primal of human activities after eating, sleeping, and sex. It is easy to imagine the earliest species of hominids swinging at each other for leftover meat or for a closer proximity to the fire, or even engaging in physical contests to decide who should lead the tribe. Although we can only speculate as to the validity of these scenarios, historical evidence exists that proves fighting indeed was practiced as sport in the ancient world. Artwork and pottery provide some of the earliest accounts of boxing and wrestling: a beautifully preserved six-teenth-century BCE fresco from the island of Santorini dubbed "boxing boys" shows two young men with long dreaded hair and small loincloths punching each other at very close quarters. Wall paintings in Egypt from 2000 BCE depict groups of men practicing various wrestling techniques. A fragment of a Mycenaean pot circa 1300–1200 BCE found in Cyprus features two stylized male figures striking at each other with extended arms.

Although this artwork reveals the long history of combat sports, early sports scholars in the twentieth century still believed that to study ancient sports, one need only look at the Greeks. The Greeks did, indeed, have a robust sports industry that seems very advanced to our modern eyes, as the story of Epeus and Euryalus reveals. The Greeks devoted time and effort to training, as well as marketing, promoting, and organizing sporting events. They also wrote a great deal about themselves, so we have numerous accounts of ancient Greek sporting practices. American and British historians, especially those working the nineteenth and early twentieth centuries, adored the ancient Greeks, which is understandable—they are a fascinating culture.

But focusing solely on the Greeks often meant ignoring or marginalizing other ancient histories—in particular, ignoring ancient histories of cultures in Africa, Asia, and the Americas, mainly because those cultures were not considered part of Europe's historical roots. That is not to say that old-school white historians were purposefully manipulating history to identify their ideal ethnic lineage, but rather that they chose to exalt the cultures that they took for their own antecedents. Because their research remains at the forefront of most scholarship, we have a surplus of information on the ancient Egyptians, Greeks, and Romans and a lack of research on other parts of the ancient world.

It is important to note that communities, tribes, and civilizations all over the world thrived during prerecorded history. From the Americas to Northern Europe, Southeast Asia to the Pacific Islands, and Australia to sub-Saharan Africa, fighting was a necessary survival skill that had to be honed in every warrior. It is a reasonable assumption that all of these cultures practiced fighting in a way that would not harm or diminish the power of their tribe, so empty-hand fighting arts such as wrestling and kickboxing undoubtedly were used to prepare for battle. Survival in the ancient world, prior to the institutionalization of governments and religions, was predicated on the ability to protect oneself from harm, not to mention safeguard necessities such as food, livestock, and other tangibles, as well as one's family and extended family.

In order to best protect one's family and their goods existing in a community created safety in numbers, but it also required that the group, or representatives of the group, be able to fight. In fact, individuals in the ancient world were more likely than in our current era to be trained in hand-to-hand combat. Being able to defend oneself from attackers had utility, be that in an individual brawl or a tribal skirmish. Weapons can be dropped from slippery hands, and distance weaponry can be difficult to deploy when in very close quarters, but for the most part, hands and feet (and knees, elbows, and heads) always are available.

Fighting sports might be delineated into several different groups, depending on their purpose and practice. Some fighting sports functioned as war games, which tribes and cultures used to prepare for forthcoming battles. These sports typically included weapons practice, although they would use blunt versions of those weapons in order to minimize injuries. There were also fighting sports as contests between individuals who represented their city, their country, or their tribe. These contests between differing tribes were not for the sake of money or celebration, but rather to prove the superiority of one group over another. Ultimately, fighting sports pitted two individuals against each other, but the fighters did not just represent themselves—they represented their country, culture, and history.

## THE MESOPOTAMIAN EMPIRE

Many scholars believe that human civilization began—or at least coalesced—in the Fertile Crescent, an area in Western Asia, today known as the Middle East. Out of this region humans invented mathematics, built the wheel, and created the first forms of writing. Writing is a technology, created and developed by humans for a particular purpose, just as the telephone, fax machine, and the internet are technological innovations. Only in the past five thousand years has writing become part of human practice. The earliest forms of writing were pictographs, drawn in wet clay with a pointed stick, and used in Mesopotamia in approximately 3200 BCE; and cuneiform, created by the Sumerians around the same time.

Cuneiform used a wedge-shaped stick, and although it started simply for the purpose of accounting and record keeping, eventually it would allow for the first written examples of literature and religious texts. This is significant because, like early computers, ancient writing was incredibly tedious, both in effort and materials, so writing was not extensive or prolific, and instead focused on documenting only the most necessary information. In its earliest iterations, writing allowed people to keep track of inventory, such as cattle or grain, and maintain certain types of balance sheets (X traded so many head of cattle for so many bushels of grain). However, as cuneiform became used more widely, and the materials of writing were more readily available, taking down religious and literary texts for posterity suddenly increased.

Eventually, humans would migrate into other parts of the world, but the Sumerians settled and built small, round houses, which became some of the first cities. The Sumerians invented cuneiform and began to document not only their public records, but also the exploits of their kings. It is sometimes difficult to distinguish Sumerian myth from reality, because many of their key figures also featured in their epic literature. In fact, the Sumerians are responsible for what is considered the first piece of literature, *The Epic of Gilgamesh*, which tells the story of Gilgamesh, who is one-third human and two-thirds god. Setting the standard for all epic tales, Gilgamesh goes on the hero's journey, fighting evil, making friends, falling in love, and, of course, fighting a particularly intense wrestling match against his future friend, Enkidu. The significance of this moment is not only about the hero's struggle with himself, but it also reveals the importance of wrestling as a symbolic gesture. The men do not run a race, or compete in an archery exhibition; they risk injury and defeat in a true match of skill and strength.

Mesopotamia's confluence of various city-states, each with its own ruler, created rivalries between the leaders of these different communities. Eventually the Babylonians gained control of the area, led by Hammurabi, who created one of the first written codes of law. Each of these city-states might have been separated by space, but they shared language, trading practices, and organized sporting events. They dedicated a month to footraces and held a nine-day wrestling tournament in Assur in which competitors were fed by temple priests and given oil to rub on their bodies before competition.

The Sumerians also practiced boxing and were depicted on one terra-cotta relief from the period wearing short skirts and hand wraps. Unfortunately, although we know that the Mesopotamians held boxing and wrestling contests, we have no information on how these bouts would have looked. Wrestling is not a definite term; wrestling could include throws or pins or submissions or even striking, depending on the rules and techniques of the people who practiced it. Thousands of years ago, boxing did not look like the streamlined and highly regulated version we see today. Boxing was a catch-all term for striking, so many ancient boxing styles had kicks, elbows, throws, and even head butting as part of the style. In the case of ancient Mesopotamia, we do not know what their fighting sports looked like, but we do know that, from a cultural and social standpoint, they were important.

*The Epic of Gilgamesh* and other royal stories reveal that wrestling was the ultimate signifier of strength and character in ancient Mesopotamia. So much was this the case that future Sumerian kings would boast of their own wrestling prowess, although whether truly earned or propaganda of the state remains unclear. But wrestling, in the ancient world, already was a device, literary and physically, for demonstrating worth. Accounts of Sumerian kings defeating foreign opponents in wrestling bouts were not fact-checked at the time, nor can they be substantiated today, and a king hardly would allow word of his defeat to be heralded in his own kingdom.

It became the practice of Mesopotamian kings to demonstrate their own physical prowess in public spectacles and celebrations, revealing their strength, speed, and agility, even if the highly scripted feats of strength were more symbolic than contested. Although we do not know exactly what these wrestling matches entailed, it is hard to imagine a Sumerian king fighting a foreign opponent and losing; the fights probably were more in keeping with the conventions of modern-day theatrical wrestling. This is not to diminish the robustness of ancient kings, who did, indeed, often have to lead armies into battle and defend the throne from a wide range of threats. Mesopotamia's most powerful neighbor to the east, Egypt, maintained a consolidated political force led by the pharaoh, who was considered not just a man but a god on earth. And like the kings of Mesopotamia, the pharaohs loved to brag about how great they were at wrestling.

## AFRICA

### Egypt

Ancient Egyptians created their own writing system around 3200 BCE, at the same time as the Mesopotamians. Egyptian hieroglyphics are logographic, an extensive form of pictographs and symbols that can be combined to create words and sentences. It is interesting that the technology of writing was not practiced by everyone in Egypt, including royalty. Only scribes, who often were enslaved, were literate, and early forms of writing always were read out loud.

The evidence of Egypt's sporting cultures exists in both written history and artwork recovered from the period. According to ancient Egyptian art, wrestling was the most popular sport; from 3000 to 1100 BCE, most sporting artwork centered around wrestling. The beautiful artwork found in the Egyptian city of Beni Hasan depicts more than four hundred wrestling scenes, laid out to illustrate a sequence of the progression of a wrestling match. This artwork, dating to 2000 BCE, contains images of wrestlers in clinch positions, performing takedowns and throws, and wrestling on the ground, attacking each other's arms and legs. Although the ancient Greek system of wrestling would focus more on throws and pins, the Egyptians appeared to do far more ground submissions.

Although careful and extensive drawings of wrestling tactics exist, the exact scoring process for ancient Egyptian wrestling is unknown.

But a piece of artwork from the twelfth century BCE shows one wrestler choking another, and an inscription underneath reads, "Take care! You are in the presence of Pharaoh!"; that indicates that choking may have been against the rules at the time.[2] However, earlier depictions show choking as part of the Egyptian wrestling system, so either it was outlawed at the time of this particular artwork, or perhaps it was gauche to choke an opponent in front of the pharaoh.

Boxing was not particularly popular in ancient Egypt, especially compared to wrestling or stick fighting. A surviving illustration depicts young men wearing skirts with their left fist in the air and the right by their hip in a type of high/low guard, but they could be dancing rather than fighting. They are considered boxers because of their proximity to another depiction, that of Egyptian stick fighting. Ancient Egypt, indeed, may have had boxing, and perhaps the recording artifacts were destroyed, but we have no doubt that stick fighting was tremendously popular. Artwork from fourteenth century BCE Thebes shows two stick fighters striking each other with a single stick that included a hand wrap and wearing guards on their non-striking arm. Other artwork from the same period includes fighters with sticks in both hands, revealing that some Egyptian stick-fighting competitions were single stick and others were double. Matches, judged by officials, could be won by submission or landing the most blows.

In addition to artistic depictions of stick fighting, the Ramesseum Papyrus, dated to 1991 BCE, describes two priests in a double-stick competition. Earlier iterations of stick fighting occur in the Old Kingdom (roughly 2900–2150 BCE) practice of fisherman jousting, in which fishermen on the Nile would joust with the long poles used to propel their reed boats. These skirmishes probably were done either in fun or in territorial disputes. Fisherman jousting was, however, the purview of laborers, whereas stick fighting and wrestling had nobler connections.

Like Mesopotamian kings, the pharaohs of Egypt used sports to demonstrate their health and vitality, both of which were symbolic of their godliness on earth. At the thirty-year mark of the pharoah's reign, he or she would perform a ceremonial run during the Sed festival at the Djoser pyramid complex in front of a tremendous crowd. The "race" required the pharaoh to run unopposed around markers set fifty-five meters apart, and it certainly was more performance than exertion. But it acted as evidence of the pharaoh's ability to rule, and even old and infirm pharaohs participated. In Egyptian pictographs portraying the exploits of Ramses III, the pharaoh is shown wrestling with foreigner combatants in competition and roundly defeating every one of them. These images serve to buttress the reputation of Ramses and Egypt as a whole, but they may have been more propaganda than reality. Egyptian pharaohs also called out their subjects, daring them to fight or race or compete in archery with their king. Of course, no subject would be so silly as to trounce the pharaoh, so he remained undefeated.

Artwork also depicts Egyptian wrestlers competing against warriors from Nubia, Syria, Libya, and other foreign lands. The diverse audience in the artwork includes noble men and women, and we even see referees overseeing the matches. At first interpretation, one might consider this an early form of international competition, but ostensibly they were highly orchestrated events for the enjoyment of Egyptian citizens because the hometown wrestlers managed to defeat every single foreign opponent. The most likely scenario is that these foreign opponents were forced to "take a dive," especially because the Nubians, in particular, were incredible wrestlers.

## Western and Sub-Saharan Africa

The historic overview of sports on the African continent has been greatly skewed by the focus on Egypt. Egypt, with its pharaohs and pyramids and connection with the Roman Empire, has garnered far more attention by Westerners than the rest of the continent. The Victorian era obsession with the ancient kingdom, and the subsequent proliferation of gentleman Egyptologists, meant that Egypt's history subsumed that of the rest of the continent. Egypt was an easier study for most Westerners, one that reflected on their own ancient roots, because the country sat at the junction of Africa, Asia, and Europe and functioned as one of the most powerful outposts of the Roman Empire. If Egypt was the seat of ancient culture, then old-school historians had no issue delineating the history of ideas and cultural practices to its roots. But this reduction discounts the numerous societies that existed at the same time as the Egyptian empire—societies that had their own languages, narratives, and cultural practices.

In the history of scholarship, we, as academics, have privileged cultures with writing even though advanced societies existed that relied on oral tradition rather than the written word. Excavating, both metaphorically and physically, the history of a particular culture group requires looking into all of the artifacts that articulate the mores of that society. Art and sculpture, architecture and tombs, songs and dancing, even fighting sports can provide historians with a depiction of a society that is rich and intricate and interesting.

In order to learn more about ancient people who did not have a writing system, scholars use artifacts and information gleaned from countries that did have writing, such as Egypt. It is important to remember that although those writings from one nation about its foreign neighbor might be a bit skewed, they still can be helpful in excavating the past. However, oral and performed history can be just as useful for scholars, because in many cultures with a strong oral history, the actions of the past are reenacted daily in art and in sport. We will discuss the more modern iterations of African fighting in future chapters, but just know that their connection to the past appears to be so much stronger because it is rooted in memory rather than in books.

In navigating the history of Africa, in particular West and sub-Saharan Africa, one must contend with the biases of those individuals, primarily Westerners, who viewed the indigenous populations as Other. Read accounts from Sir Henry Morton Stanley, David Livingstone, or even Joseph Conrad's novel *Heart of Darkness*, to see how racism permeated the writings of these early "explorers" of the African continent. In addition, the non-Egypt countries of Africa were where so many slaveholding countries obtained their slaves, and history shows no better way to dehumanize a group than to erase or ignore its history. But Africa, a tremendously vast continent that is home to numerous countries, states, cities, villages, camps, and tribes, has a history of fighting sports that is not limited to the story of Egypt.

The empty-hand combat sports of striking and grappling permeated nearly every group, large and small, in ancient Africa; and stick fighting, a sport not necessarily particular to ancient Africa (many Southeast Asian traditions include stick fighting, as do some European ancient cultures), was of tremendous importance in these lands where carrying a stick could mean the difference between life or death.

In ancient Namibia, the Kunene people trained young boys to use weapons to fight humans and to protect their livestock from predators. Known as *kandeka*, this style used sticks two feet long, one inch in diameter at one end and approximately two inches in diameter at the handle. Small children would practice stick fighting to hone their skills in combat and to become proficient at protecting cattle, the prize of their tribe, from other men or from hunting animals. An Egyptian relief of Ramses III from approximately 2000 BCE includes depictions of Egyptians competing in stick fighting with "Nubian" fighters, although the Egyptians defined any darker-skinned Africans as "Nubians," not just men from Nuba. Another fourteenth-century BCE engraving shows Nubian wrestlers competing while stick fighters stand off to one side, preparing to engage in combat themselves.

In ancient times, the Nuba of Sudan wrestled in their home territory and in Egypt using a dynamic style of fighting similar to today's free-style wrestling. The Nuba were extremely accomplished wrestlers, although a young man's competitive career would end upon his marriage. Nuba fighters continue to practice the sports of their ancestors, and through oral histories and martial arts tradition, most scholars believe that the modern iteration of Sudanese wrestling provides a general view into the ancient sport.

Boys and young men train outside their village in camps and compete at community festivals, covered in white ash as a symbol of strength. The Nuba believe that sex incapacitates fighters; thus, a young man's wrestling career ends fairly early in his life in order for him to start a family. Nubian women also wrestled once a year in conjunction with the harvest reaping. A particularly skilled woman could win acclaim from her community that sometimes included a particularly advantageous marriage, which subsequently would end her career and her husband's as well. These practices of the modern Sudanese culture are considered to be the same, or at least incredibly similar, to the traditions of their ancestors thousands of years ago. Currently, a group of people in Sudan known as the Nuba continue to have their own sport of wrestling, which includes regular competitions that are community events featuring food, dancing, and wrestling matches.

Wrestling was a widespread art in seemingly all West African groups, and many of those same styles are practiced and contested today. Some early sports historians claimed that African wrestling styles evolved singularly from Egypt's Beni Hasan wrestling system, although this seems unlikely, given the linguistic history and the archaeological evidence of various western African populations. The idea that the Egyptians somehow "taught" wrestling to the rest of Africa might have been rooted in Egyptian propaganda, or in Egyptologists' desires to read Egypt's ancient culture as the inventor of nearly everything on Earth. The fact is that wrestling is a nearly universal sport, and we probably cannot trace it to one single origin, nor would it be necessary to do so. Wrestling, like music or cuisine, is human.

Fighting sports are found in nearly every tribal community on the African continent, but every group practiced and lived its martial art differently. Fighting arts are remembered and shared as a means of protection and bringing glory to the tribe through successful application of the fighting sport's particular style. In other words, most African fighting arts were a direct corollary to combat, and they continued to prepare young warriors for battle long into modernity. Ancient African martial arts traditions have passed on, through oral history, rituals, and the actual arts themselves, through hundreds of generations—a lived history.

## The Persian Empire

The Persian Empire was founded by Cyrus the Great in 550 BCE, and eventually it would stretch from modern-day Bulgaria to Egypt. In current times, Iran dominates the modern wrestling world, and its Persian ancestors were no different. Persian wrestling was celebrated as a sport in itself, outside of military training. Wrestlers wore linen cloths and leather shoes, and covered every inch of themselves in oil in order to make themselves slippery and tough to grasp. The fighter who pinned his opponent flat on his stomach was considered the winner. Manuscripts from the Middle Ages claim that Iranian wrestling involves 360 techniques, a significant figure in Iranian numerology. Most techniques were based on joint manipulations, leg trips, and pummeling techniques to get the opponent closer for neck cranks.

Martial arts in the Persian Empire included archery and swordsmanship as well as wrestling, all of which were practiced in the *zoorkhane*, which translates to "house of strength." Fighters engaged in strength and endurance training as well as skill-building exercises. The zoorkhane includes a large pit, approximately six meters in diameter and about two-and-a-half feet deep, where wrestlers practice, overseen by a *sadat* who instructs and runs exercises, as well as a musician who plays the drum and sings religious songs. The training regimens included wrestling drills and strength training exercises, such as push-ups performed on a wide wooden plank, and steel mace swings. Northern Iran's traditional wrestling style, *koshti gil mardi*, was a precursor to modern-day MMA. Fights began with opponents punching and kicking, using footwork and head movement to get inside. Once the fighters clinched, however, all punches and kicks stopped, and both began working to throw each other to the floor. If a hand or knee made contact with the ground, the bout was over and the winner declared.

Persia famously attempted to invade Greece and was repelled in 480 BCE. In 334 BCE, Alexander the Great expanded his kingdom by invading Persia and eventually amassing one of the largest empires in history. Alexander supposedly was a fantastic athlete; he was a runner and a polo player, a sport he learned from the Persians. Yet he did not seem to enjoy fighting sports particularly, despite his own combative tendencies on the battlefield. He believed that sports should be for the enjoyment of amateurs, rather than for the benefit of paid professional athletes. His native Macedonia, a powerful region in ancient Greece, was at the forefront of the standardization of athletics and what would become the height of amateur competition in the ancient and modern worlds—the Olympics.

## GREECE

Nearly every society, existing and extinct, has a martial art or a folk fighting style that certain portions of its citizenry practiced. The ancient Greeks are trotted out most often in reference to historical fighting sports, not necessarily because they practiced them more than other nations or dynasties, but because the Greeks were prolific writers, obsessed with their own history and their place in the world. Greece rose to prominence in the late Bronze Age as the civilizations based around the Aegean Sea evolved politically, economically, and culturally. Hundreds of years before the Greeks, Crete and the Cycladic islands developed sophisticated societies that included sports contests. The famous "boxing boys" frescos in Crete, circa 1635 BCE, include images of young boys wearing caps and hand wraps and attempting to punch each other in the face. Another section of the fresco includes men training in knife fighting, and in another a man appears to have been thrown recently with his legs in the air, as if engaged in a wrestling match.

The most beloved sports in ancient Crete focused on bulls, perhaps in reference to the Minoan myth of the Minotaur. Although it is unclear precisely how such a feat would take place, Minoans apparently made a game of leaping over bulls, sometimes wrestling them to the ground. The Mycenaeans, who occupied mainland Greece from 1600 BCE to about 1200 BCE, also had bull sports, as well as running, boxing, and wrestling. Sports in the Bronze Age primarily were associated with funeral games and were not yet formalized sporting events, but that would change with the rise of the ancient Greek civilization.

Ancient Greeks, in particular, celebrated the combat sports that their athletes practiced as the embodiment of their most cherished cultural codes. Combat sports demonstrated athletic prowess, bravery, power, determination—all attributes that the Greeks prized. They did not shy away from violence or capitulate to an enemy. The Greeks referred to wrestling, boxing, and pankration as the *barea athla*, the "heavy events," because the sports were dominated by large, strong men, for antiquity did not recognize weight classes. The combat triad was also heavy in that participants engaged in the most dangerous form of athletics at the time. Death was not unheard of, and, in fact, the ancient Olympic Games held that an athlete was free of legal responsibility were he to kill his opponent during a match.

Boxing, wrestling, and pankration were three distinct sports, each with its own stable of fighters and fans. Numerous fighters, however, were multidisciplinary, competing in boxing one day and pankration the next. That is, if they were able to compete. For all three were, again, heavy, and demonstrated the cultural concept of *karteria*, meaning endurance. The Greeks loved all of their sports, but they revered the barea athla, the heavy events, because those sports embodied the ideal of karteria above all others. Because boxing, wrestling, and pankration could be dangerous, and because of the ideal of karteria, athletes would persevere in spite of pain or even death. Fighting carried risks and rewards in ancient times, when rules were not always clearly delineated, and the desire for greatness sometimes outweighed caution.

The fighters in the heavy events competed in today's version of Absolute. It did not involve weight classes, and other than divisions between men and boys, athletes could face any opponent in their sport, regardless of size. Although larger, stronger men typically excelled, the agility, speed, and precision of a smaller fighter could prevail over a bigger opponent. In addition to the lack of weight classes, none of the three sports had rounds or time limits. No points were awarded, so contests were won by knockout or submission, or when a fighter could not continue due to fatigue or injury. Admitting to either one would have been shameful and in direct conflict with that Grecian ideal of karteria, so the matches for all three sports typically lasted a very long time.

The three heavy events took place in a shared arena, the *skamma*, which was part of the running track in the event stadium. Additional sand would be laid down on the track in order to provide an extra bit of cushion for the fighters. No ring restricted the fighting space, which was about the size of a modern football field, but at times officials would cordon off an area of the skamma in order to bring the fighters closer together and diminish the amount of rest. Although judges did not call fights based on a combatant's ability to continue, the judges used sticks to poke, prod, or beat fighters who stalled, committed fouls, ran from their opponents, or just seemed tired.

Fighters from all three disciplines trained indoors, in the *palaestra*, a special training academy for top Greek athletes. But during competitions, whether the Olympics, local tournaments, or funeral games, athletes competed outside in the sunlight. Therefore, fighters worked hard to ensure that they were not staring into the sun. Good footwork was imperative, even more than strength, in this particular strategy to force an opponent to look into the sun. The heavy events of ancient Greece had much in common, from their venue in the skamma to the lack of weight classes, points, time limit, and rounds, but each also had its own rules and rituals that made it unique. And of course, all of them have their stories, the tales of athleticism, of horror and of triumph, that establish boxing, wrestling, and pankration in ancient Greece as three of the originators of today's combat sports.

## The Olympic Games

Fighting sports, along with running, have the longest history in the origin of the Olympic Games. The first Olympic Games were held in 776 BCE and featured only a single-course two-hundred-meter race, known as the *stadion*. Wrestling was introduced in the eighteenth Olympiad in 708 BCE, boxing in the twenty-third Olympiad in 688 BCE, and pankration in the thirty-third Olympiad in 648 BCE. Precisely when and why the games died out continues to be debated, as academics in the past thirty years have argued against the long-held reductionist belief that Theodosius unilaterally quashed them in 394 CE. Sports, of course, continued to be popular pursuits around the globe, but it was not until the end of the nineteenth century that a French anglophile, Pierre de Coubertin, worked to revive the Olympic Games.

Greek women were forbidden to enter the stadium to watch the games or to enter the Altis during the period of the games, although the Priestess of Demeter Chamyne, an honorary office that changed every four years, was allowed to watch the games. Seated at an altar directly opposite the chief judges, she was the only woman officially allowed to be present. In fact, penalties were severe for women who attempted to watch; offenders could be thrown off the cliffs of Mount Typaion by the Eleans (the Olympic judges) if they just crossed the river Alpheios on the days that the games were held.

However, there are several examples of girls and women who risked death, or at least castigation, in order to watch the Olympic Games. Kallipateira was the daughter, sister, and mother of Olympic victors. After the death of her husband, she took it upon herself to train her son, Peisirodos. When he won an event, Kallipateira, dressed as a male trainer, leaped over the trainer's enclosure to celebrate and somehow managed to disrobe in the process, revealing herself as a woman. In honor of her father, husband, and sons, she was allowed to go unpunished.

Boxing was considered the heaviest of the heavy sports because the fighters generally landed very hard, damaging punches from a distance, rather than the shorter strikes common to pankration. In 688 BCE, boxing became an official Olympic sport. Boxing matches were not judged on points or style, nor did a fight ever go to decision. Instead, the boxers fought until one of them could not continue due to exhaustion or knockout—or if a fighter raised his right hand in defeat, essentially throwing in the towel. Conjecture has it that this is why Sparta never sent athletes to the Olympic games—the risk that a fighter might lose or admit defeat went against Sparta's cultural ideal of death before defeat.

Boxing in ancient Greece was a bloody sport, made bloodier and more brutal by the thin leather wraps that boxers wore as gloves. The *himantes meilichai* were intended to protect the fighter's hands (although not the fingers), not the head or face of the opponent. A long-held misconception is that the Greeks used *caestus*, a leather glove studded with bits of metal and glass, apparently adopted from the Romans. But historians now challenge that the caestus ever truly was in use. Roman historian Hugh Lee argues that neither Greeks nor Romans sewed bits of metal into their gloves, and that other historians "misread the evidence to push the notion of Roman decadence."[3]

In fact, we have no need to adhere to this misleading legend: Greek and Roman boxing was violent enough without subscribing to the false idea that they intentionally made it even bloodier with the caestus. Boxers in antiquity were athletes, highly trained and valued by the culture. Although injury and death occurred in boxing, wrestling, and pankration, the sporting community would not have wanted to add unnecessary maiming with metal-studded gloves. After all, the Grecian governments needed the men to go on to fight another day, on the skamma or the battlefield.

Even as boxers and pankration fighters wrapped their hands in leather, they wore nothing while competing in the Olympics and other games. In addition, athletes of all sorts covered their bodies in olive oil; oiling rooms were specially designed to apply the slick substance. Scholars long have argued about the purpose of the olive oil, assuming the intent to be everything from hygiene to protection from the sun or the cold. Most scholars today assume that the oil was used simply to make the body glisten and look more attractive. Training and competing in the nude anecdotally are attributed to Orsippus, a runner in 720 BCE who apparently lost his loincloth, yet went on to win his race. Thereafter, his competitors ran in the nude, thinking that a nude Orsippus simply may have been more aerodynamic. Another story claims that a runner tripped on his loincloth while in the race, so officials declared the end to all clothing.

Ancient boxing matches had no ring, no rounds, no rests, and few rules. Boxers could strike while their opponent was down and fought until one of the fighters could not continue. Emperor Augustus apparently loved boxing matches, especially nonsanctioned fights used to settle disputes in dingy alleys. Amateur "street fights" may have delighted Augustus, but most men preferred to watch the trained boxers compete because they demonstrated the concept of karteria in a way that would horrify many of us today. Fighters did not show that they were injured and reportedly made no noise when they were struck or knocked to the ground. In a particularly brutal example of extreme endurance, Euraydamas of Kyrene famously won a match through a war of attrition. When his opponent hit him hard enough to break his teeth, Eurydamas swallowed them, rather than giving his opponent the satisfaction of seeing him spit them into the dirt.

Wrestling, too, made an appearance in *The Iliad* when Homer described a battle between Ulysses and Ajax that Achilles eventually stopped when neither man could lift the other. Ajax was a famously huge man, and Ulysses's inability to lift his larger opponent was par for the course in ancient wrestling. Great wrestlers were typically large men who trained, and ate, to be even stronger. Milo the wrestler famously ate twenty pounds of meat, twenty pounds of bread, and drank eighteen pints of wine every day. It is said that one time, in a particularly unique style of training, he carried a four-year-old bull around the stadium of Olympia for his cardio and strength workout, then sat down and ate the entire bull.

Like boxing, wrestling had no rounds, weight classes, or time limits. Many matches would end in a draw after seemingly hours of protracted combat. In order to win a wrestling match, a fighter had to throw his opponent to the ground three times. A successful fall typically was constituted when the wrestler's shoulders hit the ground—throwing an opponent merely to his knees would not count. In addition, the ancient Greeks did not practice pinning. However, submissions, including chokes, were legal and encouraged.

Although the matches were not as bloody as boxing or pankration, wrestlers still sustained injuries from submissions; before it was banned, a wrestler dubbed "Mr. Fingertips" systematically broke his opponent's fingers in order to win a match. With the exception of Mr. Fingertips, wrestling was the least violent of the heavy events, yet the most popular, given its prominence in antique art and sculpture. Wrestling was part of the pentathlon in antiquity as well as its own event. The pentathlon in ancient Greece consisted of javelin, discus, jumping, running, and wrestling. It is fascinating to imagine a modern athlete proficient in all of these forms, especially the widely distinct sport of wrestling.

Some of the ancient gentry practiced wrestling, more than boxing or pankration, probably because the risk of injury was relatively low. Socrates was an avid wrestler, training with two of his most famous students, Alcibiades and Aristocles, both of whom, in addition to being accomplished rhetoricians, purportedly were skilled wrestlers. Aristocles was a poet best known by the nickname given to him by a wrestling coach—Plato, which means "broad shouldered."

The Greeks practiced one of the earliest forms of MMA with pankration, which translates to "complete strength" or "complete victory." Pankration was an amalgamation of boxing and wrestling, with the added techniques of leg sweeps, kicks, and knees; the only techniques prohibited were biting and eye gouging. It is believed that the Greeks were inspired to develop pankration as a sport after the three hundred Spartans warriors reportedly resorted to hand-to-hand combat in their final battle at Thermopylae. Alexander the Great, while still believing that sport was for amateurs, apparently recruited the tough pankration fighters to his army, leading to speculation as to whether the Macedonian forces spread the art to Asia.

Pankration fighters had to be proficient at all forms of fighting, but the preferred strike was a kick to the stomach. Attacking the genitals was not off limits, and supposedly many pankrationists learned to cover their genitals in certain positions to prevent grabbing or twisting. Pankration joined the Olympic Games in 648 BCE and quickly became the most popular of nearly all of the sports. Pankration champions were elevated to instant celebrity status, and some even were worshipped as demigods. Many boxers and wrestlers were also pankration fighters, although because the pankration event took place on the day after boxing at the Olympic Games, many boxers never made it to the pankration competition due to injury.

Because the athletes had to be well-rounded, pankration fighters were typically large and powerful. They were allowed to employ a wide range of techniques, and breaking fingers and toes was an accepted and popular way to attack one's opponent. The art had four primary areas of fighting—arm techniques, such as punches, slaps, and elbow strikes; leg techniques, such as kicks and knees, throws and takedowns; and grappling, which includes holds, joint locks, and chokes. Fighters trained in a gym, the *korykeions*, with heavy bags called *korykos* suspended in the air for the students to kick and punch. It included wrestling and grappling classes, as well as gymnastics and calisthenics. Schools employed masseuses, dieticians, and coaches, many of whom themselves were former pankration champions, ready to pass on their knowledge to the next generation. Pankration was not included in Homer's *Illiad*, but still tales are numerous of fighters winning, and losing, on the field. Some athletes were noted for their strength, such as Polydamus of Skotoussa, a man so tremendously strong that he could stop a moving chariot by grabbing the wheel. Sostratos of Sikyon, in the fourth century BCE, won dozens of pankration events by bending back the fingers of his opponents.

The heavy events of ancient Greece were indeed heavy—heavy in size, bloodshed, and risk. But the risk, at the time, may have seemed nominal in light of the reality of war and the brutalities of ancient Greece as a society. Yet it was the Romans who elevated fighting sports to a new level of violence and, sometimes, cruelty.

## ANCIENT ROME

Rome, the epicenter of the world from eighth century BCE to the fifth century CE, was a vast state that spanned continents. As Rome amassed more land and peoples, it also took on many of the customs of the cultures it now controlled. Sport was one of the many things that Romans appropriated from the lands they conquered and then made their own. Rome, over the course of its history from republic to empire, to its eventual fall, assimilated the fighting sports of Greece and Etruria, to name a few, to produce a hyper-violent rendition of boxing, wrestling, and pankration. And famously, the Romans became obsessed with another type of fighting entertainment—one that made boxing and pankration, the heavy events of the ancient Olympics, look gentle, or, at least, safe. The most beloved sport in Rome was the gladiator contest—a violent spectacle that literally was used as a means of the death penalty, for which historians would forever mark the Romans as barbarians.

Describing the Romans as barbaric may seem apt, given their predilection for extreme violence and torture as a form of entertainment, but anti-Roman historians appear to have inflated some of the ghastlier stories of Roman sadism. Maligning Roman society and paganism in general after the fall of the Roman Empire was an effective propaganda tactic in the burgeoning Christian world. Early Christians had been targeted, along with numerous other minority groups, in the Roman Empire, and they suffered atrocities that were not easily forgotten. But between ancient historians' exaggerated claims of Roman sadism and Hollywood's sensational versions of semi-historical events, inaccuracies regarding Roman culture—specifically Roman gladiator events—have become deeply entrenched in our cultural imagination.

Roman culture was highly inspired by the lands and peoples it conquered, especially the Etruscan culture. Etruria had a cosmopolitan culture that greatly influenced the Roman Republic and later, the Roman Empire, but the Etruscans did not leave any written accounts of fighting sports or funeral games. Luckily, although the written word may have been destroyed, or may never have existed, the Etruscan fighting sports have been memorialized and documented in art. Vases and bronze artworks depict wrestling scenes, and tomb paintings include boxers. Etruria did not compete in the Panhellenic Games, but it had its own sporting culture that did not just mimic the sports of the larger Greek nation. In fact, Etruria's fighting sports impacted Rome's gaming culture tremendously. Boxing was a popular spectacle in Etruria, and scholars speculate that in their version of the pentathlon, both wrestling and boxing took place alongside running, jumping, and throwing the discus. Etruscan fighters, unlike their Greek counterparts, fought bare fisted during training and sparring. Only in competition would they would wrap leather strips around their hands, sometimes braided into cords, making a more devastating type of glove.

The Romans may have been influenced by the cultures they conquered, but their attitude toward sports was distinctly different than that of the ancient Greeks. For the Greeks, sport was a way for citizens to demonstrate their athleticism, determination, and prowess. In their early days, many Romans practiced and played sports, especially running, wrestling, and boxing, but as Rome became a powerful republic and then a superpower empire, sports took on the form of entertainment, best left for professionals to practice. Professional fighters who entertained the elite and the masses risked their health and their lives, but, ultimately, they were relegated to the lowest rung of the social ladder.

Roman's preferred the *munera*, the blood sports, above all events in their games. Upper-class Romans may have enjoyed practicing boxing as amateurs, but they never would debase themselves by participating in a sport in public. This tendency to leave sports, particularly the heavy fighting events, to the professionals also was adopted by upper-class Greeks in the Hellenistic period. With the exception of gladiator contests, boxing, known as *pugilatus*, was the most popular blood sport in Rome. Like most sports in Rome, it was the realm of the professional athlete, who was praised while he fought, then ostracized by the patrician class.

As previously mentioned, the story of the caestus, the ancient boxing glove studded with metal spikes, has been roundly debunked by most modern scholars as a revisionist attempt to paint the ancients as not just boorish, but as Caligula-level inhuman (although, to be fair, Caligula is a villain whose horrific exploits historians appear to have exaggerated). Most scholars believe that depictions of metal spikes in art are actually fingers, and that the knuckle-duster previously believed to be added to the top of the knuckles to tear away flesh more effectively actually was gripped by the boxer inside his fist, functioning more like a roll of quarters than brass knuckles. The fact is that fighting in ancient times was bloody, and injury was standard. Broken noses, smashed teeth, and cauliflower ears were the reality for fighters, which probably is why the Romans preferred to see professionals fight than to damage their own bodies.

Like their Greek counterparts, boxers in this period wore leather straps wrapped around their fingers. The wraps extended up their arms, allowing them to use their forearms as part of their defensive posture. The leather wraps assisted the fighters in landing particular hard punches, but their "gloves" did not provide the same type of defensive capabilities as a modern boxing glove. Instead, Roman boxers held their forearms vertically to cover their faces and the top of their head, or at a diagonal angle against straight punches to the face. Fighters could adopt a number of guard methodologies as part of their boxing game. Some fighters stood with their lead hand extended, open palm, to shove in the face of their opponent, forcing the man to move in order to punch. In addition, because their hands essentially were open and free, they could use the surface of their hands to parry or check a straight punch. This guard, with the lead hand open and outstretched, positioned the rear hand to extend quickly and land a blow. And straight punches were fighters' typical modus operandi. Strikes were aimed at the head, with body shots not really considered that impressive. Another guard was based on the *Sagittarius*, the archer, where the fighter kept his rear hand back, as if drawing a bow, to land a cross more swiftly.

Roman boxers preferred straight punches to the chin or heavy downward strikes, like overhands, in order to strike the ear. Like the Greeks, Roman fights had no rounds, no weight classes, and no breaks, unless both fighters agreed to take one briefly and go back to fighting in a very short time. Thus, Roman boxing strategy called for either knockout punches to the head or repeated strikes specifically to the nose or eyes, the areas that caused the most pain and blood. Because fights could be ended in just one perfectly landed punch, Roman boxers chose their shots carefully and fought from a distance. Their fight stance was wide, more like a modern-day MMA fighter than a traditional boxer, allowing them to use their footwork to move in and out of the pocket quickly.

Ancient Greek philosophers may have loved wrestling, but to the Romans, the relative safety of wrestling, *lucatio*, was the most boring of the ancient heavy events. However, the Romans adopted wrestling far before they took on pankration, which is surprising, given that pankration's bloodiness seems much more in line with the Romans' love of spectacle. Pankration fighters had to be the most versatile of the fighting sports' athletes, and, typically, they also were the largest and the toughest. As for the Greeks, pankration had no rules beyond no eye gouging and biting. The Spartans actually did allow both of these tactics, but because the Spartans never competed in international events because they would not risk losing to any non-Spartan, their eye-gouging and biting strategies remained legal only in their own country. Of course, rules did not preclude these maneuvers from occurring, and one pankrationist of the period noted that once fighters hit the ground, getting bitten was standard. Roman pankrationists could strike on the ground, and a favored attack was to kick from a down position. Galen, a Greek philosopher in the Roman Empire, jokingly awarded a donkey with a pankration prize because the donkey excelled in kicking.

Romans used primarily Greek terminology to describe their fighting sports, but the reverse is true of gladiator events. This lexical distinction reveals how Rome sought to mark the practices of other nations. Although historians, especially those operating in periods that are now in our own history and who sought to elevate ancient Greek culture, cast the Romans as the only nation to enjoy extreme violence, the Greeks were not averse to watching and even relishing gladiatorial spectacles. It is common practice to think of the Greeks as noble thinkers, the Romans as barbarians, but that is far too reductive. The fact is that people love violence, and the Romans merely perfected the showmanship of spectacle in the ancient world. And nowhere was the spectacle more spectacular than in the gladiator contests in the Roman Colosseum.

In another fascinating bit of lexicography, ancient Romans called boxing events matches, but gladiator events were called contests, thus firmly rooting gladiators in the world of performance, even though gladiator contests were viscerally real. It is unclear exactly which society originated gladiator contests—historians formerly believed it was Etruria, because the Etruscans greatly influenced Roman culture. But the earliest representation of gladiatorial combat comes from fourth-century BCE frescoes of the Osco-Samnites tribe, who lived just south of what is now Naples, showing armed combatants facing off at funeral games. It was not until 264 BCE that the first documented gladiator contest took place in Rome at the funeral games held in honor of aristocrat Brutus Pera. In 73 BCE, a prisoner of war named Spartacus, forced to join a gladiator school, led a rebellion with seventy other gladiators against the slave-owning oligarchy of Rome. Spartacus's story continues to be retold in popular culture, providing a modern version of violent spectacle as entertainment.

In 55 BCE, Pompey the Great hosted an extravagant event that included gladiator contests and live animal hunts in order to win over the plebeians and gain political popularity points. The crowd was not impressed, and, in fact, expressed pity for the animals in the show. Ten years later, his rival, Julius Caesar, presented an even more lavish version of Pompey's efforts, staging a mock battle scene with one thousand infantrymen, sixty cavalrymen, and forty elephants that charmed the Romans and brought Caesar great political success.

It is helpful to think of gladiator contests as serving two different purposes: as punishment and as a sport. The idea of gladiator fighting as sport may seem like a stretch, but professional gladiators, especially the well-trained ones with a fan base, were not sent to the arena so that they would be killed, but rather, so that they could fight, just as boxers and pankrationists did.

The other type, gladiator contests as punishment, was a different story. People who were forced into gladiator contests typically were murderers or men who committed arson or desecrated a temple. Two sentences were handed down: death by the sword (*ad gladium*) or by wild beasts (*ad bestias*). If a man were to survive either one of those sentences, he might be pardoned. If a condemned man did survive, which rarely happened in the ad bestias scenario, he would be able to continue his life as a gladiator, remaining at the school to do his duty to fight and, ideally, kill another criminal in the future.

Some gladiators may have been those who survived the ad gladium sentence, but the majority of gladiators in Rome were prisoners of war, recruited by their masters or gladiator trainers to fight, which to many prisoners was preferable to traditional modes of enslavement. Gladiator contests were so popular in Rome that winning fighters could achieve great stardom and subsequent financial support. They may have been considered the dregs of society, but that did not stop some Roman citizens from volunteering to become gladiators and, hopefully, attaining fame and fortune. By the second century BCE, Roman gladiators were highly trained weapons fighters who competed in public against other gladiators. Injuries were frequent, and death was a possibility that all of the fighters were willing to endure.

The Roman people treated star gladiators like gods. Many adopted pseudonyms, perhaps anticipating the twentieth-century professional wrestling conceit. One particular star gladiator, Hermes, was memorialized in a poem by epigrammatist Martial that revealed he was "both a gladiator and a trainer," skilled at not just one but three different fighting styles. He dominated other fighters with the long spear, the trident, and his own helmet. So great was Hermes that he made a fortune for ticket scalpers. The Roman Colosseum could seat fifty thousand spectators, and although some blocks of seats were free, when a big-name gladiator such as Hermes was scheduled to appear, fans would pay scalpers in order to see their favorite.

Gladiators may have been gods to some portion of the Roman populace, but they were considered, legally and morally, part of the lowest social rung, classified alongside actors and male prostitutes as *infamia* (ill-repute). However, Cicero, an attorney and Stoic in the first century BCE, believed that gladiator contests were "a noble and educational art," where the combatants showed self-control and grace in the face of death.[4] The Stoics may have admired the behavior of the gladiators themselves, but they viewed the crowds with disdain, for excitement and other strong emotions had no place in a disciplined mind.

Later Roman philosophers condemned gladiator contests as crude and harmful to Roman morale. Thus, it was a tremendous shock when, in the late second century CE, Roman emperor Commodus greatly embarrassed aristocratic Romans by appearing in public events as a gladiator. Commodus not only did not care at all for the opinions of the gentry, but he was also, by the latter part of his life, completely mad, dressing as Hercules and demanding that he be paid for his appearances in the Colosseum. Eventually Commodus was killed, not in the arena, but in his own home by his training partner, a wrestler named Narcissus.

A version of Commodus's exploits was memorialized in Ridley Scott's 2000 film, *Gladiator*, which is not known for its historical accuracy or authenticity, but certainly solidified the image of the gory gladiator contests in the Colosseum. The bloody spectacle that the film depicts may capture a version of the horror of the life of a gladiator, but it also glorifies it. The violence and the atrocities perpetrated in Rome, which the vast majority of the ancient world enjoyed, are captured by the film, and we, as the audience, participate in that violence. Perhaps that was Scott's intent—to simultaneously titillate and horrify the viewer so that we, like the Romans who sat in the Colosseum thousands of years ago, can get a charge out of the brutality we see before us.

Ancient Roman culture may be one of the most heavily replicated historical fantasies in Hollywood, although recent productions have explored ancient Viking and Celtic cultures as well. Unfortunately, we have far less historical information about those societies. Celtic society began forming in 1000 BCE, and its fighting was almost entirely military based, with swords, axes, and spears the primary focus of training. In other parts of Europe, tribes and communities formed and also needed forms of self-defense. In Ireland, the earliest mention of wrestling was in connection with leader Cu Chulainn, who apparently wrestled his son around 600 BCE. Although this might have been entirely anecdotal, Ireland did have its own ancient games that predate the Olympic Games. From 632 BCE to 1169 CE, Ireland's harvest festival games included wrestling. Fighting as a sport was most widely recorded in Greek and Roman cultures, but weapons training remained at the forefront of most ancient cultures.

## ASIA

### Ancient China

The vast majority of ancient fighting arts were predicated on the necessity for weapon proficiency rather than the standardized sports of Greece and Rome. Chinese culture, like many other ancient civilizations, practiced fighting in order to prepare its soldiers for warfare. At the same time, the performance of fighting, both wrestling and boxing as well as other martial skills such as horseback riding and archery, often were part of entertainment for the aristocracy and royalty. An enormous country with a vast history, China currently hosts hundreds of variations of its own martial arts. Each style is particular to the terrain and environment, and the families and people who developed the arts.

China's tremendous size and history mean that it has an extensive and diverse fighting sport history, although little historical documentation relates to the ancient period, for two reasons: first, many of the ancient practitioners of Chinese martial arts could not write; and second, the distinct practices often were considered secret, so those who trained would not write about their methodologies. We do know that wrestling dates back to approximately 2600 BCE and was referred to as *bo*, which means to seize or strike. Early Chinese wrestling included striking as well as wrestling techniques, making it perhaps more appropriate to call it empty-hand or bare-handed fighting rather than just wrestling. Wrestling became an official military sport in approximately 200 BCE, although it still operated as an amalgamation of modern-day wrestling and kickboxing, resembling the no-holds-barred style of twentieth-century MMA. Empty-hand fighting remained only a secondary or even tertiary practice compared to weapons-based training.

In ancient China, the term martial arts indicates the clear tie to military practices. The concept of *jiangwu* refers to the practice of training soldiers in fighting arts. In antiquity, most Chinese fighters devoted themselves to training for armed military engagements rather than sport. Chinese warriors expected all of their military exploits to be armed combat and, thus, rarely practiced unarmed techniques. However, many folk styles of unarmed fighting arts developed around parts of China differentiated not only by technique, but also by style. In the later Ming period (1368–1644 CE), forty-two different styles were recognized around the country. Most Chinese martial arts were named after animals, such as crane or tiger style, or marked by geographical differences between northern and southern China. It is hard to pin down the exact origin of these arts, outside of cultural narratives, because of the dearth of written records and the blending of styles.

The earliest indications of wrestling or boxing occurred during the Warring States Period, from 475 BCE to 221 BCE, although weightlifting was considered a much more important supplement for Chinese fighters. Strength training was of vital importance to a warrior using heavy weaponry, not only because it made it easier to don armor and heft a sword, but also because his strikes would be stronger and, thus, more deadly. Weightlifting and wrestling were considered functional military supplements, but striking empty hand was not as highly practiced at the time because warriors wore a great deal of heavy armor that no punch or kick could sufficiently penetrate or damage. In addition, the weight of the armor made it difficult for warriors to practice hand-to-hand combat, so most fight training focused on the techniques necessary for battle and the ability to move while wearing exceedingly heavy armor, rather than techniques used in a sport context.

However, Chinese martial arts did have a place apart from the battlefield. In the Han Dynasty, 206 BCE to 220 CE, swordsmanship and wrestling both became performative sports that were part of highly popular celebrations. Fighting as entertainment, outside and away from the battlefield, proliferated in the Han Dynasty, where demonstrations of Chinese dancing, music, archery, feats of strength, and displays of fighting skills were used to showcase the supremacy of the emperor's kingdom. Wrestling matches were particularly popular in the Han Dynasty, although it appears that they were practiced most widely by foreigners, brought to the royal court to entertain the aristocracy as well as the masses.

This survey of ancient martial arts, while not inclusive of every society or community on Earth, does demonstrate how fighting sports developed from the necessities of the battlefield to the entertainment of both the elite and the masses. In the twenty-first century, we benefit from the innovation of writing, which allowed some ancient peoples to document their practices, aiding in our own study of the ancient world. But we must not let ourselves forget that the vast world had many other means of recalling and sharing information. In the next chapter, we will see how world politics shaped the development of fighting sports, from war games designed to train soldiers, to defensive tactics used to combat foreign invaders, to theatrical fighting used to entertain royalty.

# 2

# PUTTING THE 'MARTIAL' IN MARTIAL ARTS

The Japanese emperor Suinin sat enthroned in his imperial palace in 23 BCE, eager for the fight to commence. Suinin had been annoyed, and he did not like being annoyed. One of his subjects, Taima no Kehaya, recently had bragged that he was the strongest man on Earth, and Suinin wanted to see the braggart put to shame. So, the emperor called on Nomi no Sukune, a potter and famed wrestler, to challenge Kehaya to a wrestling match. The men met in the emperor's palace, and as the great man, Japan's god on Earth, sat watching, the two commenced fighting. After wrestling Kehaya to the ground, Sukune kicked him in the ribs and back repeatedly, killing him in a brutal fashion sure to satisfy the emperor. This fight was an amalgam of wrestling and kicking, making it one of the earliest iterations of mixed martial arts in Asia. It also demonstrates the necessity for royalty to have a ready-made fighting force that could protect his lands and exact retribution for anyone who dared to annoy a great emperor.

In the post-classical era and the early modern period, from about 200 CE to 1400 CE, civilizations around the world became more connected through travel and trade, and empires began to consolidate through conquests attained by war or by religion. Soldiers certainly were trained to fight, but the purpose of that training was to improve their odds of survival. The art of fighting, which, in turn, could be applied to the combat in war, was not terribly important if the supply of peasants to conscript for battle was almost endless. Sports, including fighting sports such as boxing and wrestling, certainly never disappeared from practice, but competition, especially large-scale events such as the Olympics, were a frivolous part of the pagan, ostentatious past during the post-Roman Empire eras.

This chapter traces that evolution, from the dearth of fighting sports in the Byzantine Empire to the popularity of the masters of defense in Europe in the Renaissance. As the large-scale wrestling programs of ancient Persia and Greece gave way to modern military training, certain parts of the world no longer saw fighting as sport—only fighting as conquest. In other parts of the world, however, sport remained a fundamental part of the human experience. This chapter examines the fighting sports of many African communities prior to European invasion and the horrors of slavery that disrupted cultural traditions. Finally, we will look at many of the folk styles of wrestling and striking from around the world, including wrestling in Europe, the striking arts of the Angkor empire, and fighting in the Amazon.

## THE ROMAN EMPIRE

The Middle Ages in Europe often are described as dark times marked by a dearth of philosophy, of learning, of general culture. Thus, the Renaissance, a renewal of all of those things, was celebrated and continues to be celebrated today as Europe's rise out of the dark ages. And the Middle Ages, indeed, were rather crude times, in which illness ran rampant, illiteracy was common, and the church, as the arbiter of Europe's entire social structure, eradicated the pursuit of art for art's sake as extravagance. The Crusades, an atrocity fueled by religiosity and xenophobia, may be in their own way the apotheosis of the Middle Ages. Yet in this time of dank living spaces, poor hygiene, forced religiosity, and baleful delight in the macabre, some European martial artists developed the first formalized schools for fight training. These masters of defense were elite swordsmen with a passion for improving martial arts pedagogy and standardizing combat training.

But why did martial arts proliferate in the medieval and early Renaissance period in Europe after being seemingly forgotten in the ensuing eight hundred years after Rome fell?

The phrase "fall of Rome" technically is a misnomer, because only the western half of the empire collapsed in 476 CE. Innumerable reasons explain the decline and subsequent end of the western portion of the Roman Empire, ranging from invasions by the Visigoths from the north, to economic hardship, to natural disasters, to the hubris of overreaching territorial conquests. As the West weakened, the eastern portion of the empire grew stronger; and when the collapse of the West finally occurred, the East continued, operating as the new iteration of the Roman Empire. Now referred to as the Byzantine era, the Eastern Roman Empire remained a dominant force in Europe and Asia Minor for the next thousand years. As an extension of the Byzantine reign, many Roman and Greek traditions were upheld by the citizenry, although the primary religion went from the polytheistic pantheon of Roman gods to the singular Christian god.

Most historians believe that after the fall of Rome in the fifth century, Europe devolved into a nearly constant state of battle as the Teutonic tribes invaded and fought throughout various parts of Europe and as many of the Christian nations engaged in warfare with the Islamic nations in the Middle East. Europe certainly was fighting in the post-Roman Empire eras, but the art of fighting and the application of fighting methodology, practiced as sport, gave way to constant battles on the front lines. No time remained for sports such as boxing, wrestling, and even stick fighting when one constantly was conscripted into war. In addition to the need for men to act as soldiers rather than athletes, ideology shifted as the Roman Empire and its culture of violence and excess became subsumed by the sedate, yet militaristic, Byzantine Empire.

Emperor Constantine, the first major world leader to convert to Christianity, not only ended the persecution of Christians in the Roman Empire, but he founded, in essence, the Byzantine Empire in 330 CE as the "new Rome." Byzantium consisted of the East Roman Empire, spanning, with changing borders of its thousand-year existence, through most of Asia Minor, Greece, Italy, and the Mediterranean. When the Western Roman Empire fell in the fifth century, the eastern portion continued as the Byzantine Empire for another thousand years. Byzantium was a Christian state, and the art and architecture reflect that influence. Christianity impacted the political, social, and cultural climate of the Byzantine Empire tremendously, and in the beginning, as

Rome fell and the new Byzantium held on for power, pagans and their lifestyles became a scapegoat for the decline of the Roman Empire. Alexander the Great previously had expanded the Macedonian empire far into Europe, but when the Roman Empire tumbled, many of the European tribes thrived.

When not faced with the tremendous numbers that substantiated the Roman war machine, Germanic and Celtic tribes began their own campaign to colonize other tribes and peoples. Most European tribes warred constantly, so expertise in weaponry was imperative for survival. Both longbows and crossbows were common, as were broadswords and short swords. Heavy weapons, such as hammers, axes, and maces, were used to smash through armor; spears were used to take down horses and warriors; and short daggers were used in close contact to pierce vulnerable spots in a knight's armor.

Unarmed combat was practiced regularly, for close-quarter battles often meant fighting to disarm an opponent or dealing with being unarmed oneself. Although punching someone wearing full knight's armor might not seem particularly effective, that blow could help create a space to slip in a dagger. The utility of striking, however, was not nearly as useful as wrestling, which always could be useful in a struggle. Although this book is not a history of armed combat, in this era, it is hard to separate the history of sport without referencing weapons-based training. In the medieval period in Europe, fighting schools emerged, led by self-described "masters of defense," who taught their pupils the intricacies of swordsmanship, as well as wrestling and boxing maneuvers. In the lead-up to the cultural Renaissance that would erupt in Europe, the Middle Ages heralded the forthcoming era with highly organized and carefully crafted martial arts schools that harkened back to the days of the ancient Greeks and looked forward to an era of enlightenment.

## THE BYZANTINE EMPIRE

A thousand years of Byzantine culture, religion, politics, and warfare cannot be condensed into a pithy statement or two, but the period marked an interesting turn in the historical trajectory of fighting sports. The ancient Greeks loved celebrating athleticism and prized the heavy events of boxing, wrestling, and pankration as a national symbol of strength and skill. Ancient Romans also enjoyed fighting sports and treated them more as a form of spectacle, as an opportunity to see violence as entertainment. The Greek heavy events also were part of Roman sport, but their favorite combat sport was the gladiator contests that took place in the Colosseum.

The Roman elite displayed some concern, though, that gladiator events were problematic. Although gladiator events were seen as a way of hardening the men who would make up Rome's infantry, they were barbaric, and the men at the forefront of Rome's philosophical human-ist movement found their depravity to be both sad and disheartening. Seneca, a philosopher in the first century of the modern era, wrote of visiting the Colosseum one day, wanting some mindless entertainment, and discovered instead men being thrown to lions and gladiators fight-ing to the death. But the worst part for Seneca was that the stadium was nearly empty, as if this form of spectacle were old news to the hardened Roman masses. "I came home more greedy, more cruel, and inhuman," Seneca confessed.[1]

In the coming years, more Greeks began to eschew Roman gladiator events, banning them outright in Athens and Corinth, although the heavy events of boxing, wrestling, and pankration remained. The strongest objections to gladiator events came from followers of the new-est, and fastest growing, religion in town—Christianity. Christians had good reason to despise the brutality of events featured in the Colos-seum, for early Christian adopters had been thrown to lions regularly and struck down by gladiators for following their new religion. In 404 CE, gladiator contests officially were banned, primarily because the powerful Roman Empire was in steep decline and in dire financial straits. The third century would see the final ancient Olympic Games, as interest waned and financial support disappeared in the shadow of the Roman Empire's failure and the rise of Byzantium as the new power.

The Byzantines, to be somewhat reductive, were not terribly keen on sporting events. Athleticism was important only for the benefit of generating mobile and skilled soldiers. In the eastern half of the Roman Empire, fighting was part of the culture, and it was a warring culture rather than a sporting one. But the rise of Byzantium did not entirely wipe out the pursuit of fighting sports. Pankration continued in parts of the Byzantine Empire in the first few centuries. The capital city, Constantinople, hosted athletic events; but by the time Christianity was firmly situated as the primary religious authority, fighting sports such as wrestling, boxing, and pankration, which were synonymous with paganism, were no longer tolerated in the new cultural climate. Not only were competitions prohibited, but the Byzantine Empire discouraged the practice and transmission of fighting sports because of their association with pagan traditions.

When Constantine the Great ruled the Roman Empire very early in the fourth century, he decreed acceptance for those of the new Christian faith, to the ultimate destruction of pre-Christian Roman traditions. In 393 CE, Emperor Theodosius I eradicated all pagan festivals in the empire. Although the Theodosian code never explicitly discussed fighting arts, it did seek to eliminate all traces of paganism, which primarily would focus on the festivals and general gatherings associated with the sporting events of the ancient world. Thus, boxing, wrestling, pankration, and gladiator fighting no longer operated as large-scale entertainment; and, as a consequence, the systemic practice of training in fighting sports diminished. The only sport that the Byzantines truly embraced was chariot racing, which continued through the late Middle Ages.

In the ensuing years, Augustine of Hippo, now known as Saint Augustine, began pronouncing the new ideologies and moralities that would rule the Roman Empire. Saint Augustine decried paganism and pointed to the horrors of gladiatorial combat in the Colosseum as the embodiment of paganistic excess. So, with the growth of religiosity and the embargo on traditions of the past, by the fifth century fighting as sport nearly disappeared in Europe and Asia Minor. Byzantium, while subsumed with war and religious conflict, no longer considered fighting to be sport or entertainment. Byzantium rose from the Greek and Roman traditions, but unlike its predecessors, who happily engaged in both war and sport, the Byzantines dismissed sport as frivolity and, instead, concentrated all of their athletic prowess on creating a strong fighting army. They had no time, no energy, and no tolerance for petty games when they had holy wars to fight.

The Byzantine approach to warfare, which would remain nearly unchanged for a thousand years, prioritized minimizing human loss and maintaining the borders of the empire against invading armies. The

Byzantine military strategy operated in units, called themes, of approximately ninety-six hundred men and included cavalry and infantry that were mobile and ready for battle. Generals were not averse to retreating if it meant minimizing loss of life, especially because troops stationed in local towns and villages could swiftly come to their aid. This system organized Byzantium's military force around the functionality of the group and the efficacy of the theme, rather than any heroic ideology that may have propelled soldiers under the former Roman Empire. Perhaps it was due to the religiosity of the Byzantines, who fought for the glory of God rather than any vainglorious conceits.

The Byzantine Empire perfected the institution of the military, maintaining a standing army of 150,000 men for more than four centuries. Emperors emphasized the training and the general health of its army, providing medical service not only to those wounded in battle, but also to men who became ill. Illness was rampant in the close quarters of ancient and medieval militaries. Army camps did not just include the military; civilians followed the military to provide services and/or conduct business, and nowhere was that transaction more prominent than in the attachment of prostitutes. Through prostitution, communicable diseases, such as syphilis, spread through the military. Later, when plagues swept across Europe, the armies of many nations would be hit particularly hard due to the close proximity of large populations of men.

Plagues, of course, did not impact only the military. The infamous Plague of Justinian devastated Byzantium in 541 CE, killing an estimated twenty-five million people in its initial outbreak. The Byzantine military could not combat this disease, but the institution of specific military medical care did help ameliorate the effects of many communicable diseases and elevated the care of soldiers, instilling an ethical prerogative for the empire to value its soldiers as men and not just fodder.

The Byzantine Empire shifted in power and in the amount of land it controlled over its thousand-year reign. In the late ninth century, the Macedonian empire established its place as head of Byzantium; and under its control, the Byzantine Empire flourished, sparking a revival in arts and culture as well as expanding the empire's territories. Interestingly, this revival included an apparent reintroduction of competitive fighting sports. Basil I, the first Macedonian ruler of the Byzantine

Empire, reportedly won the respect of Emperor Michael III when, as a young man, he competed in a wrestling match against a Bulgarian challenger. Basil was from humble origins, and after making his way to Constantinople for an opportunity to better his circumstances, he found himself working as stable master for one of the emperor's courtiers. When Byzantium needed a champion to fight the Bulgarian wrestler, Basil was brought to the palace and, to the delight of Emperor Michael and the rest of the empire, he easily defeated the Bulgarian fighter. Basil eventually would become emperor of Byzantium, murdering the very man who admired his wrestling prowess in 867 CE. Despite his ruthless accession to power, his reign marked the beginning of the Macedonian period in the Byzantine Empire and the cultural and political renaissance that followed.

The cultural renaissance included a turn toward pedagogy in the art of war. The Byzantines created a system of cavalry fighting that, while not negating the necessity of foot soldiers, focused on the efficacy of fighting on horseback. Emperor Leo VI, who ruled the Byzantine Empire from 886 to 912 CE, produced the seminal text, *Tactica*, which outlined the most proficient way to deal with a multitude of specific enemies in battle. *Tactica* advocated for soldiers to use sticks to practice swordsmanship and longer poles for the spear, and suggested war games where teams would practice fighting each other. This text, written (in full or in part) by the Byzantine emperor, was a precursor to the flood of martial arts texts that would be produced in the Middle Ages.

The Byzantine Empire also eventually would fall, and in the last few centuries preceding its end in 1453 CE, military stratagem shifted, as it often does, back to the prowess of the individual. The focus on the individual soldier may have been an amalgam of ancient Rome's pugilistic past and the efficacious militaristic strategies of the glory days of the Byzantine military. The Byzantine Empire demonstrated the cultural prerogative of valuing efficiency and skill in the pursuit of military might. Soldiers no longer were fodder for opposing armies; instead, they were valued as a skilled unit. In the nearly eight hundred years following the fall of the Western Roman Empire, fighting had focused on the military and the necessity of group fighting rather than on the individual's pursuit of skill. But in the Middle Ages, as disease and filth ran rampant, fighting literature moved away from the large military treatises and focused, instead, on the individual's attainment of fighting mastery.

## EUROPE

One particular by-product of the competent and puissant Byzantine era was the formation of guilds, composed of skilled swordsmen, that created clear guidelines to what constituted an expert fighter in the Middle Ages. These medieval guilds functioned as small-scale versions of the Byzantium theme, yet instead of being charged with protecting a specific military border, these men, known henceforth as masters of defense, created a system of close-quarter fighting, using weapons and empty-hand approaches. Their goal was to inject rigor into the transmission of fighting arts and to establish an accredited group of martial arts instructors—no charlatans accepted.

Nearly every country in Europe, including Greece, Spain, Turkey, Germany, Scandinavia, the British Isles, Russia, and the Baltics, had masters of defense, fighting experts who worked to proliferate an integrated approach to fighting that included both armed and unarmed types of martial arts. Not only were these guilds organized and professional, but the masters wrote combat manuals that continue to be studied today. At a time when most writing was liturgical in nature, masters of defense across Europe, such as Byzantine emperor Leo VI before them, produced fighting manuals and dedicated their time to developing their combative skill.

In the thousand years after the Western Roman Empire collapsed, fighting as sport nearly disappeared as war became the only prerogative to fight. It is a fascinating stretch often glossed over in fighting scholarship that skips from the Roman Colosseum to seventeenth-century English pugilism. Fighting sports did not truly disappear as much as they were put on the back burner, waiting for the luxury of free time when individuals could afford to fight for sport rather than fight for their very lives. The Byzantine Empire may have put an end to the Greek and Roman traditions of fighting for sport, yet it also inculcated a culture of precision and pedagogy that eventually would translate into an explosion of elite fighting scholars. It would not be until the thirteenth century that the masters of defense would emerge, across multiple European nations, and create a codified fighting system centering not on the military and the army but rather on the individual and his pursuit of excellence.

## Italy

The fall of the Roman Empire did not mean the death of martial arts in Italy. Romans were adept at blade fighting, and, in fact, many of the medieval masters used the Roman knife-fighting traditions in their own systems. In the Middle Ages, every man, especially those who had obligations as part of the feudal system, would be required to be proficient at fighting. Those skills were taught on a local level, handed down from generation to generation, and practiced as part of a community, tribe, farm, or family.

Between the thirteenth and seventeenth centuries, fighting changed drastically in Italy and the rest of Europe due to a number of factors. The expanding use of firearms in warfare negated the need for the military to rely on the more antiquated fighting styles of medieval and ancient armies. This does not mean that battles in the Renaissance era were fought solely using guns, but rather that firearms and cannons changed the range of fighting in the sixteenth century. Across Europe, the demand for a scientific and scholarly approach to fighting increased, and in lieu of specific military training, expert swordsmen, referred to as masters of defense, provided martial arts training to gentlemen and military officers. These masters of defense were martial arts instructors of the highest pedigree, and their fighting tactics represented a cultural shift in the countries in which they lived. In Italy, masters of defense wrote expansive manuals on their fighting techniques, operated fencing schools that included conditioning and sparring, and created a style that would be studied by other fighting art enthusiasts, although criticized by masters in other European countries, especially England.

As the dark Middle Ages came to an end and the Renaissance loomed on the cultural horizon, the study of swordsmanship became a gentlemanly pursuit rather than a military one. Masters of defense taught tactics that were more likely to be used in fights between two individuals than in an engagement between armies on the battlefield. In the 1400s, the demand for formal fight training exploded, and Milan, Venice, Verona, and Bologna all had schools where masters of defense taught. Under the masters' tutelage, combat methodologies became more sophisticated and streamlined, due in part to technological advances in combat weaponry and armament, as well as the proliferation of firearms and an increasingly armed and educated middle class. Using new materials and construction, swordsmiths produced weapons lighter than their medieval predecessors, so the rapier became the primary sword type that the masters of defense used. Because of its light weight and exceedingly thin body, the rapier moved sword fighting from large, broad strokes to the finer, more accurate thrusting approach. A precise hand was needed to land a thrust correctly.

Fighting manuals that masters of defense produced exploded from the 1200s to the 1600s, first by hand and later by the printing press. Interestingly, the popularity of training with a master of defense initiated a debate that continues in online forums and on YouTube today. In the late sixteenth and seventeenth centuries, and continuing on for many years, arguments raged as to whether one could truly learn the intricacies of fighting through the written word. Ideally, of course, a student would dedicate himself to a master of defense, but not all those interested in fighting arts had access to such a teacher.

Masters were unanimous that students should learn in person, but a demand for texts that detailed specific techniques, formations, and theories that one could study and implement in practice remained. This demand, coupled with the renaissance in learning that coincided with the advent of the printing press, required that masters of defense be able not only to teach students in person, but also be able clearly to articulate their expertise in writing. This new requirement of martial arts instructions via belles-lettres, called *la communicative*, recalling the Socratic methodology. Masters of defense sometimes would write their treatises as if they were an actual training session, providing a dialogue where the pupil would ask questions of the teacher. Nearly every master experimented with the art of explication in his own written work, although the most effective approach seems to be the universal clarity of diagrams and drawings rather than text alone.

The fascination with the varied techniques of swordsmen across Europe meant that masters of defense would publish their combat manuals in their own language, as well as provide for translation of their text into other languages. English practitioners were especially invested in learning the "foreign" fighting methods, so masters from Italy, Spain, and Germany had their treatises translated, often rather poorly, into English. Although the English studied foreign fighting manuals, they did not always agree with their approaches. But this act of translation was prescient, as martial arts became increasingly translated (and transformed) through globalization.

Although nearly every European country had its own coterie of experts, the Italian and Spanish masters were in vogue among trendy and young middle- and upper-class men, especially in England. In Shakespeare's *Romeo and Juliet*, first published in 1597, Juliet's cousin, Tybalt, is described as adept in the new Italian style of fighting. Shakespeare picks up on this difference between the English and Italian approach, as Mercutio describes Tybalt's fighting style to Romeo's cousin, Benvolio:

> He fights as you sing prick-song: keeps time, distance, and proportion. He rests his minim rests, one, two, and the third in your bosom. The very butcher of a silk button. A duelist, a duelist. A gentleman of the very first house, of the first and second cause. Ah, the immortal passado! the punto reverse! the hay! (II.iv.19–23)

In this exchange, Mercutio pokes fun at Tybalt's Italian training by quoting an English master of defense, George Silver, who in his treatise on swordsmanship criticized the Italian style. To Shakespeare's audience, Tybalt's Italian swordsmanship reveals the Capulet's otherness, whereas the Montagues, even though technically Italian characters themselves, are aligned with the solid (if stolid) combative style of the English.

The English had their own cohort of masters of defense who, not surprisingly, were not enthralled with the Italian combat craft. But many of the Italian masters are remembered today as the arbiters of scholarship in the quest for fighting prowess. The Iberian Kingdom, which is now modern-day Spain and Portugal, had a robust military training protocol that included boxing and wrestling, in addition to practicing gymnastics for calisthenics and running. Catholic Iberia warred constantly with the Germanic Visigoths, and eventually it was invaded and controlled by Muslims in 790 CE. Nearly seven hundred years later, the Iberian Peninsula again was under Catholic control and one of its most famous sons, Pietro Monte, would revitalize Iberian wrestling and change the face of martial arts across Europe.

Pietro Monte (sometimes spelled Monti) was a fifteenth-century swordsman and master at arms who taught fighting arts to gentry across Italy and Spain. Monte wrote numerous texts on martial arts and general military strategy, as well as treatises on the benefits of exercise. Leonardo da Vinci, while considering the trajectory of javelins thrown from a sling, wrote a note to himself to ask "Pietro Monti" for his thoughts.[2] In addition to being a friend of Leonardo da Vinci, Monte instructed Galeazzo da Sanseverino in wrestling. Sanseverino, a member of Milan's famous Sforza family that ruled during the Renaissance in Italy, was praised for his athleticism and skill in handling a number of weapons, all taught to him by Monte.

Monte himself came from a long line of Italian fighting masters, many of whom were scholars outside of the fighting world. Master Filippo di Bartolomeo Dardi operated a fencing school in Bologna, Italy, where he was a professor of mathematics and astrology at Bologna University in the early fifteenth century. Bologna was also home to Fiore dei Liberi, master of the long sword and author of the 1410 illustrated combat manual called *Flos Duellatorum*, which in Latin means "Flower of Battle." Dardi originally studied martial arts under the German masters, but in his nearly fifty years as an experienced swordsman, he created his own approach to the long sword that would become synonymous with the Italian school of fighting.

Fiore's *Flos Duellatorum* contained strategy for fighting in a number of different configurations with assorted weapons, including knife fighting, knife-versus-empty-hand strategy, spear-and-staff systems, two-handed sword techniques for knights, and empty-hand combat. Fiore discusses two different approaches to wrestling, that for recreation or sport, and wrestling that should be used in "anger," when one's life was truly at stake. In the case of the latter, he instructed readers on the intricacies of locks (*ligadure*) to subdue an opponent or breaks (*roture*) to destroy an arm or leg.

Fiore's wrestling instruction, which includes his methods for unarmed defense against an opponent with a knife, is thorough and brutal. His techniques are not just wrestling, but more what we would refer to in the modern vernacular as self-defense. His treatise includes neck breaks, groin shots, and driving one's palm into an enemy's nose and then immediately clawing his eyes. All of his techniques also include a counter, and a counter to the counter. *Flos Duellatorum* was one of the only Italian texts of the period to include unarmed combat techniques. The English and Germans both produced many more manuals on unarmed combat, yet it is the Italian Pietro Monte who is remembered as one of the most famous masters of defense of the period, and one of the few who taught a holistic approach to martial arts training.

Monte believed that wrestling was the foundation of all martial arts, and because all weapon systems that he taught included techniques to disarm an opponent, he felt that his practitioners should understand the basics of wrestling so that if they were unarmed, they could still defend themselves. Monte's most interesting text, *Exercitiorum Atque Artis Militaris Collectanea*, or "Collected Martial Arts and Exercises," also known as *Collectanea*, is particularly useful to fight historians because it includes his writing on fitness as well as martial arts techniques. A product of his time, Monte promoted general health using the humor theory of the Middle Ages to articulate his approach. The four humors were elements that made up the body—phlegmatic, choleric, melancholy, and sanguine—and dealt with different aspects of the human condition. He argued that not only should one's humors be in balance for health, but that a skilled fighter would particularly need to be balanced in order to avoid making mistakes by being too aggressive, impetuous, or passive. Monte's approach, which epitomized the Italian style, emphasized light footwork, requiring that fighters be lean and supple rather than large and muscular. Perhaps this is what disgusted the English masters, that a man essentially should be small rather than brawny.

Not all Italians were built this way, nor did all Italians necessarily revel in the delicacy of rapier fighting. Emperor Maximilian I, who ruled the Holy Roman Empire from 1493 to 1519 CE, is depicted in his autobiography as participating in what appears to be a kicking contest in which his Holiness eschewed rules or decorum by stomping on his opponent's calves, kicking him in the knee, standing on his feet, and punching one man in the face. Interestingly, the emperor's aggressive style was more akin to the fighting modes of the masses rather than the elite.

By the mid-sixteenth century, the Italian cities of Venice and Pisa, as well as some smaller hamlets, became renowned across Europe for their violent mass fighting events, known as *battagliola*. These "war games" were designed to be both practice for battle and a cathartic experience for the lower classes to blow off steam. The first and most popular version of the Italian *battagliole* consisted of mass stick fights, known as the *guerre di canne*, which took place between two large factions who would fight for the conquest of a bridge. The battagliole was, at times, an orchestrated brawl involving city magistrates and aristocrats designed to entertain visiting men of note, including England's King Henry VIII, who disdained the fights as not quite war but too bloody for sport. The other, more frequent iteration of the battagliole was spontaneous, where men would gather at the bridge, sticks in hand, and fight, with no rules or regulations, or even, to some spectators, a purpose.

The games easily could turn deadly if fighters morphed their sticks into spears, which they did by sharpening the ends and soaking them in boiling water to harden. To ward off the fatal blows, the men would don an assortment of body armor that consisted of antiquated suits of iron, handmade leather torso covers, or odd pieces of chain mail. Protected by shoddy armor, wielding sticks, and fighting for what seemingly was an unknown purpose, the battagliole appears to have been a pastime to medieval Italians in various cities, a social cathexis that, although popular, eventually became too violent (and perhaps pointless) for city administrators. By the end of the sixteenth century, the *guerre di canne* was banned (although it still continued in underground brawls), only to be replaced with the *guerre di pugni*, mass boxing matches.

The guerre di pugni had more in common with Pietro Monte and other Italian masters of defense than it did with its weaponized cousin, the guerre di canne. The pugni fighters, although unarmed, were faster and more precise. In some battagliole, pugni, and canne, fighters would end up facing each other, whether by design or by disarmament. The pugni reportedly were able to overcome the canne fighters most of the time because they were not encumbered with heavy weapons or body armor. The Venetian pugilists in particular were said to be skilled in throwing straight jabs and crosses, which apparently baffled fighters untrained in empty-hand fighting. Swinging roundly, the untrained boxers quickly were put down by the Venetian pugni. Even soldiers who joined in the battagliole and were adroit in handling swords and spears, though not at empty-hand combat, were at a loss when faced with the accuracy of a well-practiced Italian boxer. The best of the guerre di pugni were, in their own way, the everyman version of a master of defense.

Fighting in medieval and Renaissance Italy was as striated, it seems, as social class in general. The middle and upper echelons sought the chic, perhaps foppish approach to combat that the masters of defense taught, while the lower classes fought in the streets and sometimes, en masse in battagliole, with sticks and fists. Both groups, perhaps, were training for the version of fighting that they most likely would encounter in their lifetime. The middle and upper classes prepared for single-opponent combat and the exactitude required of fighting a gentleman's duel. Working-class men, meanwhile, lived in congested areas and were exposed to riots and brawls, as well as the likelihood, if conscripted, of serving as part of the infantry in Italy's frequent wars. Regardless of social standing, Italian men seemed to have revered fighting, as a science or a scrap.

The Italian Renaissance not only brought about a rebirth of art, music, and culture, but also a renewed interest in the science of fighting. The masters of defense are remembered today as the scholars of the period, sharing their knowledge with students who had the time and money to pay for combat education. But even the poorer men of Italy experimented with combat methods, testing their fighting techniques in the laboratory of the street fight rather than the controlled sparring of a fencing school. And in their own way, all seemed to have come to the same conclusion: that proficiency can triumph over strength, brains can beat brawn, and unarmed styles such as wrestling and boxing are necessary skills for any fighter, regardless of social standing.

## Germany

When one thinks of swordsmanship, one typically thinks of the Japanese warrior, wielding a katana, or perhaps a Celtic warrior swinging a broadsword. And empty-hand fighting largely is attributed to British boxers or Cornish wrestlers. But in the Middle Ages, Germany surpassed itself as the European epicenter of knowledge in the martial arts. More than any other nation, Germanic martial artists wrote prodigiously on the subject of fighting arts, producing fencing manuals and other seminal texts that defined the German style of defense. As Europe slowly emerged from the dark, oppressive cocoon of the medieval period, a renewed interest in science and reason sparked a revival, be it very small initially, in learning. This metamorphosis eventually would lead to the first codified fighting system in Europe. Although the German military would remain in disorder until Frederick the Great took the helm in the mid-1700s, the German masters of defense cultivated a system of learning, and of language, that all Europeans could celebrate as the new scholarship of fighting.

In ancient times, Germanic tribes passed down fighting styles by having their most experienced warrior teach the youth. Tribal communities lived in sects, and the familial aspect of that culture made learning martial arts a social function, learned within the confines of the group. Training was based on the tribe's young men, and sometimes women, learning under the tutelage of the best warrior. Martial arts were taught in person. No written accounts record how that training progressed, although we have some documentation from the ancient Romans about the efficacy of Germanic warfare.

Generations of this type of pedagogy by proximity forged a strong fighting culture, which continued even as political and military action altered the borders of the European landscape. In the Middle Ages, what previously had been the purview of individual warriors teaching random flocks of young men who might eventually become soldiers changed when Germanic fighting experts began to produce manuals describing their system of fighting arts. Although by the Middle Ages the technology of writing certainly was not new to Germanic peoples, the subjects they penned moved beyond religious and political dictates. By the thirteenth century, German masters of defense began drafting some of the first martial arts textbooks in Europe.

Of all of the European masters of defense from the Middle Ages through the Renaissance, the German masters were the most prolific writers of fighting arts from the mid-fourteenth century to the early sixteenth century. Germany also was home to many fighting schools, called *fechtschulen*, where individuals could go to learn under the great masters and exercise—an early version of the German *turnverein* (gymnasium). Fighting schools were organized and operated by guilds such as the *Marxbruder*, the Brotherhood of Saint Mark. Guilds were populated by soldiers and regular citizens and specialized in particular weapons, such as the two-handed sword or the short knife.

Fencing schools were not always considered socially acceptable in Germany. A 1464 CE engraving depicts a German fencing school and fitness center alongside a brothel cum bathhouse, indicating that to participate in martial arts training was to be involved in an activity comparable in morality to prostitution. Germans in the Middle Ages may have enjoyed, or at least tolerated, fencing guilds, but they did not tolerate fools or pretenders to teach fighting arts. The Germans had no patience for charlatans, creating a clear lexical distinction between actual masters and those who performed fighting as part of theater, the *leichmeistrere* (a snide reference to a dance master) and the *klopffechter*, which translates to clown fighter.

Interestingly, it is language and the creation of a fighting lexicon that makes the German masters of defense such a fascinating study for fighting historians. The German masters created a specific nomenclature for every move, and in fact, even named every opportunity in which one could attack. The *nachraissen*, attacking after, indicates the Germanic version of counterpunching in which a swordsman would invite an opponent to attack in order to follow with a specific counter. The most famous of the German masters, Johannes Lichtenauer, referred to these types of returns or after attacks as the *meisterhau*, the master's cuts, and they became a central tenet of his style and that of the numerous masters who followed in his footsteps and expanded his work.

Johannes Liechtenauer, known usually as Hans, was the father of Germanic martial arts, the *fechtmeister* or fighting master of his time in the 1250s. In 1389, Hanko Döbringer, a priest who studied under Liechtenauer, compiled his master's work into a fencing manual, known as a *fechterbuecher* (fight book). Keeping with the fashion of the time, Döbringer wrote the entire treatise in rhyming couplets. The work was translated in the twentieth century, and it provides insight into the German fighting art philosophy, which is, in essence, effective and to the point, without any unnecessary movements. Although masters of defense in other countries may have practiced or even taught fighting suffused with style, the German master taught fighting without flourish. In the very beginning, Döbringer instructs that one should "strike or thrust in the shortest and nearest way possible" without any "wide or ungainly parries."[3]

Liechtenauer's student and amanuensis, Hanko Döbringer, produced the text that, in 1389 CE, would remain the foundation for German weapons fighting for the next three hundred years. He also instilled the notion of naming each particular movement with a specific name rather than trying to describe a technique by what it does. Although it may seem like it would be terribly confusing, it was easier, once conversant in Liechtenauer and other German masters' lexicon, to understand instructions using specific names such as *Zwerchhau*, which meant side cut, rather than to read "side cut" in conjunction with other instructions on footwork or movement.

As mentioned previously, one problem that plagued all instructors was transmitting information via the written word, known as *la communicative*. Ideally, one should train martial arts under the direct tutelage of a legitimate master of defense, but if no instructor could be found nearby, or if one wanted to study the works of a master in another land, written treatises were available for the avid pupil willing to learn via text. The precise articulation of fighting techniques irked many medieval and Renaissance era masters, but those who tackled the problem of enunciating their movements often employed artists or engravers to provide images to accompany their words, which helped in some cases. Not every manual proved to be a reliable or even effective source of martial arts material. Many of the German treatises required that the reader be aware of preexisting techniques and have knowledge of the clunky, if interesting, lexicon that some masters used. The expansion of Liechtenauer's methodologies culminated in an insanely dense, and no doubt heavy, text Paulus Hector Mair produced in the mid-1500s. His prodigious work was overshadowed by his own misdeeds when Mair was hanged for embezzlement in 1579 CE. But Mair's death did not diminish the enthusiasm for fighting texts.

Like Italian master Pietro Monte, German fencing masters regarded wrestling as foundational to all fighting arts, although Monte apparently disdained German wrestling because it practiced fighting on the ground. Monte believed that a fight was over once one person was thrown to the ground, and he did not see any reason to practice ground fighting as the Germans did. Regardless of Monte's sneers, the German masters provided some of the only empty-hand fighting treatises to be published in the Middle Ages. One manuscript, *Ringen im Grüblein* (Wrestling in the Little Pit), describes a wrestling sport that required one opponent to keep a foot in a small, shallow hole while his opponent, who had to hop on one foot, apparently as a way to even the playing field, attempted to force him out—literally wrestling in a pit. According to Fabian von Auerswald, medieval wrestling master, "it calls for great skill, and is enjoyable to watch."[4]

Von Auerswald produced his own manual in 1539 CE and described wrestling as a sport rather than an approach to combat. In describing one particular maneuver that sounds similar to an arm drag, he explained that it could produce a "terrible dislocation" that, although effective, was "something for rough folk and is not convivial."[5] Yet von Auerswald also offered readers a technique in which one grabs an opponent "between the cheeks of his arse," or wrenches the testicles.[6] Perhaps it was these techniques that, although not "convivial" by our standards, did allow von Auerswald, depicted in his text as a rather wrinkled old man, to best his younger opponent easily. Although wrestling at the time seemed to strive for sport, other masters included techniques that were more lethal combat maneuvers. Christian Egenolff's 1531 CE treatise, *Der altenn Fechter*, contains instructions for head butting, strangleholds, and a "back breaker."

The most famous wrestling treatise to emerge from the Renaissance was Nicolaes Petter and Romein de Hooghe's 1674 CE text, *The Academy of the Admirable Art of Wrestling*. This text offered "clear and homely instruction" on the ways in which a fighter, with his newfound knowledge of the human body provided by the text, can avoid any attack using wrestling.[7] Petter and Hooghe's methods, however, appear largely to be reiterations of the works of those masters who came before them, but it was the articulation, the very clear language, and wonderfully illustrated engravings, that made this book the apotheosis of German wrestling instruction.

Petter, a wine merchant and wrestling aficionado, reportedly died in 1672. His wife doggedly pushed to publish his text, and with the help of de Hooghe, an expert engraver, Petter's treatise was released just two years after his death. The techniques include a variation of holds and throws, including a particularly brutal maneuver that can be described only as a hair throw. Petter relied on letters for naming the participants in a certain technique. In this example, the first man, D, secures his grips by grabbing the hair of his opponent, E, in his fingers, then twisting his elbows inward so that they are parallel and inside of E's arms.

> Then D pulls E backwards by the hair, turning him around, placing his elbow on his spine, which allows him to strike E on the face from behind with his other hand.
>
> E being inconvenienced thus, still being held by the hair, D turns around so that D and E are back to back, D then places his behind

against the behind of E, and pulls him with great force, as a result of which E will fall over the head of D.[8]

In this somewhat convoluted maneuver, D ends up throwing E by his hair, yet E is not vanquished, despite this painful insult. According to the plates, E leaps up and "grasps D behind the sleeve or arm, and grasps with the right hand the right wrist of D, forcing this grasped arm of D inwards, and places his left foot on the back of the right knee of D, thus forcing him to fall."[9]

Petter's methodologies vacillate from their appropriateness for sport to deadlier techniques against knife-wielding opponents. One engraving shows the unarmed man stepping on his opponent's foot and simultaneously punching him in the face, apparently as a method of disarmament. He also provides techniques to break the hand holding a blade, a disarming method that makes the holder stab himself, as well as a maneuver that seems straight out of Hollywood where one kicks the knife out of the hand of the bumbling, would-be assassin. Many of Petter's tactics seem impossible to deploy, at least to one relatively experienced in the actuality of blade fighting, yet others seem perfectly probable. Whether or not Petter was the greatest master of defense in Germany, his tome provided martial arts enthusiasts, both in the seventeenth century and today, with wrestling tactics often ignored, disdained, or neglected in an age dedicated to rapier and sword fighting.

## Northern Europe

From the eighth to the eleventh century CE, the Vikings dominated Northern Europe and practiced wrestling in addition to weapon-based martial arts to prepare for battle. This wrestling style, known as *Glima*, primarily is a standing wrestling style in which one opponent tries to throw another to the ground. The first to hit the ground loses the match, reflecting the belief that in battle, a downed fighter is doomed. The origins of the sport are outlined in Icelandic epic literature and records from the medieval period. In Norse mythology, the god Thor wrestles an elderly woman, Elli, who represents old age. Although the woman appears infirm and frail, Thor cannot throw her to the ground and, indeed, ends up on one knee, at which point Loki, who is refereeing the match, declares Elli the winner. The fact that Thor loses the match when one knee touches the ground reveals that in this mythical text, the wrestling match ends when any body part other than the foot touches the ground. It also symbolizes the reality that no one, not even Thor, can avoid growing old. Despite Thor's loss to Elli, he was celebrated as the god of wrestling.


## England

After the fall of Rome, warring tribes battled over the area now known as Britain. In 1066 CE, after the Battle of Hastings, Britain became a formal nation, although families would continue to war for hundreds of years over who would rule her. In England, schools of defense in the early thirteenth century were not always as popular as they were in other parts of Europe. King Edward II banned fencing schools in 1286 CE in order to "prevent criminal mischief."[10] However, by the fifteenth century, defense schools popped up around London, and the English joined their European brethren in systematizing fighting arts. Elizabethan-era master of defense George Silver criticized other fencing schools for not including empty or "bare-hand" fighting, such as wrestling or "wrastlings," as he described it. Silver argued that "all-in fighting," the colloquialism for unarmed combat, was necessary for a well-rounded combative education. According to Silver, a true master of defense, his students should be able to fight, subdue, and even kill an enemy with his bare hands. Sir Thomas Elyot argued that wrestling was particularly useful for boys, although they should have someplace soft to train so that "in falling theyr bodies be nat brused."[11]

In the English countryside, festivals included wrestling matches featuring the champions of each village or neighborhood. In London, wrestling matches were typically sponsored by noblemen or guilds, who organized the match and provided the purse, which was usually a ram. Betting was a significant sideline part of English wrestling, so much so that street riots reportedly broke out in the aftermath of some matches in the thirteenth century.

England, Scotland, and Ireland exhibited many variations on wrestling, differentiated mainly by nuances and places of origin. The Scots practiced back-hold wrestling, a style where wrestlers each put their left arm over their opponent's right arm, and their right arm under the left arm, then clasp their own hands together in the back, typically in a gable grip. Fighters remain in this grip while trying to trip or throw each other to the ground. The first one to hit the ground with anything other than his feet would lose the match. Fighters traditionally wore kilts, so the throws were spectacular visually as kilt fabric flew in the air, typically known as "birling." Although it might seem fun for spectators to watch the kilts creating sails in the air, it apparently impeded the view of referees who had to decide whether one fighter landed on bottom first or both at the same time (known as a "dog fall"). Apparently, this distraction was so common that the phrase, "watch the wrestler, no' the kilt, Sonny!" became a somewhat standard refrain.

One of the most famous wrestling matches in history pitted two styles of European wrestling against each other. In 1520 CE, twenty-nine-year-old King Henry VIII of England challenged fellow monarch King Francis I of France to a wrestling match at the historic "Field of the Cloth of Gold" meeting. Although Francis was able to throw the older and larger Henry to win the match, the two were said to have left the meeting as friends, despite Henry's historic bad temper and the ever-present enmity between England and France.

Europe was run by three young men in 1520 CE: Henry VIII of England, Charles V of Spain, and Francis I of France. Two years earlier, Henry, Charles, Francis, and other princes of major European countries signed a peace treaty in which they agreed to join each other to battle the growing Ottoman-Turkish Empire and end fighting in the constantly warring European nations. In 1519 CE, nineteen-year-old Charles was elected Holy Roman emperor, and in an effort to maintain a balance of power in Europe, Henry (twenty-nine years old), and Francis (twenty-three) agreed to meet in a neutral location to pledge their friendship and brotherhood, as only young, ludicrously rich men knew how.

The illustrious meeting, organized by the ever-conniving Cardinal Wolsey, was to be a spectacle of epic proportions, celebrating the signing of the Treaty of Universal Peace two years prior. Charles lingered in the background, conferring with Wolsey, who assured the new Holy Roman emperor that the event was more a show of friendship than an alliance against Spain. Meanwhile, Henry and Francis worked to outdo each other, each demonstrating his own power, wealth, and virility.

The event nearly bankrupted the two countries, not surprising given that Henry commissioned a temporary palace built for him, ostenta-

tiously filled with the trappings of a royal Christian court. Golden stat-
ues of the saints stood next to a crucifix festooned with pearls. Henry,
still married to his first wife, Catherine of Aragon, ensured that his
quarters were suitable to his queen, with real glass in the windows and
fully outfitted kitchens to cook decadent feasts. Francis's quarters were
as luxurious as his fellow monarch's, with rich blue velvet walls embroi-
dered with France's gold fleur-de-lis.

At the heart of the Field of the Cloth of Gold was an attempt, by
both men, to simultaneously express their kingly kinship and to demonstrate more implicitly to the other the might of his fighting force. Ten
days of sporting events ensued, and knights competed for both country
and honor. Not to be eclipsed by their men, Francis and Henry also
participated in the games, culminating in the wrestling match that was
no mere kerfuffle, for it was not just a bout between two men, but
rather, a harbinger of hostility between England and France.

Henry was a huge man—in the sixteenth century, the average height
of European men was five feet four, and Henry stood a towering six feet
one. Although he often is portrayed as fleshy, even obese, by popular
culture, it was only near the end of his life that Henry became corpulent
and sickly. An avid athlete, Henry Tudor jousted and hunted, threw the
javelin, and excelled in archery. He was skilled at double-ax fighting and
played bowls. And Henry practiced, and apparently excelled, in a style
of wrestling indigenous to the Cornwall region of England, known as
Cornish wrestling. The practitioners wear short jackets, which their
opponents can grab, hold, and manipulate in an attempt to throw each
other to the ground, where the match ends. It includes no ground work,
only a series of highly dynamic flips, sweeps, wrenches, and trips to take
an opponent off his feet.

Francis, like Henry, was highly educated in a wide range of academ-
ic disciplines and showed particular skill in military strategy and combat. He hunted, played tennis, and wrestled in his country's style,
known as Breton wrestling. Breton wrestling (sometimes known as
Gouren) is similar in approach to Cornish wrestling; the primary difference between the two styles is how tight the jacket is worn. The Breton
wrestler wears a tight jacket, and the Cornish wrestler wears it loose.

The Field of the Cloth of Gold focused on the efforts of the French
and English knights as they sought to best each other in numerous
tournaments and contests. On the third day, Henry defeated Francis in

an archery contest, and by all accounts, Francis good-naturedly congratulated him. As the day (and the drinks) wore on, Henry challenged Francis to a wrestling match—a true hand-to-hand competition. Francis initially demurred, not wanting to risk his friendship with Henry, who was an egoist at best and a narcissist at worst. But Henry persuaded Francis, and the two men set out to a flat, grassy area for the match. Francis eventually managed to outmaneuver Henry and using a technique known as the Breton trip, the king of France tossed the king of England to the ground.

This infamous bout between the Cornish and Breton styles of wrestling is emblematic of many differences in wrestling approaches across Europe. Wales had two styles of wrestling, known as *cwdwm braich* and *cwdwm cefn*. Cwdm braich wrestlers grabbed each other's arms and tried to kick the feet out from under each other. In cwdwm cefn, fighters tried to grab each other around the waist; from descriptions, it sounds as if the goal was to achieve underhooks. Neither style remains much in use today, but their unique approach shows the Welsh community's desire not only to compete and play, but also to create two wrestling protocols in which to compete.

Despite many masters of defense, who argued the necessity of wrestling for all martial arts training, wrestling's reputation in Europe still was as a provincial fighting sport. Mostly practiced in rural areas, wrestling was the activity of farmworkers and day laborers, who, after a hard day in the fields, may unwind by attempting to throw each other to the ground. Boxing would not have been a viable option for many of these groups simply because they needed to be able to wake up and work the next day without dealing with the aftermath of a boxing match. Whereas wrestling and swordsmanship dominated the martial arts practice in the postclassical, early modern, and Renaissance eras, boxing would become the English obsession in the 1700s, just as the monarchs of Europe turned their attention away from their own kingdoms. But before the era of European imperialization, all over the world indigenous cultures had their own fighting traditions, some based on combat application and others focused solely on sport.

## THE OTTOMAN EMPIRE

The Ottoman Empire was one of the longest and wealthiest empires in history, from its founding in 1200 BCE to its collapse in 1922 CE. The Ottoman Empire comprised numerous places and spaces, which shifted through time as cities were conquered and other lands lost. The primary areas of the empire were from North Africa through Mesopotamia and included a large expansion when the empire aligned with Europe. The Ottoman Empire was a warring nation, primarily practicing martial arts for use in battle, focusing on archery over empty-hand fighting styles. However, the oiled wrestling style, often referred to as Turkish wrestling, became widely practiced in sporting and ceremonial settings. Fighters were covered in oil and wore leather pants, called *kisbet*, which allowed competitors something to grab because the rest of the body was greasy and difficult to control. Wrestlers typically represented a wealthy or politically connected patron, making the competition about much more than individual prowess. The winner of a wrestling match could bring honor to his patron, and a loss might heap criticism and abuse on his head. Ultimately, however, the Ottoman Empire prized victory on the battlefield over victory in sport.

## ASIA

### India

Wrestling and stick fighting linked the various tribes and communities in South Asia, from India, Bangladesh, Nepal, and modern-day Pakistan. Strength training played a particular role in Indian society, as men sought to demonstrate pure strength and health through physical appearance. Push-ups, squats, and clubs called *mugdal* contributed to strength training, as did the practice of wrestling and stick fighting. Sanskrit texts from the eighth century CE mention wrestling, and another twelfth-century text discusses how court wrestlers trained and ate for their athletic endeavors. Indian wrestling, sometimes known as *kushti* or *pehlwani*, is very similar in rules and approach to freestyle wrestling. Indian wrestlers tend to wear small shorts and sometimes compete in sand or dirt pits. One fascinating aspect of the history of

Indian wrestling is the emphasis on creating a well-rounded and appropriately fueled athlete, which seems obvious to our modern understanding of athletic training but was not standard at the time.

Historically, Indian wrestlers stuck to a stringent diet, focused on recovery and health, trained in the gymnasium, and performed rigorous strength-training exercises. In addition, fighters remained celibate while competing, focusing their entire energy on their training and competitions. Because India had a highly developed patronage system, wrestlers worked closely with their teachers to be at their personal best at competition time in order to better represent their royal benefactors. Southeast Asian martial arts also have a strong religious element, using the ancient Ayurvedic texts as a guide to training, nutrition, mind-set, and spirituality.

Medieval texts from the eighth century reveal the nutrition and training habits of wrestlers, but lack extensive detail on the actual techniques used in competition. Although modern-day Indian wrestlers typically eat a vegetarian diet, these medieval texts suggest eating meat, despite Brahmins' usual aversion to meat. In some places, the wrestlers would rub a mixture of dirt and ghee on their bodies and toss a handful on their opponents to make them easier to grab.

India also is home to an early form of mixed martial arts, called *vajra-mushti*, where fighters wore studded knuckle-dusters, typically made of ivory, on their right hand. Fighters could strike with elbows, knees, and punches, although all strikes were supposed to land on the chest or above. The goal, however, was to use takedowns or throws to wrestle an opponent to the ground, then submit them using joint locks. Fighters wore very small shorts and would shave their heads on the day of a match, leaving a small circular tuft on top of the head. The first written reference to *vajra-mushti* occurs in a twelfth-century *purana*, or ancient book, but it appears that matches took place long before the writing of that ancient text.

## Japan

Despite its small size, Japan's martial arts are vast and encompassing, partly because of the history of the samurai and the desire of modern Japanese teachers to keep their arts alive. Japan has numerous weapon-based systems, such as aikido and kendo, and the wrestling systems include different iterations of jujitsu and judo. Jujitsu was one of the eighteen martial arts that comprised the training and expertise of the samurai warrior. In their earliest iterations, Japanese fighting arts combined grappling and striking arts in order to target an enemy's weak points, but eventually the styles became distinct arts in themselves. Because jujitsu was practiced in order to prepare samurai for warfare, the art was designed to accommodate the heavy armor they donned for the battlefield. Punches and kicks, originally part of early jujitsu training, were made fruitless by samurai armor, so the emphasis was placed on grappling. The techniques were designed to finish off an enemy, either by throwing him on his head and breaking his neck, or pinning him to the ground and stabbing him. Throws and trips made use of gaps in the armor or places where one could better grab, so the art was truly martial rather than sport. Most of the training was practiced alone as a *kata*, or form, because the movements were deadly and difficult to practice without hurting fellow warriors. However, wrestling competitions in antiquity were designed to instill work ethic and promote the might of Japan's male citizenry.

In the seventh century, Japan's emperor held a wrestling tournament that brought together fighters from all over his kingdom. Once assembled, the wrestlers weree organized into groups and then practiced for a multiday, single-elimination tournament. The fighters sought to wrestle each other to the ground or throw each other from the ring, but little action followed once the wrestlers were on the ground. Watched by two referees, who stuck arrows into the ground to tally points, the fighters continued until one was declared victorious. When a wrestler won his bout, he returned the following day to fight until only two champions were left.

After the eighth century, wrestling tournaments died out in Japan as the shogun warlords saved all of their fighting for the battlefield. Nearly eight hundred years later in the sixteenth century, tournament fighting resumed with a much more formalized approach. The rules clearly defined which techniques were allowed, and the emperor authorized one particular family to act as official wrestling referees, an honor that was passed on throughout the generations.

## China

Like many ancient cultures, early Chinese sports were functional contests for normal and necessary practices. Archery, chariot racing, and wrestling competitions were analogous to the actuality of everyday life; sports were, in essence, the game version of daily activities. Although Asian martial arts have had a profound impact on international fighting sports today, we do not have as much information about their ancient practices as ancient Greek and Roman fighting sports, although the Chinese had a sophisticated writing style and even invented a printing press long before Gutenberg in 1440 CE.

In the first century, the *Han History Biographies* listed boxing and wrestling as military skills for "practice in using the hands and feet, facilitating the use of weapons, and organizing to ensure victory in both attack and defense."[12] In the early days of Chinese martial arts, the distinction between boxing and wrestling was not as clear. Early Chinese martial arts, called *bo*, which translates to striking, consisted of boxing methodologies as well as grappling techniques. Practiced primarily to develop the type of martial skills a warrior would need in a feudal state, bo prepared practitioners for hand-to-hand combat but apparently also could be implemented successfully against a weaponed fighter.

During the Han Dynasty (206 BCE to 220 CE), Buddhism was introduced in China, most likely by Indian practitioners who came to China via the Silk Road. The adaptation of Buddhism included not only the religious orthodoxies, but also the mind, spirit, and body connection. Chinese martial artists focused on the internal health and creating a balance between the four elements of earth, water, fire, and wind. As martial arts and the internal health of the mind and body became inextricably linked in Chinese martial arts, so did fighting become part of religious orthopraxy. Buddhist monks living in monasteries practiced, developed, and perfected their martial arts, in part to help support the new emperor of the Tang Dynasty (618–907 CE) and in part to find equilibrium between the mind, body, and environment. The monks of the Shaolin monastery focused on the external training of their bodies by hardening their bones and muscles through exercise and regulating their breathing, even during stressful training, while internal training sought to find mental stillness and vital energy.

In China and many other parts of the world, especially Europe, people considered "lowborn" could become educated if they joined a religious order. Chinese men who opted to become Buddhist monks studied literature, philosophy, mathematics, and martial arts. The monks of the famous Shaolin monastery assisted Emperor Li Shimin, founder of the Tang Dynasty, in securing his throne; thereafter, they were granted rights to own property and protect it using their highly effective martial arts.

The Shaolin monks were not the only practitioners of martial arts in China, and, indeed, much of Chinese martial arts are differentiated by the region in which they were developed. Traditional wisdom claims that those living in the wide expanse of northern China developed a style based on distance empty-hand fighting that included lots of kicks and acrobatic movements. Those living in the South, which was much more congested in the cities and in rice pastures, often worked in trades such as fishing, used more upper-body movements exemplified by close-quarter fist strikes and short-distance kicks. Although it may be reductive to organize the Chinese martial arts in this way, it is true that those living in the North would have had to wear heavier clothing during the cold months, which might have restricted the movements of their arms, while those in the South might have had to fight in close quarters, in cramped alleys, or on the deck of a boat.

In the Tang Dynasty, China formalized wrestling and boxing into separate activities, primarily associated with military training. However, whereas wrestling was not supposed to contain any striking, the *Tang History* references particularly bloody wrestling matches at the Imperial Palace, where broken bones and smashed skulls were frequent. In fact, one Tang emperor so loved the sport of wrestling that he regularly challenged his guests to impromptu matches with lavish prizes—if they could defeat him. Apparently, he was defeated once, and his opponent was awarded a governmental position of authority. China hosted exceedingly popular wrestling matches in Hangzhou, which featured both male and female fighters. However, when a high-ranking government official noticed that the women fighters wore less clothing than normal while wrestling, he petitioned the king to eliminate female fighters from the proceedings, fearing their presence might impact public morale.

When China was ruled by the Mongolian Empire from 1206 to 1368 CE, martial arts and fighting sports were banned, although they apparently were included in some theatrical performances. In the aftermath of Mongolian rule, during the Ming Dynasty (1368–1644 CE) fighting arts returned to the military. The southern coastal parts of China frequently were attacked by Japanese pirates, so the villagers began training with a legendary martial artist, General Qi Jiguang, to protect their families and livelihoods. So successful was this volunteer fighting force that the general created his own standardized training program, which he outlined in his book, *New Book of Effective Discipline*, published circa 1561 CE. Boxing was a foundational part of the training, although General Qi believed that boxing operated best as a confidence booster rather than as an effective tactic against armed opponents. So martial arts became firmly rooted in Chinese daily life, and, indeed, it was exceedingly rare for young boys to be unfamiliar with wrestling, boxing, and weapons-based tactics—not only because they would prepare them to be soldiers, but because martial arts already were inextricably linked to the health of the mind, the body, and the soul.

## Mongolia

Nestled between Russia and Northern China, Mongolia has a vast history of warfare and military conquests, rooted in "three manly games" of archery, horse racing, and wrestling. So dependent were the Mongolians on horsemanship that their wrestling style includes no groundwork, for a soldier who ended up on the battlefield inevitably would be trampled by horses, obviating the need to practice fighting on the ground. Instead, Mongolian wrestling involves trips and throws to get an opponent to touch his elbows, knees, or back to the ground. Mongolian soldiers may have practiced wrestling to prepare for battle, but the competitive sport of wrestling was its own practice. Today, Mongolia continues its wrestling tradition with large events where fighters perform ceremonial dances before bouts emulating a bird in flight, and celebratory dances after victories.

Mongolian wrestling is known for its elaborate traditional costuming, which features a long-sleeve top cut away to show bare chest, and very short briefs. A legend states that the top became standard after a woman concealed her gender, beat numerous opponents, then ripped open her top to reveal her true sex. The story may be apocryphal, but the open top now allows for no such gender-concealing prank. It seems that some Mongolian women continued to practice wrestling, despite the exclusion of female wrestlers in tournaments. Marco Polo noted in his travelogue written circa 1300 that the daughter of Kaidu Khan claimed she would marry any man who could best her at wrestling, but no man ever was able to do so, because the daughter was a serious practitioner. She remained single for the rest of her life.

## Korea

During the Koguryo Dynasty (3–427 CE), Korea stretched into Manchurian China and left an impact on China's folk customs. Murals created during that time depict men in loincloths wrestling one another and sporting long hair, goatees, and mustaches. The artwork represents the predecessor to Korea's traditional grappling system, called *ssireum*, where wrestlers fight to force each other to touch the ground with any body part above the knee; no chokes or locks are allowed. The fighters wear sashes, called *satbas*, that wrap around the waist and the right thigh, which are gripped and used to set up takedowns and throws. Ssireum is believed to have originated as an ancient method of defending oneself against other tribes. Although anecdotal, it does fit into the assumption about all fighting styles—that they evolved from the basic necessity of self-protection. In sixth century CE, ssireum became a more formalized military art and, eventually, a pleasurable pastime, although not always considered appropriate.

In the early fourteenth century, King Chunghye of the Yi Dynasty was reprimanded for delegating his kingly duties in order to train in ssireum. By the eighteenth century, however, the practice of ssireum became decidedly a lower-class activity, far removed from the aristocracy. When the Japanese occupied Korea from 1910 to 1945 CE, the sport had a resurgence, probably because the Korean wrestlers provided competition and practice for the Japanese sumo wrestlers. Although little is known of ssireum's practice in North Korea, it continues to thrive in South Korea, although it has not caught hold in other parts of the world.

Korea also has a unique fighting style, *Taekkyon*, which focuses primarily on leg-based attacks, emphasizing footwork, kicks, trips, and sweeps. Fighters use their fast footwork to set up jumping kicks and only use their hands to initiate sweeps and trips, although they can do open-hand slaps and finger rakes, with hammer-fist punches the only closed-hand strike. Korea's most well-known and exported martial art is tae kwon do. In fact, tae kwon do is one of the most popular and practiced martial arts in the world; we will discuss it in a later chapter.

## Southeast Asia

Southeast Asian martial arts often are grouped together rather than differentiated by country or people, which has led to contention between many countries and their individual fighting sports. A search for Cambodian or Laotian martial arts frequently conflates the traditions in those areas, and nowhere is this tension more apparent than in the identification of the original striking art in Southeast Asia. The reason for contention lies not only in nationalism and heritage, but in the history of occupation, war, and prominence on the world stage. Thailand, Cambodia, and Myanmar all have their own iterations of striking as sport, although Muay Thai is certainly the most well-known worldwide. Rather than engage in the current debate about whose version came first, we will explore each country's striking art, and, in later chapters, consider how they contributed to our modern version of MMA.

## Thailand

Muay Thai is the national sport of Thailand, formerly known as Siam, and one of the most respected and beloved fighting sports worldwide. Texts from the Ayutthaya period, circa 1351–1767 CE, mention Muay Thai as a prizefighting event associated with festivals and, of course, gambling. Unfortunately, many records were burned by Burmese occupiers in 1767 CE, so little written information survives about the early formations of Muay Thai. The legend of Muay Thai's origin dates to the eighteenth century, when Siamese soldier Nai Khanom Tom was captured by the Burmese. In this origin story, Nai Khanom Tom was imprisoned and forced to fight ten Burmese fighters in competition, all of whom he defeated. He then was granted his freedom, along with the freedom of his fellow Siamese soldiers. This story might be apocryphal, but it remains part of the legend of the sport, with March 17 designated "Boxing Day" to celebrate Nai Khanom Tom's victory.

As military tactics evolved in Southeast Asia, Muay Thai shifted to a more specific sport format, contested during times of celebration and always with musical accompaniment. In the eighteenth century, matches were arranged between fighters of similar body type, rather than weight, and ropes laid on the ground demarcated the "ring" space. In order to keep time during the rounds, rather than fighting to knockdown like English pugilism, a rather ingenious device was used. A coconut shell with three holes drilled into it was placed in a bowl of water. As the shell slowly filled with water, then sank, the round ended. The fight rounds would go on until one fighter could not continue.

Like many Chinese martial arts, Muay Thai instruction frequently was housed in Buddhist temples, taught by warrior monks. Fighters wore cloth wrapped around their bare fists, and if both opponents agreed, these wraps could be covered in glue and dipped in ground glass. As a fighting sport tied directly to the might of the kingdom and the representation of masculinity, with the addition of the glass Thai fights were seen as even more heroic. Grappling, biting, gouging, and kicking a downed opponent were banned, but otherwise, the fights had few rules. The tactics, however, always were focused on kicks, knees, and elbow strikes. Until the introduction of some Western fighting methods in the mid-twentieth century, lead-hand striking was rare. In 1939, the country officially switched from the Kingdom of Siam to the Kingdom of Thailand, marking a period of fierce Thai nationalism that was embodied in the intense Muay Thai fights. Muay Thai became Thailand's official sport, further connecting the heroism of fighters with the might of the Thai Kingdom.

## Cambodia

Stone reliefs in the Banteay Chhmar temple in Cambodia, created during the Angkor empire (802–1431 CE), depict armed warriors engaged in battle, as well as empty-hand fighters. Images show flying knees, kicks, and elbows, the ultimate weapon in Kun Khmer, also known as *Pradal Serey*, Cambodia's brutal striking art. Developed during the reign of the Angkor kingdom, the empire that controlled Cambodia, Thailand, Vietnam, and Laos, Kun Khmer appears to have been formalized as a sport, with some ancient engravings featuring fighters with a third person acting as referee. Although Kun Khmer is not well known outside Southeast Asia, it is extremely popular in Cambodia, and knockouts from elbow strikes are particularly valued in competition.

Alongside the engravings of Kun Khmer in the Banteay Chhmar temple are depictions of wrestling, the ancient art of Bok Cham Bab, which also was featured in the eighth-century CE artwork. Cham Bab begins with ceremonial dancing and music, then the wrestlers attempt to throw each other on their backs. The wrestler to win two of three bouts was declared champion. Ancient artwork and oral tradition reveal that both men and women competed in Cham Bab, and prowess in wrestling often translated to leadership positions in the tribe and office in the military.

## Myanmar

Burma has three primary forms of unarmed martial arts—Bando, Lethwei, and Naban. Bando is more akin to self-defense, perfecting an amalgam of striking and throws, as well as footwork for avoiding contact. The Burmese fighting art, Lethwei, is one of the most brutal traditional styles that endured and then exploded in the twenty-first century, achieving prominence in part due to the emergence of social media. Seemingly developed simultaneously with Muay Thai and Kun Khmer, Lethwei includes similar strikes, but with the addition of head butts, making it the art of nine limbs instead of Muay Thai's eight. Historically, Lethwei matches had no time limit, but instead used their "yoe-yar" rules, which means a fight can only be won with a knockout. Many historians believe that Burmese martial arts were highly influenced by its two largest neighbors—India and China. Although the Chinese may have inspired some elements of Burmese martial arts, Burma's wrestling style, Naban, seems much more similar to India's wrestling systems. Naban is unique in that it allows for joint manipulations, such as arm bars and leg locks, as well as chokes. In Naban, fighters seek to get their opponent to the ground and win by submission.

## Indonesia

Indonesia and Malaysia are also said to have been heavily influenced by Chinese martial arts and have their own wide range of unique weapons used in warfare and defense. Indonesia's Pencak silat is an empty-hand style that differs according to the region in which it is practiced, as well as the ancestors of those who practice it. In some parts of Indonesia, it includes boxing and kicks; in others, grappling and wrestling. Although the historical antecedents are unclear, most theories point to the sixth century and the necessity for royal bodyguards as the origin of Pencak silat. The term silat is rather ubiquitous, like wrestling, in many parts of Southeast Asia. Malaysia and the Philippines also use the term silat to refer to some aspects of their fighting styles; the story of Filipino martial arts will wait until the next chapter.

## OCEANIA

Not every culture had an extensive empty-hand fighting system if weapons were their primary form of self-protection in battle. Aboriginal communities in Australia operated in nomadic tribes and did not go to war to gain property, so military training was rare. Skirmishes sometimes arose between tribes; and fighting between individuals happened, but nearly all of it included weapons, although one must imagine that if a warrior lost his weapon in the heat of battle, he would defend himself and continue to attack his enemy despite his empty hands. Some tribes in New Guinea were found to smother their enemies by holding their hands over nose and mouth; another more painful method was to break the enemy's ribs, legs, and arms, and leave him to die in agony. In these tropical climates, even the smallest wounds could become infected and lead to death.

Polynesian culture, which spread across New Zealand, the Solomon Islands, and other places in the Pacific, primarily practiced weapon-based fighting, although wrestling was part of celebratory events. The *haka*, a ritualistic dance designed to frighten one's enemy, evoke ancestral blessings, and demonstrate the physical prowess of the performer through body-slapping, stomps, jumps, and loud chants, preceded battle and, eventually, would become a traditional performance before sporting events, especially rugby and wrestling. UFC heavyweight Mark Hunt frequently makes his walk to the octagon performing the haka with his crew, demonstrating the cultural significance of the performative dance as both ritual and inextricable from war—even if that skirmish takes place in a highly controlled and regulated environment rather than on a battlefield.

The Caroline Islands had a warrior caste who specialized in fighting with weapons, such as clubs and spears, as well as an empty-hand system that emphasized fighting in close contact during a skirmish. The techniques focused on disarming opponents, eye gouging, choking, striking and kicking, and throws or trips that could ground an aggressive opponent.

Tahiti also used weapons in its warfare, but it had a formal wrestling style that functioned as an exhibition at celebrations or festivals. Frequently tribes and clans would compete against each other, surrounded by their supporters, in a thirty-foot diameter circle of grass or beach. While instruments were played, the champions would enter the ring, sometimes as individual opponents and sometimes in groups of six or so. Once in the ring, the wrestlers, each wearing a belt and frequently covered in oil, would walk around, beating their chests and sides aggressively. This would produce a loud, hollow noise and sometimes cause bruising or even blood. Some wrestling began in a clinch setup, where one arm was placed around the opponent's neck and the other arm wrapped around the waist. The objective was to throw the other person to the ground. In other types of wrestling, the opponents would grab and attempt to throw each other on their backs. Men and women competed in these events, and sometimes women and men would wrestle each other.

Although wrestling was a widespread activity, boxing, called *motoraa*, was a more elite practice because of the religious beliefs of boxers. Boxers served the god of war, Oro, and were part of a secret society that, in addition to their boxing training, abstained from sexual activity. Boxing matches had no time limits; instead, they went until one opponent quit or no longer could get up off the ground. Other peoples of Oceania included combat training as part of their communal life, but weapons remained the focus, for both self-protection and tribal power.

## SOUTH AMERICA

There are few written accounts of South American sports history prior to European colonial efforts. In Bolivia, an annual festival at the end of

May, known as *Tinku*, brings together villagers in a large-scale street brawl. Tinku apparently originated when Spanish conquistadors forced the indigenous people to fight each other to the death to amuse their occupiers. However, the festival also is associated with a celebration of Mother Nature, with the blood of fighters cut in combat used to enrich the soil and generate a good harvest that year. Perhaps the Spanish merely took this indigenous practice and made it more deadly as a form of entertainment, but the event continues in modern times. Men drink grain alcohol, meet in the streets, and fight, taking time to eat or sleep over the three days of festival. In 2010, two men died after participating in Tinku. This obviously is not a fighting sport, and it appears not to require formal training, but rather is an opportunity for grievances to be aired and the catharsis of violence in the aftermath of the battles.

Deep in the Amazon rainforest, the Kamayurá tribe, an indigenous people of Brazil, maintain an ancient form of wrestling known as *Huka-huka*. The Kamayurá are prolific wrestlers who practice every day and follow a strict training and diet protocol. The Huka-huka begins with two fighters circling each other, then either one or both drop to their knees. From there, they can jump back up or grab and throw the opponent to the ground. In 2012, Anderson Silva famously trained with some of the Kamayurá tribe and was bested by the tribe's champion.

The Guarani, another indigenous tribe of Brazil, also wrestle; and, indeed, children begin practicing at a very young age and continue throughout adulthood. No records indicate just when the Kamayura and Guarani invented their wrestling systems or the details of how it changed over time. However, these considerations truly do not matter because wrestling for these tribes is a lived history rather than a rhetorical one.

## AFRICA

Much of our information about precolonial Africa was collected and disseminated by Europeans, some of whom were government officials who came to sub-Saharan Africa to look for resources to benefit their home countries or their own private enterprise. Other accounts were written by missionaries, who arrived in Africa for the sole purpose of preaching their belief in the superiority of both Christianity and European social practices. Anthropologists also visited Africa and other parts of the non-European world to collect information and then write titillating accounts of what they saw as exotic, irreverent, or taboo behavior. Although these accounts can be useful, we have an abundance of information on African martial arts, found in the oral tradition and in the articulation of fighting sports themselves, rather than through the lens of white outsiders.

African martial arts were particular to each tribe and practiced primarily in preparation for skirmishes with neighboring tribes and for ceremonial or ritual purposes. The communal aspect of fighting sports is exemplified in the dance rituals that many African tribes developed. Warriors would enact fighting moves in rhythm to drums and other instruments that their fellow tribe members played. Essentially shadowboxing to music, the fighters who practiced their skills used the beat and rhythm to help develop timing.

Historians used to scoff at oral tradition as an effective mode of passing information, but practicing movements in conjunction with music, as a dance, made it an exceedingly efficient way of teaching and practicing necessary fighting skills. The memorization was not rote, but rather, it was something that each fighter could embody, replicate in practice, and then apply in battle. Fighting sports are an ancestral practice in much of Africa and other parts of the world; martial arts were handed down through the generations, both in familial training and in the oral tradition of storytelling. Practicing the throws and trips, kicks and strikes of an ancestor functioned as worship and a way to continue familial traditions.

Wrestling as a competition was standard in nearly every African tribal group, often performed ceremonially as part of a seasonal occurrence, such as harvest, or community celebrations, such as weddings, funerals, or coming-of-age rituals. In most scenarios, wrestling was practiced by boys or young men and was part of the transition from childhood to adolescence, marking the journey from pre-sexual to becoming of marriageable age. The proximity between communities meant that regional competitions occurred.

Chinua Achebe's seminal novel, *Things Fall Apart*, includes a description of a grappling contest in Nigeria in which young men competed for their village while the entire community sang and danced to ceremonial drumming. Achebe's novel focuses on the Igbo people (formerly referred to as Ibo), who had two forms of wrestling: the general style of *mgba* and the *ebenebe*, which included ankle picks. Early Western ethnographers attempted to define the Igbo's wrestling compared to the wrestling styles of their own communities, but most were unfamiliar with Greco-Roman or Lancashire wrestling, so their comparisons do not provide sufficient descriptions. One thing that distinguished the Igbo's wrestling style from that of other ancient communities in their area was that the mgba allowed reaping, hooking, and sweeping with the feet, whereas their neighbors, the Hausa, did not allow wrestlers to use their feet to sweep or reap.

The Hausa of northern Nigeria have two traditional fighting sports: the striking art of *dambe* and the *kokawa*, a wrestling style. Both arts continue to be practiced today, but their history, passed down through generations of fighters, is embodied in the unique styles and the music that accompanies it. Like many fighting arts to arise out of tribal cultures in Africa, the kokawa fighters credit their ancestors and the spirits of the Earth for their athletic prowess.

The most prolific African wrestling tradition is the Senegalese art of *laamb*, which dates back thousands of years into the tribe's history and stretches from the Senegal River to the Kwanza River. It often is compared to Greco-Roman wrestling—as most wrestling styles are to those not necessarily fluent in the nuances of grappling. In laamb, the match ends when one fighter manages to land his opponent's head or back on the ground. Today in Senegal, laamb has become tremendously big business and is as popular as football (American soccer) in both practice and in fandom. Laamb was historically open for women to compete in, but when the sport came under the direction of officials in the twentieth century, women were banned (this is a common methodology in marginalizing women in sports around the world). In the twenty-first century, however, Senegalese women began participating in the sport.

The Kel Faduy tribe of the Taureg people in south-central Sahara continue the ancient tradition of celebrating female wrestlers with a ritual contest to honor the coming-of-age with the birth of a woman's first child. The village women compete in fierce wrestling matches that demonstrate female power rather than appeal to the men in the audience. Sometimes women in their seventies will wrestle with very young women, and boasting typically precedes all matches. Although many other African traditions include female wrestling, the Kel Faduy are unique in that their modern culture is Muslim, yet they continue the tradition of their ancestors, providing women with an opportunity to compete and celebrate female power.

The Khoikhoi of Southwest Africa practiced a type of no-holds-barred wrestling that looked much more like Greek pankration than modern freestyle wrestling. The line between grappling and striking was not always as clear in African fighting sports as in the Greek separate arts of boxing and wrestling. And in many African boxing styles, punching was not the only striking allowable.

The Hausa of Nigeria have a complete striking system in addition to their wrestling style. Dambe is one of the more unique forms of traditional boxing in that the fighters primarily use their power hand to strike and their lead hand to defend themselves. This guard often is referred to as the spear and the shield. Some historians note that the style of dambe resembles the images of ancient Egyptian boxing, as though the style evolved or somehow was influenced by that ancient civilization's art. The assumption that the Hausa's fighting art evolved from Egyptian boxing could be correct in part, but it is another example of how Western scholars often attribute all innovation to Egypt rather than recognizing the autonomous, unique histories of the numerous civilizations throughout Africa. The striking spear hand is wrapped in cloth (*kara*) and bound in a knotted cord (*zare*). Dambe fighters also can kick, but their primary weapon is that rear hand, always ready to deliver a heavy, club-style blow while using their lead hand to parry their opponent's "shield" hand. Traditionally, dambe boxers wore loincloths and sometimes in their hands clutched amulets and other charms that tribal medicine men gave them. A resurgence in dambe boxing in modern Nigeria has modernized the sport, and amateur fighters no longer are allowed to carry or wear charms on their bodies.

Many martial arts, especially those that evolved from farming cultures, have movements based on functional actions. For example, the Madagascar striking style, Moringy, includes typical jabs and hooks, as well as the *vangofary* punch that imitates cutting sugarcane, much like an overhand punch. In some harvest festivals, boys and girls would wrestle each other, in a kind of sporting metaphor for the creation of food and abundance. But because many cultures only participated in wrestling as a pre-sexual practice, the bouts between boys and girls could foreshadow the future, when both reached marriageable ages. In many cases, wrestling matches allowed boys and girls to assert their social rank and display their status among the tribe. For boys especially, victory in wrestling could mean attaining a leadership position later in life.

In Gambia, wrestling on high holidays required preparation that feels similar to anyone who has ever trained for a formal event. The young men and women, typically between the ages of sixteen and twenty, trained and fed themselves liberally to be as strong as possible for their bouts. Each fighter represented his kin, and thus was decorated and celebrated by his family. In these traditional bouts, fighters started with one knee on the ground, trying to grab each other's hands. Then one would spring up and try to grab a leg or pick up his opponent in order to slam him on the ground. In some cases, a male champion and female champion would marry, perhaps producing the next generation of super wrestlers.

The Bachama tribe of Nigeria hosted tournaments to celebrate the harvest and invited neighboring villages to bring their best wrestlers to compete. Wrestling was not just a sport or performance; warriors trained in wrestling along with their weapons in order to prepare for warfare. In the event of a hand-to-hand combat scenario, warriors from any tribe would need to know how to protect themselves sans weapons.

The ancient Kunene people of Namibia created a fighting system that other communities in the surrounding areas replicated. It consisted of two parts, the *engolo* and the *kandeka*. The kandeka consisted of stick fighting and slap boxing, both of which were used to train boys and young men in combat. The engolo was a much more brutal hand-to-hand fighting system that originated out of the need to protect the tribe against raids from other tribes.

Slap boxing was also a pastime of young Kunene men in the villages; and, indeed, matches were part of ritual displays to lead up to the more popular art of engolo. Songs were played, with a young man stepping into the center of the circle and raising his open hands, challenging all who were present, until another young man stepped in to accept. Slap boxing matches consisted primarily of open-hand strikes to the face and body, as well as footwork and head movement to dodge the blows. The fight continued until one boy gave up, then another challenger would come in for his turn to spar with the champion. The kandeka developed coordination in young men and provided them with an outlet in which they could hone their skills with a stick and learn range for empty-hand striking. Slap boxing was a safe way for boys to practice combat strategies before engaging in the harder prospect of engolo.

Engolo is an acrobatic fighting style that the Kunene used as sport and duel, for contest and combat. In the realm of contest, engolo provided young men with an opportunity to test their skills in preparation for deadlier combat in the future. The "sport" version of engolo primarily used kicks, which often were thrown from an inverted position where the fighters' hand or hands touched the ground while the kick was thrown. In the combat version, however, head butts and knee strikes became part of the fighting protocol. For the Kunene, engolo is a sacred art passed down from the ancestors. The cosmology of ancestor worship, embodied in the ludic enactment of engolo, made the place where matches took place, the engolo circle, a sacred space. Linguistically, engolo may be tied to the zebra (*ongolo*), a highly regarded animal that also uses kicks to defend itself or attack a rival. The engolo requires speed and agility; and the zebra, in Kunene culture, is a symbol of nimbleness. Tribal members became *engolo* masters through a sacred ritual (*okukwatelela*). A line was drawn across the fighter's face using white powder (*ompeyu*), which symbolized the portal to the ancestor realm.

Engolo is a striking style that primarily consists of kicks thrown from an inverted position. When the Portuguese kidnapped African civilians and took them to Brazil for slave labor, engolo became the basis for *capoeira*, the Brazilian fighting system that the enslaved population hid in dance. The impact of the African diaspora will be explored in chapter 3, but suffice it to say that ancient African fighting sports and the martial arts have numerous connections that arose in slaveholding countries hundreds, even thousands, of years later. But perhaps the most fascinating aspect of many of the fighting sports discussed in this chapter is how relevant and practiced they still are today. The masters of defense in Europe may have written the most about fighting, but in Asia, South America, and Africa, ancient fighters and their progeny lived and propagated their arts by doing them, not writing about them.

This chapter reveals the unique cultural traditions of numerous civilizations across a wide swath of time, before the interruption and intervention of European imperialism. Although most of the cultures, in one way or another, regularly interacted with their neighbors through trade, travel, warfare, and exploration, many parts of the world remained if not insular, then at least indifferent to the social practices of other countries. But that tolerance was about to change radically. Widespread colonization in the sixteenth, seventeenth, and eighteenth centuries fundamentally altered the world, generating a history of often violent cultural homogenization leading to the evolution of new, hybrid forms of fighting sports that are still practiced today.

# 3

# COLONIZING MARTIAL ARTS

George Dixon stood across the ring from Jack Skelly, blinded by the indoor electric lights. This fight was historic, not only because it was the first use of electric lights to showcase a fight; it was the first legal public championship fight featuring an interracial match. Dixon was a featherweight fighter, slim and fast, and black. His opponent, Jack Skelly, was white. Dixon was by far the more experienced fighter; in no way should the amateurish Skelly have faced him. But in the American South in 1892, most white people believed that any white man could defeat any black man. They were wrong. By the end of round eight, Dixon had so punished Skelly that the latter's head lolled helplessly on his neck. Dixon knocked out Skelly, and his four hundred black fans in the crowd of four thousand white men cheered him on gleefully. After that night, no interracial matches were held in the South for a very long time.

Dixon's victory at the end of the nineteenth century was emblematic of the changing face of fighting sports. In ancient and medieval times, people were more isolated and rarely had the opportunity to face fighters outside of their communities. Between the sixteenth and twentieth centuries, people became more connected globally through the process of colonization. The globalization of fighting sports was a process that would irrevocably change the way martial arts were practiced and contested around the world and eventually lead to the ultimate amalgam of fighting culture, mixed martial arts.

Globalization is an ongoing process, not a recent phenomenon, as is the act of empire building. Although the sixteenth to twentieth centuries are recognized most widely as the "age of imperialism," it is important to remember that imperialism existed long before the Spanish and British jumped in their boats, and plenty of other countries conquered and colonized their neighbors. But the age of European expansion, starting in the late sixteenth century and continuing for nearly four hundred years, is perhaps the most aggressive, systemic, and radically devastating process of colonization in history. Africa, Asia, Oceania, and the Americas were divvied up between the European hegemonic powers, their lands stripped of natural resources, their traditional customs banned, and, in many cases, the indigenous people forcibly kidnapped and used as slave labor. The European occupiers attempted to supplant local customs with their own practices, but thousands of years of traditions could not be eviscerated completely. This was especially true for the fighting practices of people around the world.

Whereas the previous chapters in this book focused on people and customs in their places of origin, this chapter looks at the act of translation and adaptation as people began to move from place to place. We will look at Irish martial arts in Ireland, England, and the newly formed United States; at African fighting styles in Brazil, the Caribbean islands, in the American North and South, and in England, as colonization supercharged the process of globalization. We will face the many systems that subjugate people even today, including racism, sexism, classism, xenophobia, and ethnocentrism, and how those systems of oppression impacted fighting sports.

This chapter will not focus on what we might think of as the "formal" process of colonization—the political, economic, religious, governmental, and linguistic acts of imperialism. Instead, we will look at how European rule impacted occupied nations socially, and, in particular, how imperialism changed the practice of fighting sports. In many, many cases globalization meant a change in the rules and techniques allowed in fights, and in the ways those contests were organized and won. Imperialism impacted many sports in that very Victorian approach of creating formal organizations to codify the rules of the sport. These rules not only created a clear set of guidelines as to how sports should be played, but they also systematically upheld European masculine ideals. Women almost unilaterally were excluded from participating in sports, which reinforced the concept of protected male space, safe from female incursion, and ensured that women would remain passive and amenable to male power. People of color also often were banned—if not from participating, then at least from playing with white athletes.

One reason why sports' rules became so codified in the 1800s is that European expansionism brought Western sports in contact with the sporting practices of cultures all over the world. In the late 1500s, seafaring European nations took their ships around the coast of Africa and across the Atlantic Ocean to the Americas. The kingdoms of Portugal, France, Spain, England, the Dutch Republic, and France sought to expand their trade with foreign nations and conquer new lands believed to be rich in resources.

At the same time, the European cultural renaissance was in full swing back home. The ideals of the Renaissance as a return to classical Greek art, architecture, rhetoric, and beauty were not universal. Most people did not have the time to indulge in creating artwork, or the literacy necessary to read ancient Greek. In the Middle Ages and in the early modern period, most European royal powers operated under the auspices of the church, but the sixteenth century marked a period of strong monarchies that, for the most part, still followed church dictum but made decisions for the good of their own rule rather than that of the pope. Luxuriating in their successes at home, European monarchs stretched out their jeweled fingers for new lands to conquer and inhabit.

## EUROPE

### England

Although all European nations engaged in imperialism, England seems to have made the most indelible mark on the world, perhaps because one of its largest colonization attempts backfired, maybe due to dominance of the English language. But before we launch into the many colonial efforts of England and other European powers, we will look at fighting sports on European soil during the time period.

Boxing was a favorite English pastime, although it was not always considered a very proper undertaking. The English Restoration released the puritanical restrictions on public entertainment lingering from the Middle Ages and allowed for various types of spectacles to be performed in designated areas around London and other cities. Boxing emerged as a popular spectacle during the Renaissance along with cockfighting, bearbaiting, and the theater. Britain's *Protestant Mercury* newspaper, in 1681 CE, was the first to report a boxing match, with the Duke of Albemarle's attendance evidence of the sport's growing acceptance. The aristocratic support of the sport hit an apex in 1723, when King George I ordered construction of a ring in Hyde Park. The king's support of boxing fostered an environment in which fighters received patronage from wealthy nobles, who supported their training and made heavy bets on the pugilists.

In 1801, Joseph Strutt published his history of British sport with the expansive title, typical of the time period, of *The Sports and Pastimes of the People of England, Including the Rural and Domestic Recreations, May-Games, Mummeries, Pageants, Processions, and Pompous Spectacles, From the Earliest Period to the Present Time.* This epically named tome organized and categorized sporting practices in England according to the class of people who either played or watched them. Pugilism is listed as a lively spectator activity for gentry and commoners alike. The year 1813 CE was a banner year for pugilistic scholarship; Pierce Egan published his famous volumes, *Boxiana*, and an anonymous writer produced the lesser known, but by no means less interesting, *Pancratia: A History of Pugilism. Pancratia* primarily consists of stories of various pugilistic encounters and is a wealth of information about how fights occurred in the eighteenth century. *Boxiana* generally is considered the foremost source of pugilistic history of the Regency era, and Egan is a particularly thoughtful and detailed scholar, especially in his portrayal of fighters who were shunned in basically every other facet of British life.

In the early eighteenth century, pugilists took advantage of England's increasingly literate population and the proliferation of newspapers to promote themselves in the press. Fighters called out future opponents and advertised their upcoming bouts. James Figg, who the International Boxing Hall of Fame calls "the father of boxing," was the champion of his day and opened Britain's first legitimate fight gym. His School for the Manly-Art of Self-Defense taught boxing, fencing, and cudgel fighting. Figg used the newspapers of the time to insult his opponents, remind readers of his undefeated career, and promote his gym as the ideal training academy. One of his students was Elizabeth

Wilkinson Stokes, who would become known as the "Championess of America and of Europe" in her short but dramatic fighting career.

Fighters during this time used the ubiquity of the printed word to call out opponents and issue challenges in the many newspapers. Unfortunately, these papers were not yet providing coverage of actual fights in the early 1700s, when Elizabeth Stokes was actively fighting, but her challenges and the results of her skirmishes were shared in major publications. In 1722, Stokes fought Hannah Hyfield and defeated her twenty-two minutes into the fight. Surprisingly, a newspaper, the *London Journal*, published the results without criticizing the female fighters:

> Boxing in publick at the Bear Garden is what has lately obtained very much amongst the Men, but till last Week we never heard of Women being engaged that Way, when two of the Feminine Gender appeared for the first Time on the Theatre of War at Hockley in the Hole, and maintained the Battle with great Valour for a long Time, to the no small Satisfaction of the spectators.[1]

In Egan's *Boxiana*, the author praised the fighters as examples of British national pride. Quoting the exchange between Elizabeth Wilkinson and Hannah Hyfield in a section called "Female Pugilists," Egan wrote, "even HEROINES panted for the honours of pugilistic glory!"[2]

After defeating Hannah Hyfield, Elizabeth fought semi-regularly under the tutelage of her husband, fellow boxer James Figg.

In 1728, Elizabeth exchanged words with fellow female boxer Ann Field, which resulted in a match on October 7 of that year. First, Ann challenged Elizabeth in the newspaper:

> I, Ann Field, of Stoke Newington, ass driver, well known for my abilities in boxing in my own defence wherever it happened in my way, having been affronted by Mrs. Stokes, styled the European Championess, do fairly invite her to a trial of her best skill in Boxing for 10 pounds, fair rise and fall; and question not but to give her such proofs of my judgment that shall oblige her to acknowledge me Championess of the Stage, to the entire satisfaction of all my friends.

Elizabeth responded:

> I, Elizabeth Stokes, of the City of London, have not fought in this way since I fought the famous boxing woman of Billingsgate 29 min-

utes, and gained complete victory, (which was six years ago;) but as the famous Stowe Newington ass-woman dares me to fight her for the 10 pounds, I do assure her that I will not fail meeting her for the said sum, and doubt not that the blows which I shall present her with will be more difficult for her to digest than any she ever gave her asses.[3]

Elizabeth Stokes set the standard not only for female boxers, but also for media trash-talking. Over the next several hundred years, and into our digital media today, fighters use self-aggrandizing talk to bolster their confidence, infuriate other fighters (as well as many fans), increase awareness of upcoming fights, and even create a "brand" through which they can gain sponsors and other lucrative partnerships. This might seem like a new conceit, fueled by social media, but it is, in fact, as old as fighting itself.

The late eighteenth century and early nineteenth century constituted Britain's golden age of boxing, where the sport became both a "science" and a "manly art." The golden age coincided with Britain's Georgian era and Regency period, approximately 1720 to 1820 CE, a time known for the rich pageantry of the upper class and abject poverty in the squalid lower classes. As the upper classes became more involved in the sport of boxing, numerous attempts began to establish clear rules and protocols for matches. In 1743 CE champion boxer Jack Broughton, often considered the "father of English boxing," created a rule set that remained in place until 1838.

Broughton, who was protected by the patronage of the Duke of Cumberland, outlined rules that specified round times and rest breaks, the conduct of fighters and corners, and how the purse should be split. Broughton operated his own training gymnasium and used quotes from the *Aeneid* to entice British men to reconnect with the masculine practices of their Greek and Roman predecessors. He specifically targeted upper-class men by offering a training environment that would appeal to the aristocratic Englishman. His school excluded women and gambling, and it provided an early form of gloves, known as "mufflers," so that gentlemen boxers could engage in combat while protecting their faces. And in referencing the classical era of ancient Rome and Greece, Broughton created the image of an educated man following in the erect footsteps of his celebrated stoic ancestors.

This connection between boxing and idealized masculinity transformed the concept of pugilism from the realm of back-alley brawls to the codified sport of boxing, beloved by gentlemen set on disengaging from what they saw as foreign effeminacy. As England became more culturally and ethnically diverse in the eighteenth century, some men feared the intrusion of foreign practices that might somehow diminish their own masculinity. And English boxing seemed to be the perfect antidote, although in reality, many of these new occupants of England dominated the ring.

In 1838 CE, Britain's Pugilistic Society published an updated set of rules, which built on Brighton's guidelines but focused more on safety. These rules clearly barred head butting, kicks, biting, eye gouging, throws, and hitting a downed opponent. At the time, these bouts were still bare-knuckle, but the 1866 CE "Queensberry Rules" would change that. The "Queensberry Rules" actually were written by John Graham Chambers, founder of the Amateur Athletic Club. Chambers enlisted support for his guidelines from the twenty-four-year-old John Sholto Douglas, also known as the eighth marquess of Queensberry. Chambers's rules, as published under the name of his patron, focused on boxing skill and technique, required the use of gloves, created set rounds of three minutes with a one-minute rest, allowed a downed fighter ten seconds to return to standing, and banned any wrestling techniques in the ring. These rules clearly delineated the sport of boxing and firmly separated it from other forms of fighting sports, especially wrestling.

Establishing the rules and technical guidelines of a sport make it both much easier to control and much easier to exclude certain participants. Although Egan and other educated men celebrated the reinvigoration of what they saw as a formerly gelded masculinity in England, the real work of British pugilism was enacted by lower-class men who, technically, were not even British. The process of colonization combined with the necessity of work made England's population increasingly diverse, including people from around the world and of numerous ethnicities, racial identities, and class positions.

Several of the greatest fighters of Britain's golden age of boxing were "foreigners"—specifically, Jewish, Irish, and African men who were marginalized and often ignored by the very men who would praise the sport in which they excelled. The poor immigrant population in England may have been considered the dregs of society, but bruisers with prizefighting potential had little difficulty finding a wealthy patron. Jewish, Irish, and African populations were some of the most discriminated against at the time, yet fighters could attain greater social and economic status in the ring than in any other profession.

England may have not had slaves at home, but abroad, in their vast colonies, the British enslaved Africans and used them, harshly, for labor until the Slavery Abolition Act of 1833. But England's cities, especially London, had a large African population. In 1772, around fifteen thousand Africans were living in England, the majority of whom were former slaves from British colonies or the American South, or their descendants. Africans were restricted to certain types of employment in England, so many continued to work in domestic service unless they could raise enough money to apprentice a trade. Enterprising men saw a future for themselves in the ring as prizefighters, which would provide them with an opportunity not only to make money, but potentially to gain patronage and protection from a wealthy aristocrat.

The first African fighter to gain true fame and a simulacrum of prestige was Tom Molineaux, a late-eighteenth century prizefighter born a slave in New York in 1784. He later went to Britain and fought an epic battle with Tom Cribb, a white Englishman then considered the world champion, in 1810. But before Molineaux reached the limelight, his own teacher, another African, entered the forefront of British boxing. Bill Richmond was born in New York and later was employed by the duke of Northumberland. He trained as a cabinetmaker, but in 1804, he entered the ring. Although he, too, would lose to Cribb, he won his next eleven fights and went on to become a boxing instructor.

Thomas Molineaux, sometimes spelled Molyneux, undoubtedly is the most famous boxer of African descent in the nineteenth century. Molineaux's antecedents are the story of legend, but what is best known about the man comes from Pierce Egan and his tireless coverage of Regency-era boxing. When Molineaux arrived in England, Richmond saw potential in the man's five feet nine, 195-pound muscular frame but wanted to break Tom of his bad "American" fighting habits. According to Richmond, Molineaux often threw "hammer"-style punches at a downward angle, a striking tactic undoubtedly passed down through African lineage. Richmond allowed Tom to fight one of Cribb's pupil's, Jack Burrows, a giant at six feet one and 210 pounds, but Molineaux destroyed the bigger man. Tom continued fighting Cribb's men while calling out the champion. In London, he enjoyed celebrity status, in part due to his boxing prowess and bravado, in part due to his good looks. English women were particularly fascinated by Tom, and he began to drink and womanize more than a future champion should, spending his earnings on fancy clothing and not training nearly enough. As the excitement and fervor surrounding Molineaux increased, Cribb finally agreed to a fight, pending both men getting back into shape.

It was a cold, rainy day on December 10, 1819, when a crowd waded knee-deep on a clay road in Copthall Common, a neighborhood thirty miles from the city of London, to watch Thomas Molineaux face Thomas Cribb in a prizefighting match for the ages. Egan described both fighters as "claim[ing] peculiar notice from their extraordinary efforts."[4] Both men, in other words, were at the top of their game that day, although by the nineteenth round, Egan noted that "to distinguish the combatants by their features would have been utterly impossible, so dreadfully were both their faces beaten."[5]

Fight day was particularly dreary, with freezing cold rain pouring over the two as they battled for forty rounds. For the first twenty-nine rounds, Molineaux was roundly beating Cribb. To the crowd, this fight symbolized a battle for the bragging rights of a nation, the struggle for supremacy between the mother country and her naughty, prodigal child. Cribb's seconds were able to pause the fight on a technicality, and in the time that intervened, Molineaux is said to have caught a chill while waiting for the fight to resume in the icy downpour. When the men were finally called back to their feet, the American reportedly was numb, thoroughly chilled by the English rain. In the following eleven rounds, Cribb made his comeback, and in round forty, Molineaux was finally vanquished.

The two men met again the following year, but Cribb rather quickly defeated Molineaux in the ninth round. They did not fight a third time, but Molineaux continued his prizefighting career until he lost to George Cooper in 1815. Sadly, he died destitute in Ireland in 1818, his decline reportedly exacerbated by alcoholism. But Thomas Molineaux would forever be remembered for his fierceness, his bravery, and for opening up a new space for African men to excel in prizefighting in England. Pierce Egan rather elegantly summed up Molineaux's career in the estimable *Boxiana*:

> Molineaux came as an open and bold competitor for boxing fame;
> and he challenged the proudest heroes to the hostile combat. Such
> declaration was manly, fair, and honourable, and entitled to every
> respect and attention among the pugilistic circles.[6]

Egan noted that much of the criticism of Molineaux came from his
ambition, his threats to "wrest the laurels from the English brow and
plant them upon the head of a foreigner."[7] Molineaux was unwilling to
approach his boxing career with the obsequiousness required of a ser-
vant or slave because he was not one. Despite his position in society and
the color of his skin, he was a man who demanded respect; and, from
his performance in the ring, he earned it.

At the turn of the eighteenth century, the city of London had between fifteen and twenty thousand Jewish immigrants. Daniel Mendoza
was one of the first Jewish prizefighters to make a name for himself,
both as a fighter and as a boxing instructor. Mendoza was small in
stature, and his style of quick footwork and fast hands would engender a
new style of boxing that differed greatly from the bruising power and
hulking size of most Regency-era fighters. Mendoza trained other
prizefighters in what was called the Mendoza school, or, revealing the
vernacular of the time, "the Jewish school of prizefighting." His style
sometimes was considered cowardly because he used his footwork to
evade heavy bruisers rather than exchange blows standing still, like a
turnip. When he won his first professional bout in 1787, he was presented to King George III, providing the monarch with his first opportunity
to speak to one of his Jewish subjects. Mendoza's prowess in the ring
won him the ultimate royal patron in the prince of Wales, who later
would become George IV after his father succumbed to illness/madness
(thus the name of the Regency period, marked by the prince of Wales
acting as prince regent in his father's stead).

Mendoza began his fighting career under the tutelage of "The Gentleman Boxer," the famed prizefighter Richard Humphries. But something later broke the relationship between the two men, and in 1788,
they met in the ring before sixty thousand to settle the score. By all
accounts, it was a tremendous event, but Mendoza slipped in the twen-
ty-eighth round and twisted his ankle, ending the fight. Humphries
taunted his former protégé, calling him a coward, and the following
year, the men met again, this time with Mendoza as the victor. But like
many rivalries, especially those in which each fighter won a match, it

called for a third fight, a reckoning to determine who was the greater man in the ring. Egan, of course, detailed the importance of that third fight in *Boxiana*:

> The awful set-to at length commenced, and every eye beamed with anxiety; the moment was interesting and attractive, and each party was lost in suspense. The combatants were heroes of no common stamp, and feint was regarded with respect and attention; money was a secondary consideration in this case; towering fame was attached to the issue of the contest; and the proud title of conquerer rested upon its termination—they both felt its consequences, and were determined to gain or lose it, honourably. [8]

Mendoza defeated Humphries in just fifteen rounds, and the triad was complete. Mendoza would go on to fight and to teach, and, of course, to be praised by Egan and other boxing enthusiasts. His last match was in 1820, when he fought at the established, if somewhat elderly at the time, age of fifty-five. In 1990, he was inducted into the International Boxing Hall of Fame, a legendary pugilist in spite of his marginalized position in society as a Jewish man and criticism of his quick-footed style.

## Ireland

Ireland is an old country, settled thousands of years ago and becoming a bastion of Christianity in formerly pagan Europe. In the *Annals of Ulster*, a historic text that covers the operation of the country of Ireland from Saint Patrick's arrival in the mid-fifth century CE to sixteenth century CE, the people who occupied Ireland, known as the Celts, maintained an agrarian lifestyle frequently interrupted by both local skirmishes and international warfare. In the ninth century, the Vikings began their invasion of Ireland, intermingling with the now occupied Irish, until they were defeated and essentially driven out of Ireland by Brian Boru, the famed Irish king, in 1014 CE. Irish autonomy would be short lived.

In the twelfth century, the Normans invaded Ireland, beginning the reign of the English in Ireland. Henry VIII named himself king of Ireland in 1541, and less than one hundred years later, under the reign of his daughter, Elizabeth I, the country was ripped apart through harsh penal laws and the persecution of Catholics. As rulers changed, politics evolved that continued to reduce Irish autonomy on a grand political scale; yet, as is so often the case when comparing history on a micro rather than a macro level, individual Irishmen and women asserted their individuality, not in their politics, but in their fighting.

Ancient Irish warriors used a great number of weapons, including swords, spears, and sticks, which were in common use by all of their neighbors. In Ireland, fighters routinely adorned their swords and other weapons with jewels and gold, although the vogue in ancient times was to festoon one's sword with the teeth of large sea animals, known colloquially as *claideb dét* or "sword of teeth." The use of weapons in ancient Ireland and in historic Europe in general advanced and changed as warfare evolved. Ancient Irish fighters used carefully hewn stones as weapons, throwing them with apparently expert precision at enemy combatants at surprisingly far distances. The English and other groups roundly ridiculed the Irish, comparing their attack to small boys throwing rocks, but these throwing stones were no mere pebbles. Carved to fit the thrower's particular style and imbued with mystical power, Irish throwing stones still were being used, with accuracy, in the nineteenth century. Irish warriors also created slings and other projectile apparatuses to fling their throwing stones farther with significantly more power. But Ireland's most famous weapon was the shillelagh.

An Irish shillelagh is approximately one meter in length and constructed only from woods of oak, ash, crab tree, hazel, or blackthorn, the most prized of the Irish woods. They typically have a knob at the end, made for crushing craniums, and double in functionality as a walking stick. Shillelagh fight culture evolved over hundreds and thousands of years, forming an implicit set of protocols that reveal the rather organized nature of street fighting, most likely assisted by the structural nature of the factions, or gangs, that ruled the country's underbelly. Prearranged fights between individuals or factions could be organized by the length of the *bata* and whether the stick had a knob at the end. In ancient days, fighters tended to use longer sticks or staffs, most likely because they were more similar in use to a fighting spear or broadsword. As time progressed, sticks became shorter, most likely to accommodate the close quarters of street fights in packed urban areas.

Due to the surplus of weapon options and the personalization of fighting styles, not every shillelagh fight entailed a specific set of movements, although today, various organizations that host Irish stick-fighting tournaments dictate clear rules and structures. The stick typically was held in the right hand; six inches or so extended past the base of the hand, and the remaining three feet or so extended upright. The left arm could be used for blocking strikes, throwing a punch, or, once in close quarters, grabbing an opponent's stick to attempt a disarm. The first objective, especially in the seventeenth and eighteenth centuries, was to knock the hat off the head of one's opponent, both as a sign of disrespect and to make the skull more easily accessible. A heavy blow from the side removed the hat, and the follow-up strikes, hopefully, were blocked by the bottom part of the stick. As the distance between fighters decreased, the tip of the stick, on both ends, but especially by the bottom of the hand, could be used to jab and strike. As fighters lost their weapons, they would then move to wrestling, attempting to throw each other to the ground so that the final stomping could commence.

The typical shillelagh fight went through three stages: stick fighting, collar and elbow wrestling, and stomping. Shillelagh fights began with both fighters using sticks to strike each other. Fighters often would lose their weapons as the fight progressed, either from being disarmed or sometimes due to injuries that made it impossible to grip their sticks. The combatants would then grab each other in the typical Irish collar-and-elbow style, sometimes with one or both sticks being employed in the grappling. When a shillelagh fighter was able to get his opponent to the ground, he (sometimes joined by his fellows) would stomp the downed fighter, often while wearing hobnail boots. Worn by nearly every Irish laborer, hobnail boots had nails or spikes protruding from the bottom to provide the wearer with increased stability while traversing Irish bogs and fields.

Outside of shillelagh battles, the Irish had several distinct wrestling styles, including collar and elbow, square hold, scuffling, and back-hold wrestling. Irish boxing, known as *Dornálaíocht*, was part of the *Gráscar Lámh*, the Irish hand-to-hand fighting styles, and was very similar to what the British practiced. Shin kicking (*Speachóireacht*) remains a part of the Irish martial arts, and, rather tellingly, is referred to as Irish shin kicking or English shin kicking, depending on one's perspective and, no doubt, nationality. The Irish did far more wrestling than boxing on a communal and cultural level, although individual Irish boxers certainly made names for themselves as they fought against British pugilists, especially in countries, such as Britain, where boxing was far more popular and profitable.

The Irish, perhaps, were the most despised class in England, stemming from the huge influx of immigrants streaming into England starting in the early seventeenth century, long before the potato famine began in 1845. The Irish were considered a threat to the very livelihood of the Englishman, who believed that the Irish would undercut the English laborer. The Irish also were stereotyped as barroom brawlers, which was not true unilaterally, although certainly young Irish men were eager for gainful employment through prizefighting.

Numerous Irish fighters were successful, but one of the most famous was Jack Power, a plumber and champion pugilist. Celebrated as a scientific boxer, Jack Power was born to Irish parents in England in 1790 and began his fighting career at the bright age of fourteen. Many of his fights were with other Irish working-class pugilists, including a butcher, a tailor, a saddler (one who makes saddles), and a blacksmith, all of whom, in their nonworking hours, sought money and bragging rights. Power, according to our friend Pierce Egan, was "one of the most accomplished boxers of his day, viewed either as a practical fighter or an elegant *setter-to.*"[9] He fought against men from around England, sending them to the hospital with devastating injuries and nearly killing a man from Birmingham.

At an exhibition event in Salisbury, Power went to corner for a fellow fighter, while Tom Molineaux offered to take on any comers in an exhibition sparring match. A belligerent blacksmith who had a reputation for violence wanted to fight Molineaux, and the impression was that he really wanted to kill Molineaux for being black, not spar according to the rules of the time. Molineaux literally locked himself in a room and refused to come out, lest the blacksmith attack him. The blacksmith then turned to Power, swaggering and yelling, and finally striking Power in the head. Power stripped off his clothes and set upon the blacksmith. Within fifteen minutes, Power knocked out the blacksmith, and the man was carried away, his two front teeth missing. The villagers were so delighted to see the town ruffian vanquished that they paid Power handsomely.

Power made his career as a plumber, which, at the time, was a dangerous endeavor that eventually would damage Power's ability to perform in the ring. It is said that plumbers at the time would drink large quantities of castor oil to mitigate the effects of lead fumes, although perhaps adding to their overall level of dehydration due to the tremendous purgative property of castor oil. On November 16, 1812, Power met Jack Carter in the ring for a hundred-guinea purse. Whether it was his lungs, a reported ruptured blood vessel, or the act of fighting in the freezing English rain wearing nothing but a thin pair of breeches, Power did not fare well in his fight with Carter. His constitution, significantly weakened by inhaling lead fumes as part of his work as a plumber, impacted his overall performance in the ring, and though he lost, it was considered a manly, scientific battle.

Like many lower-class men of his day, Power lived a rough life in the streets of London. His dual careers as pugilist and plumber were enough in themselves to lead to his eventual decline in health, but according to Egan, Power also lived hard. Egan explained,

> Alas! possessing a gaiety of disposition which could brook no restraint: the fascinating charms of company, and the enlivening glass, proving too powerful for his youthful and inexperienced mind to withstand, he entered precipitously into excesses which produced debility and a bad state of health.[10]

But, given his druthers and the prospect of a life of poverty, it seems that Jack Power rather enjoyed his life of fighting, womanizing, drinking, and partying, being willing, after all, to forgo his health for the celebrity life of a Regency prizefighter. His success encouraged other Irish boxers to try their hands, literally, at prizefighting and attempt to secure some semblance of respectability.

Molineaux, Mendoza, Power, and Stokes exemplify the lives of immigrants and other outsiders living in England during the Regency era. Egan's book *Boxiana* provides sketches of hundreds of boxers, but these three men not only embody the experience of the immigrant, they also reveal the harsh reality of eighteenth-century boxing. Elizabeth Stokes, meanwhile, represents a largely ignored and maligned history of women's fighting in Europe. Interestingly, while boxing at the time was terribly brutal in length, ferocity, and even the natural elements (Power and Molineaux both lost while fighting in the rain), for all of these pugilists, fighting was a way out of poverty and, more important, an opportunity for each to represent his or her community in spite of racism, xenophobia, and sexism.

## India via England

England's influx of foreign fighters changed the landscape of pugilism and solidified the country's place as a mecca of fighting sports. British imperialism also meant occupation abroad, and few countries experienced the power of England's imperialistic forces more than India. After decades of operating under Afghan rule, Britain slowly and methodically occupied India through the East India Company. India contained numerous natural resources that the British were eager to export and exploit, and offered an opportunity for the import of British goods. India was occupied first by the East India Trading Company, a British company backed by the government. Official British occupation, known as the British raj, began in 1858 and ended in 1947. During that time, Indian rulers brought back the pageantry of old, offering lavish wrestling events that celebrated Indian masculinity. Training centers opened in the urban areas, and an emphasis on physical fitness returned, focused especially on middle-class men who were separated from their strong peasant roots but unable to reach the exalted position of an upper-class man.

Manipuri, India, is home to a unique martial art known as *Thang-Ta*, a style that includes weapons and empty-hand tactics. In the sixteenth century, Thang-Ta had a strict code of ethics required of warriors, even in warfare. One manuscript described the process by which combatants would have an official fight, and whoever bled first was considered the loser. Both men would then eat and drink together with their wives, and the victor would cut off the loser's head. During British occupation, Thang-Ta officially was banned, although it was practiced in secret through the use of ritual dance. This is a common practice in occupied nations: when martial arts are banned, people shift their practice by hiding the movements and techniques in dance.

Although wrestling was considered a safe form of physical fitness for Indian men, Thang-Ta was far too risky for the British occupiers or for the Indian maharajas. The unarmed version of Thang-Ta is designed to be used against another unarmed opponent, or one wielding a weapon. Striking attacks using punches and kicks were designed mainly to be defensive. In fact, this version of Thang-Ta, called *sarit-sarat*, sometimes was performed in a theatrical venue where a woman being attacked by a man would defend herself using sarit-sarat tactics. After the end of British occupation, Thang-Ta slowly emerged from hiding, although it has survived primarily as a form of dance, a lasting legacy of imperialism.

England's power stretched across the globe during the age of imperialism, and its lasting impact, both at home and abroad, led to many martial artists coming into contact with other fighting styles. Between warring with their new subjects abroad and battling their neighbors on the continent, English traditions and customs spread around the world and contributed to the formation of fighting arts in the new United States of America, and Britain's oldest enemy, France.

## France

France was the second largest colonial power in the age of imperialism, right behind its British neighbor. French territories spanned the world, from the Americas, to Africa, to Asia and Oceania. Their biggest impact on martial arts took place in their own country, inspired by some of the martial arts of their territories in Taiwan, Laos, Cambodia, Vietnam, India, and parts of China. Whereas English boxing developed after the history of Greek and Roman fighting, the French style of *savate* was unusual in Europe for its highly acrobatic kicking style. Savate has some similarities with Cambodia's Kun Khmer and Thailand's Muay Thai, and may even have been inspired by the two, given France's occupation of Southeast Asia in the imperial age. Savate started primarily as a kicking-dominant system and included inverted kicking techniques with hands on the ground, similar to engolo. Eventually, it evolved to include punches, inspired by a bout between a British boxer and a French savateur.

The French lived in politically and socially tumultuous circumstances from the 1500s to the late 1800s, but that did not stop development of the much-beloved sport of savate. Initially it was a substitute for dueling with weapons, which were banned, restricting irate Frenchmen and women to the use of their hands and feet to settle scores. The first savate school, or *salle*, was opened in 1803 CE in Paris by Michel "Pisseux" Casseux. Casseux taught fifteen kicks and fifteen cane techniques, codifying the long-practiced *canne de combat*, a fighting style using a staff or cane, which remained popular through the early twentieth century.

Casseux's most famous student, Charles Lecour, tested his savate skills regularly, fighting against any style. He fought against British boxer Owen Swift using savate, but the fight ended in a draw. Swift's legs were damaged from Lecour's kicks, Lecour's face bruised from Swift's punches. Lecour then spent a few weeks in England with Swift, working on his boxing, which he eventually would incorporate into his fighting style. Lecour's amalgamated style was christened *Boxe Française*.

The origin of savate is unclear, although the word savate refers to shoes that workers wear, indicating that the sport originated in the working classes. However, the sport became popular when French writer, poet, and fighting enthusiast Théophile Gautier suggested teaching savate in schools and changing the name from its rather rough antecedents to the more eloquent "French boxing." As it grew in popularity, French boxing had three iterations—an acrobatic version performed as theater in entertainment halls, a self-defense version, and a true sport version. Today, savate has three levels of competition: assault, precombat, and combat. Assault savate involves light sparring, and fighters are judged on technique and amount of touches landed. Precombat is similar to amateur boxing or kickboxing. Fighters wear headgear, soft shoes, and other standard protective gear and can win by knockout or a judge's decision. In full combat, savate fighters wear gloves, a mouthguard and groin protector, and the standard savate shoes but no headgear or shin protection.

The sporting version was based on fencing rules, in which the first person to land a strike won that point; therefore, speed was of the utmost importance, rather than power. One unique and rather delightful addition to French boxing was the practice of a fighter being required to say, "Touche!" if he was struck first, regardless of whether the blow did any damage. Savate has many of the same rules as kickboxing, and in the twentieth century, savate fighters often fought other styles in early mixed-match bouts. Savate fighter Gerard Gordeau famously fought Royce Gracie in the first UFC event (see chapter 4).

## Russia

The vast Russian empire had a variety of wrestling styles that differed from village to village, where the local wrestling champions might fight neighboring champions or soldiers from armies passing through. One version of Russian wrestling competition had matches that ended only when one person overcame the other with a joint lock, and fights could go on for hours until that goal was achieved. The Mongolian Empire invaded Russia in the thirteenth century, and Siberian wrestling took on aspects of the Mongolian style, in particular the use of short jackets. When the Russians fought off the Mongols and expanded their own empire into parts of Asia, they were introduced to other wrestling styles, elements of which made their way into Russia's folk wrestling. Stick fighting also was popular in Russia, and prior to Peter the Great's rule, beginning in 1682, fights often ended in severe injury. Peter wanted his men ready to fight on his behalf at any time and outlawed stick fighting in order to ensure that his army was healthy.

In other parts of Europe, the boundaries between countries and traditions were less defined than those of England and France. Folk-style wrestling was practiced ubiquitously and contested between villages and tribes. Many of these arts had similar approaches, such as back-hold wrestling of England, Scotland, Iceland, and Serbia, while Mongolia, China, Turkey, Devon, Cornwall, Siberian Russia, and Sardinia had jacket and/or belt-hold wrestling.

The similarities between folk wrestling traditions across Europe, Asia, and North Africa reveal that trade does not just occur in the marketplace. It takes place in sporting events held in cities or at rural festivals, between conquerors and the conquered, and enemies as well as friends. And, so, as globalization brought together fighters from differing backgrounds, information was transmitted, and fighting arts evolved. During this age of imperialization, borders changed and regimes rose and fell, and all the while, people continued to fight, in order to survive and to prove their own national superiority.

## AFRICA AND THE AFRICAN DIASPORA

In 1627, the Portuguese began systematic raids into the Kunene region of Namibia, where more than one thousand people were captured and enslaved. The Kunene people, who were adept at the arts of engolo, which we discussed in the previous chapter, as well as the bow-and-arrow and the stick-fighting style of *kandeka*, fought bravely against the Portuguese military. In fact, in 1639 CE the Kunene warriors killed the leader of the Portuguese kidnapping campaign along with all of his men. The Portuguese, however, continued their onslaught of the western coast of Africa, transporting thousands of Africans to the Americas. Many captives from West Central Africa were transported to Brazil to work on sugar plantations. Between the sixteenth and nineteenth centuries, more than 5.8 million enslaved Africans were transported to Brazil. [11]

The Kunene who were forced into slave labor in the Americas continued their tradition of practicing engolo and passed the movements on to their children born into slavery. As those children interacted with enslaved people from other parts of Africa, engolo spread further and evolved into an iteration that could survive the brutality of Portuguese rule. Slave masters feared any type of combative training, so the descendants of the Kunene hid their fighting art in the dance of capoeira. Capoeira combines acrobatics and kicks with footwork, all practiced to music, and described as a game or play rather than a fighting bout.

"Playing" capoeira may have seemed innocuous to Europeans, but the movements could be translated when needed and even used with weapons for self-protection. For a time, capoeira was associated with street gangs in Rio, although the relationship between the martial art and crime probably was exaggerated to generate fears of roving African criminals in the hearts of white Brazilian elitists. When slavery was abolished in 1888 CE, alarm about African uprisings continued, and the art of capoiera was banned in 1890. Banning capoiera was part of a systematic campaign to destroy the African cultural practices that had not been diminished even during the horrors of European slavery.

The African diaspora generated new fighting styles in the Caribbean islands. In Cuba, fighting sports and dancing combined to create a unique cultural practice. *Juego di maní*, also called *bambosa* or just *maní*, means "game of war." In this creative environment, players move in a circle and deploy punches, forearms, elbows, and head-butt strikes, as well as sweeps and throws, to demonstrate their prowess. Interestingly, this dancing fight style is more in line with modern MMA than many of the component martial arts, such as boxing or wrestling, that often are ascribed as its foundation. Some versions of maní include the use of weapons, such as machetes, to symbolize the agricultural-based foundation of the art. Haiti also has a dance form of martial art using weapons, as do Trinidad and Barbados, which refers to stick fighting as stick licking. Many of the arts are hybrids of traditional African fighting arts, the fighting styles of the indigenous populations, and the structures that European colonizers imposed. Even after the end of formal European occupation, local celebrations include demonstrations of these martial arts, ensuring that the history of imperialism and the cultural traditions that evolved continue to survive.

## The Canary Islands

The Canary Islands, located off the coast of Morocco, consist of seven small islands that, prior to the Castilian conquests of the early fifteenth century, largely were populated by the Guanches. The indigenous people had a stick-fighting system, used foremost for fending off animals, as well as tribal sport and warfare. The Guanches also had their own wrestling style, which remained part of their cultural practices even after the Castilian invasion. Although the Castilian rulers did not like the idea that their newly acquired "subjects" practiced fighting with weapons, even sticks and stones, they had no issues with continuing wrestling competitions. The Castilians embraced the Guanches' wrestling because it was a sport both cultures shared. Stick fighting frightened the occupiers because of its novelty and easy translation to combat, but wrestling was neither confusing nor threatening. The universality of wrestling actually connected these two seemingly different cultures and, because of that connection, the sport thrived. In addition, the Castilians wrote accounts of sporting events, so we have textual descriptions that were heretofore absent because of orality Guanchen culture.

The Guanchen wrestlers came from modest backgrounds but obtained the sponsorship of wealthy businessmen, the support of fans, and, eventually, the attention of the press. The nineteenth century began a trend that eventually would bifurcate the sport of wrestling between the sport and the theatrical. Performative wrestling, frequently known today as "professional wrestling," became exceedingly popular in the Canary Islands in the mid-nineteenth century. Performing wrestlers, known as *luchadas*, eventually would bring their skills to other parts of the world through emigration.

## Madagascar

Moraingy, a folk striking style, originated with the Sakalava community, which occupied the western coast of Madagascar. Moraingy probably existed long before the arrival of the Portuguese in 1500 CE, but it spread across the Sakalavan territories and became practiced in the Seychelles, Mauritius, La Réunion Island, and the Comoro Islands. The sport celebrates Sakalavan cultural legacy and is designed to instill traditions of hard work and respect in every fighter and in the fans. Fighters always hug each other after the fights, and everyone in the community cheers equally for the winner and the loser of a bout.

Traditionally in Moraingy, bouts last until one of the opponents cannot continue due to fatigue, injury, or if the referee decides that the contestants show a tremendous skill imbalance. Fights primarily are boxing based, with straight punches, hooks, uppercuts, and a punch similar to an overhand. Kicks also were allowed, but because Moraigny traditionally was fought between villages and representatives from different family units, the rules in the eighteenth and nineteenth centuries were not firmly established. Today, Moraigny continues to be part of traditional Madagascar culture, celebrating the traditions of the Sakalava and instilling respect in those who participate.

## NORTH AMERICA

When colonials set out to inhabit the New World, they found vast lands occupied by indigenous tribes, each with its own culture and social structure. But as we have discussed previously, some themes in human play extend across time and place, and several of the games that the indigenous peoples of the Americas practiced were strikingly similar to the sports played in Europe. Stick and ball games (specifically the antecedents of lacrosse), an early form of football, wrestling, and boxing were part of some tribal cultures, although the context of sport differed from European practices. For Europeans, sports often went hand in hand with leisure time, but for many Native American tribes, sport acted as war games and coming-of-age practices, as well as entertainment.

The Iglulik tribe in the far north played a unique boxing game where one competitor would punch the other in the shoulder or temple, taking turns until one declared himself defeated. Like many of the island and African cultures, most Native American tribes communicated their histories orally, so we have little written documentation on the actual movements and techniques of various indigenous American sports. In addition, the vast spaces and varying topographies of North America meant that each tribe would have its own iterations of sports.

Several European powers colonized North America, although the British certainly had the largest hold on this newly discovered property. Of the many groups leaving Europe for the promise of a new life, the Puritans were the most doggedly invested in creating their heaven on Earth. The Puritans were a thorn in the side of King James of England, who was considered a somewhat crass man. James loved sports and even published a *Book of Sports* in 1618 CE. The king believed that sports had tremendous nationalistic value and provided individuals with an opportunity to blow off steam that could otherwise contribute to a political coup. But the Puritans objected to sports and, in particular, sporting events, much to James's annoyance. Sporting events, especially fights, often included alcohol and gambling, which further ruffled Puritanical ideological feathers.

The Puritans were not the only group in the New World who objected to fighting. The era of colonization coincided with what later would be called "the Age of Enlightenment," a rather quixotic movement for reason and humanism. Colonization and Enlightenment are rather strange bedfellows, because the former frequently stripped indigenous people of their basic human rights. But many luminaries of the Enlightenment made their way to various colonies, advocating rationality and challenging long-held beliefs based on prior knowledge. Thomas Paine, whose 1775 pamphlet "Common Sense" would help galvanize the American Revolution, was part of the Enlightened movement in the colonies, as were Benjamin Franklin, James Madison, and Thomas Jefferson. And when the United States became its own country independent of British rule, one key tenet of the American Enlightenment was distancing the new country from the old. Thomas Jefferson wrote that an English education corrupted young American men by introducing them to "drinking, horse racing, and boxing," which leads to a fondness for "European luxury and dissipation."[12] Enlightened men should not participate in these brutal acts, nor should intellectual men take pleasure in watching a boxing match.

Yet many of the Europeans who flocked to the New World brought with them their own cultural traditions, including wrestling and boxing, which could be practiced in times of leisure. The Puritans linked work to godliness, and any type of recreational activity with devilment, making sports antithetical to their religious and moral ideals. Many other religious groups immigrated to the colonies, seeking distance from religious persecution in Europe and finding the tendency toward boisterousness in some of their new neighbors a bit frightening. Not only had individuals seeking religious and political freedom come to the New World, but those looking for adventure and perhaps a bit of lawlessness. In the South, a fighting style emerged that would remain popular even after the Revolution.

In 1806, Englishman Thomas Ashe wrote an account of his visit to Wheeling, Virginia, where he witnessed a fight between two working-class men that he would remember for the rest of his life. The men, one from Kentucky and one from Virginia, argued over who had the better horse, a somewhat standard debate in the booze-filled outskirts of small towns. Not willing to acquiesce to a difference of opinion, the men, along with the Englishman Ashe and a large portion of the town, took off to a track to test the speed of the two beasts.

Apparently, the race was inconclusive, but the two men, unwilling to end their feud, challenged each other to fight. They agreed to "tear and rend" rather than "fight fair." Ashe watched in astonishment as the man from Virginia took the Kentuckian to the ground and from a mounted position, grasped his hair and stuck his thumbs into the man's eye sockets. Kentucky recovered and rolled Virginia off of him. Once on top, Kentucky leaned over and bit off the nose of the man from Virginia. But the fight was not over. The man from Virginia took the Kentuckian's lower lip between his teeth and ripped it down to his chin. Then, the fight was over. The man from Virginia, sans nose, was carried off in victory while the Kentuckian headed to the doctor, his eyes damaged from the attempted gouging and his torn lower lip flopping around his chin.

This fight was not an anomaly, but rather a tradition of fighting that was particular to rural southern areas of the young United States in the eighteenth century. "Rough-and-tumble" was the name given to no-holds-barred fighting in the southeast region of the newly formed America. Betting was prevalent, rules nonexistent. Contestants could kick a down opponent, knee to the groin, bite, and even scratch each other with fingernails sharpened just for the purpose. Eye gouging became the ultimate finish in rough-and-tumble, disfiguring many men for life. Fingernails, sharply filed and coated in wax, dug into an opponent's eye socket, attempting to literally rip out the eyeball and hold it aloft before a screaming crowd. How frequently this feat occurred is unknown, as many accounts merely speak of that being the goal rather than an actual result, although an unsubstantiated folktale in North Carolina told of eyeballs littering the ground after a mass rough-and-tumble fight. Eye gouging may have been the preferred coup de grace, but fighters had numerous ways to maim an opponent and earn the approbation of the crowd. Biting off ears, lips, fingers, and the nose were popular moves, as was head butting and, of course, testicle tearing.

American men in the mid-eighteenth-century southeast territory apparently took great umbrage at any insult thrown in their direction. The journal of one Philip Vickers Fithian, a tutor from New Jersey working for an aristocratic family in Virginia, provides one of the most detailed accounts of a rough-and-tumble bout. Fithian wrote that two men would meet at a space, surrounded by a cheering (and typically inebriated) crowd, and start off boxing. However, the fights quickly would deviate from the standard rules of boxing to the anything-goes nature of the rough-and-tumble. If one man fell to the ground, the other man could kick, stomp, strike, or gouge. In rough-and-tumble fights, no-holds barred was part of the "gentlemanly" agreement.

Started in the rural Carolinas and western Virginia, rough-and-tumble expanded in popularity in the late eighteenth century into Kentucky and Tennessee. These sparsely populated areas lacked those two dueling American ideologies, Puritanism and Enlightenment, that in cities and urban areas deemed boxing gauche. Boxing at least had rules and limits, but rough-and-tumble undoubtedly was the most violent form of fighting in the United States at the time.

Because rough-and-tumble fighting was a conceit of rural communities, most of which did not have newspapers that wrote about the fights, accounts of "gouging" typically come from travelers visiting Virginia and the Carolinas who wrote about their misadventures. Many of these accounts were carried in British newspapers and clearly are exploitative, presenting Americans as backwoods folk heroes, albeit barbaric ones, and the Brits could read these narratives, aghast but pleased to see their former colonies in ruin. To many British readers, American democracy gave autonomy to those who did not deserve it, such as the savages in the Deep South, and gouging was merely a sign that independence was not meant for all.

As the eighteenth century came to a close, and a cultural shift toward perceived refinement moved through the American South, rough-and-tumble fighting and the injuries associated with it became less a sign of masculinity and more a symbol of old barbarism. In this new, seemingly genteel society, differences were settled with dueling rather than tearing off another man's testicles. Men in the middle and upper classes began to train in the art of pugilism, and rules became part of gentlemanly culture. It seems as if the heatedness and the frenzy of rough-and-tumble is what most southern men truly deplored. A true gentleman should be calm and aloof, always adhering to decorum, even when agreeing to fight another man to the death. These formal duels did not always succeed, and sometimes, heated tempers led men back to the rough-and-tumble. U.S. senator James Jackson famously resorted to biting the finger of Robert Watkins, a politician from Savannah, when Watkins attempted to gouge Jackson's eye.

Although rough-and-tumble fighting never would become an organized sport, the sport of prizefighting evolved along with the founding of America. Prizefighting was the American term for professional boxing, where competitors fought for financial gain, whether it be a purse filled with coins, a silver chafing dish, or a cow. The American boxing obsession began in the early nineteenth century with the 1816 fight between Jacob Hyer and Tom Beasley, although undoubtedly bouts were fought prior to that date. At the time no formal governing body had been established to enforce official rules, but the bout was described as maintaining some attempt at structure, with Hyer winning. He was never challenged again, so Hyer retired undefeated. In 1841, his son Tom defeated George "Country McCloskey" McChester in a 101-round barn burner, initiating the first real prizefighting craze in the United States. In 1849, Tom Hyer fought the Irish-born Yankee Sullivan in a highly publicized match. Hyer's victory was of such great importance that the story was telegraphed to New York City newspapers, making it the first sports story to be shared via telegraph.

Although the puritanical and enlightened powers of early America might have wished to separate the New World from the barbaric practices of Europeans, many early Americans had rather boorish tastes. Spectators flocked to watch illegal "blood sports," such as bullbaiting, bearbaiting, and rat baiting, dogfights and cockfights. Prizefighting in the United States was a popular form of mass entertainment in the 1800s, but it struggled to equal the British golden era, due in no small part to the many critiques of the sport in general and the athletes, most of whom remained thoroughly ensconced in the lower classes. Indeed, by the middle of the nineteenth century, prizefighting was illegal in many parts of the United States, decried by politicians and religious officials as barbaric. In addition, prizefighting correlated directly with gambling, a sin to most religious people. Unlike the boxers in Europe, whom aristocratic men often backed, just as royalty once supported Shakespeare and other playwrights, the fighters in the United States had no upper-class individuals to overrule the prudish morality of middle-class Americans. Thus, prizefighting was a crime, albeit one rarely indicted.

Although American prizefighting did not have royal backing, it did have a large contingent of some less than savory supporters, including gamblers, politicians, and a group of boxing enthusiasts known as "the fancy." This fraternity of sporting gentlemen escaped their Victorian existences as husbands and fathers to join each other in a male-dominated space. The fancy met in saloons, where prizefights typically took place in an attempt to escape legal jurisdiction, to play dice or cards, bet on prizefights, drink heavily, and perhaps visit a brothel. In the aftermath of the infamous 1842 fight between Thomas McCoy and Christopher Lilly, in which McCoy died in the ring, having drowned in his own blood in the 120th round, New York cracked down on prizefighting.

But within a few years it was back again, reinvigorated when Thomas Hyer and Yankee Sullivan fought in 1848. Newspapers carried coverage of this and other prizefighting events, presenting them as stories of depravity to be abhorred by the American reader, yet salaciously detailing every moment of the bloody battles. Most media outlets openly criticized prizefighting (even as they spared no obscene punch in their stories), but one publication became its champion.

The middle to late nineteenth century could be a rather dreary time; and despite Queen Victoria's firm fixture in England, her legacy spilled over to the American continent, creating an atmosphere of prudishness that permeated both English and American societies. The blanding of American culture, focused on conservative middle-class values, decried the activities found on both ends of the class spectrum, including the luxurious excesses of the wealthy and the lively pastimes of the poor. The *National Police Gazette*, founded in 1845, was the prototype for the tabloid, the sleazy dime papers with screaming headlines printed on garish pink paper. The *Gazette* would not become the popular purveyor of spicy gossip and gristly gore until Richard Kyle Fox took over the failing publication in 1877. Fox was a poor Irish immigrant who, in his own way, would invent not only the modern tabloid, but also the American approach to sports journalism. Fox's *Police Gazette* sought to appeal to both conservative values and American bloodlust, shilling stories about violent crimes and the heroics of the police force, as well as coverage of pugilism. The *Police Gazette* pandered to the desire for blood and flesh that the religious and the intellectual communities of the time decried. While priests condemned lust and intellectuals disavowed desire, Fox's publication delighted in the orgiastic violence of fighting, from cockfights to pugilism.

Fox's approach to journalism shocked priggish readers and engendered a new type of American media that entertained while it informed. True to its name, the *Police Gazette* covered the police beat, often in horrific detail that glorified violence and sensationalized crime. Headlines fairly shouted at readers and provided them with stories that seemed exotic and illicit. In the late nineteenth century, prizefighting largely was illegal in the United States, and promoters, fighters, and spectators could be arrested for attending illegal fights. Of course, this did not stop boxing matches altogether; it merely created an environment where the lower classes were at risk of arrest, while upper-class men who enjoyed boxing could attend these illicit events with impunity.

Fox felt that prizefighting should be legalized in America, and he sought to legitimize the illegal sport by creating fighting events that the paper sponsored and providing coverage of the fight in a somewhat fair, unbiased voice. Of course, Fox's efforts to legalize and legitimize prizefighting were not entirely altruistic; it was an ingenious way to sell more papers. The *Police Gazette* exuded sensationalism on every page, but for Americans that is exactly what made it a popular read. Fox promoted fighters from a variety of backgrounds, including black fighters and female fighters such as Hattie Leslie and Gussie Freeman. But his objective, always, was to write content that presented sensationalized news to America's reading public, who hungrily devoured the blood, grit, sex, and violence Fox and his *Police Gazette* provided. Richard Fox's publication also contributed to the emerging commodification and eventual corporatization of sports in the United States, even sponsoring fighting events.

Interestingly, although John L. Sullivan might be one of the most famous nineteenth-century fighters in American history, Richard Fox antagonized the champion ceaselessly in his publication. Whether it was out of actual animosity or simply the desire to create controversy remains unclear. Fox purportedly wished to speak with the fighter in a loud bar, but Sullivan, a notoriously heavy drinker, refused the invitation and thus offended the newspaperman's sensibilities.

After that, Fox regularly put up challengers against the undefeated Irishman, and Sullivan just as swiftly dispatched them in the ring. One of Fox's protégés, Jake Kilrain, agreed to take on Sullivan, but John demurred. Fox pounced immediately, claiming that Sullivan's refusal meant he vacated his title as the "champion of America." Sullivan's prolific drinking and lack of training caused his weight to shoot up from 195 pounds to 240 pounds, which the *Gazette* gleefully reported to readers. Finally, Sullivan acquiesced to the fight, taking several months to slim down and get back into fighting shape. When the two men finally met on July 7, 1889, fight fervor reached a fever pitch, and police in four different states declared their intention to arrest everyone involved. Nevertheless, the men fought in the heat of a Richburg, Mississippi, summer day. The mayor of New Orleans refereed the bout, which would be the last official bare-knuckle championship fight.

The rules of this fight were not based on the Marquess of Queensberry rules, so there were no gloves and no time limit on rounds. When one man hit the ground, the round ended, and both men stood to go at it again. Although Kilrain controlled the action in the first few rounds, the fourth round lasted fifteen minutes, and Sullivan regained his footing. The fight continued as the men each inflicted and sustained damage, their ribs and faces bruised, eyes swollen, and skin burned from the hot Mississippi sun. After two hours and sixteen minutes, in round seventy-five, Kilrain's manager threw in the sponge, conceding the victory to John L. Sullivan.

Sullivan's victory was short lived as he and Kilrain both were arrested and stood trial in Mississippi. Sullivan was sentenced to a one-year jail term along with fines, but his fame and the fact that several jurors actually went to the infamous fight led the charges to be dropped. Several years later, Sullivan attempted a return to the ring and was roundly beaten by the far younger and much better conditioned "Gentleman Jim" Corbett. Sullivan's antagonistic relationship with Richard Fox, however, did much to promote prizefighting in the United States. And even though Sullivan was a notorious racist, his name in the *Gazette* helped sell papers, which, in turn, aided fighters Sullivan himself would have dismissed.

In fact, the *Police Gazette* supported fighters routinely ignored or vilified by the rest of the country. Women have boxed and wrestled since the origin of those sports, even if they seem constantly to be considered the first of their kind. In the nineteenth century, a time when prudish Victorian ideals dominated, the *Police Gazette* covered female prizefighting and even sponsored several women-only tournaments. In 1892, the *Police Gazette* published a lengthy article praising three female fighters, Lib Kelly, Hattie Stewart, and Hattie Leslie, and their Amazonian performances in the ring. The *Gazette* treated all three of these women as legitimate athletes, even while their fights were sensationalized in other articles.

The *Police Gazette*'s positive treatment of female fighters was rare in America. In 1888, Hattie Leslie and Alice Leary agreed to a fight, both dressed rather vulgarly for the time in tights, thin sleeveless tops, and wearing riding gloves with the cording removed. Twenty years old, standing five foot ten and weighing in at 168 pounds, Hattie had a tremendous size advantage over the 148-pound Alice, but finding another woman to fight in 1888 was a difficult undertaking in New York. In the first round, Hattie landed a sound right cross on Alice's nose, but that worthy immediately responded with a hard punch on Hattie's cheekbone. As the fight continued, both women struck often, landing body shots as well as punches to each other's arms, and finally in the fourth round, Alice punched Hattie in the teeth and drew blood. Then Hattie flurried, and Alice turned to avoid the blows, getting punched in the throat and side of the head instead. After the sixth round, Hattie's corner wiped sweat and blood off her face and told her to stop being so nice. The bell sounded, and Hattie pummeled her opponent furiously until time was called. Alice's corner threw in the sponge, conceding the victory to Hattie Leslie.

The *Cincinnati Enquirer* published the account of Hattie Leslie and Alice Leary's battle, calling the "disgusting spectacle" between two "female brutes" an example of "terrible depravity."[13] This was not the first time that women fought publicly in the United States, and it certainly would not be the last for Hattie Leslie, who went on to have a short but prolific career, competing in prizefighting and in wrestling bouts. The *Enquirer* may have found this example of female pugilism to be depraved, but the many witnesses to the spectacle cheered at the bout, and the *National Police Gazette* would praise Hattie as an accomplished prizefighter. While many other newspapers criticized and condemned female pugilists, the *National Police Gazette* celebrated the women who entered the ring, and through tournaments sponsored by Richard Fox, made the fighters, and the newspaperman, a great deal of money.

In 1884, the *Police Gazette* published a surprisingly positive article about John L. Sullivan and the popularity of pugilism in the United States of America. The article glorifies the muscular male physique, embodied, of course, by the highly successful Sullivan. The paper credits Sullivan with the growing popularity of boxing, which apparently was unknown in the United States until Sullivan's fame made headlines, undoubtedly aided by the *Police Gazette*'s efforts. The article claims that because of Sullivan, fights increasingly are between various types of pugilists,[14] from heavyweights and lightweights, to child boxers, and "women boxers of every degree of size, weight, and color." This might have been true, in terms of size and weight, but the color issue in the United States still was highly contested in 1882; and even after the end of slavery, African American fighters contended with racism, in and out of the ring.

The horrors of slavery in America cannot be understated, nor can the irreparable damage to a culture be ignored or brushed aside. African men, women, and children were sold into slavery against their will and taken across the vast ocean to a new world, only to be starved, worked to the bone, assaulted, violated, and killed. There is no space to excuse slavery, or to talk about plantations where slaves were "treated well," because without the right of autonomy, a person cannot be free.

Certainly other groups in the young United States lived in abject poverty and had a terrible existence, but it is inappropriate to attempt an equivalence between the life of a poor white man and the reality of an African slave, who was roundly dehumanized and demoralized for the benefit of white upper- and middle-class society.

The atrocities perpetrated upon the enslaved African community are so vast and so varied that one book cannot suffice to explore them adequately. Instead, this section focuses on how the Middle Passage did not completely destroy the culture, history, practices, customs, or unique traditions of the African men, women, and children who were enslaved. History books frequently reduce the lives of slaves to hollow experiences, focusing on dates and wars, and ignoring the everyday life of the people who lived as slaves in the United States. But it would be another form of erasure if we did not recognize the significant impact that the wide range of African traditions had on American culture. African people brought with them food, music, art, and dance customs specific to their communities, creating an amalgam of traditions that would eventually be reduced to that of a singular representation of Africanism. Despite the horror of slavery, many newly imported African slaves were able to retain aspects of their culture and pass them down through the generations, creating a new community with shared, if varied, traditions and customs.

The slave trade routes did not randomly distribute Africans in the Americas, but instead brought slaves from one part of Africa directly to specific ports in the Americas. Therefore, a large majority of people from a specific community or tribe might be ensconced in a particular plantation. The concentration of slaves from a shared background aided in the collective remembrance of their culture's beliefs and practices.

In South Carolina, enslaved people transported from Central Africa brought with them their own martial arts traditions. Out of this amalgamous collective of various African communities and tribes, the art of "knocking and kicking"—a fighting art that consisted of kicks, strikes, and head butting—was born. The Angolan practice of head butting became the "knocking" in this new composite style, where fighters would deploy a head butt like any other strike or grab their opponents by the ears and slam into their heads until they submitted. The *knock* of "knocking and kicking" purportedly is from the sound that the fighters' heads made when they crashed into each other. Kicking, meanwhile, grew, in part, from the engolo tradition of foot sweeps and high inverted kicks. "Knocking and kicking" was practiced as sport and ritual dance, both of which were used, along with wrestling, against rivals, slave hunters, and foremen.

African wrestling in enslaved populations came from a variety of traditions, including the Nigerian style of mgba and the Sengalese art of laamb, and it often featured leg-wrapping techniques, which marked its distinction from the collar-and-elbow style that the growing Irish immigrant population in the United States practiced. African "wrasslin" took the form of sport and play, and in many circumstances, slaves would wrestle each other, as Frederick Douglass wrote, to "win laurels" and display their physical prowess to any young women watching.[15] Douglass noted that sports also were encouraged by plantation owners, including wrestling and boxing, which Douglass deemed "wild and low sports peculiar to semi-civilized people," but that "rational enjoyment" was not.[16]

Douglass felt that by encouraging the slaves to participate in "low" sports, they would crowd out exploring more important pursuits, such as reading, writing, or perhaps, planning a rebellion. He explained that plantation owners encouraged fighting because it was "among the most effective means in the hands of the slaveholder in keeping down the spirit of insurrection."[17] Douglass saw plantation owners manipulating martial arts competition for their own benefit, which seems like a just assessment. But for many boys and young men, wrestling and boxing were ways to connect to their heritage, retain the traditions of their ancestors, and create new forms of agency despite their current circumstances.

Even as enslaved Africans brought their martial arts traditions with them, the South was becoming enamored of English boxing. In the early eighteenth century, wealthy families would send their sons to England and other parts of Europe for their education. Although young men from the North and the South made the journey to England, the vast majority of them were southern, due in most part to the surplus of wealth found in that plantation-rich part of the country. The young men would be schooled in academics, art, and culture, and, typically, would sow their wild oats amid the vast cultural diversions of the old country. British pugilism was just entering that golden age of fighting, when the working class and the elite both pursued the sweet science. Young

American men of a certain personality type learned to box from British pugilism instructors and took their knowledge back with them to the more puritanical America. But they found their choice of opponents was lacking. They turned to a seemingly abundant source of punching bags—or so they thought. If the young southern gentlemen thought that they would find easy targets in the men they kept enslaved, they were very wrong.

As with any group of people who practiced a martial art historically, fighting sports functioned as a means of self-protection when a trained individual found himself or herself in dire circumstances. Many enslaved Africans called upon their training when faced with atrocities to be perpetrated upon themselves or their family members. Enslaved women frequently put their cultural martial-arts training to use in order to defend themselves from rape. They also practiced the fighting arts of their ancestors, and those techniques were put to good use when faced with rape or brutality. Silvia Dubois, an African woman whose mistress routinely assaulted her, took her revenge by beating her mistress so severely that the white people who watched were shocked into inaction. Silvia took advantage of their momentary dumbness to flee her oppressor and escape her bonds.

The results of slavery are far reaching and have had a significant, lasting, and insidious impact on American culture today. One tendency is to think of slavery as the complete dehumanization of the enslaved, but that misconception does not recognize the communities that people create out of trauma and necessity in order to maintain their humanity. Sharing traditions and customs across ethnic lines, and through generations, the enslaved African population in the American South retained a sense of self, both collective and individual. The collective trauma of slavery generated a need for African fighting arts to endure and grow, and today the many styles of martial arts practiced in the United States and abroad contain elements of those traditions, although they are not given due credit. We often equate fighting sports to either European or Asian tradition, which ignores the vast history of martial arts across all peoples, especially those who systemically were subjugated and oppressed.

The enslaved people who did fight in the style of English pugilism, especially in the late eighteenth and early nineteenth centuries, may have had more opportunity to change their circumstances, but the United States, even in the North, was not the ideal place for them to show-case their talents. African men had opportunities to fight and create careers for themselves in Britain, and so the few African American pugilists who succeeded in the United States found ways to move to England.

Bill Richmond and Tom Molineaux both were born enslaved and after becoming free, moved to New York and then to England. It is unclear in the records just how both men went from enslaved to free-men, despite conjecture that they earned it via their pugilistic endeav-ors. Richmond was a freeman before he was employed by the duke of Northumberland and taken to England with his new master to work on his own as a cabinetmaker and a boxer. One legend, although unsub-stantiated and perhaps embellished over time, claims that Molineaux won his freedom after his master won $100,000 in a bet on Tom's success in a boxing match, and a version of this could be true. The most important takeaway from stories about both Richmond and Molineaux is that despite their dominance as pugilists in the United States, given the opportunity, they left as soon as they could for better lives in Eng-land. Even when African men and women technically were free in the United States, their lives were still harsh and tainted by racism and hatred in the country that neither they, nor their ancestors, chose for their own.

African boxers were not the only ones to set sail for England. White American pugilists also saw England as the preeminent location for aspiring champions and their departure, along with African fighters, left the United States bereft of some of the best talent. Meanwhile, those men and women still enslaved in the South sought to create their own fighting traditions, carved out of the customs of their ancestors. Fight-ing sports in enslaved populations in the United States functioned as ritual, as performance, and as communal bonding. The continuation of African traditions in their current, dire circumstances provided African men and women with a chance to remember and celebrate their heri-tage through song, dance, and sport.

In the years after the Civil War, attitudes toward prizefighting shifted, especially with the adaptation of the Queensberry rules that enforced safety protocols. Fitness clubs became popular in New York, Boston, Philadelphia, and other larger cities as men looking to learn the "manly art of self-defense" began to train in studios for the new gentleman athlete. In the late 1890s, gymnasiums for women opened, offering to help patrons slim down to the idealized body type of the time. Boxing was a favorite among young women and upper-class matrons, all of whom seemed to find it invigorating and great for both blowing off steam and working out their arms. Many of these gyms included sparring, where young women would don boxing gloves and fight each other just as aggressively as their male counterparts, training down the street at their own "self-defense" gymnasiums. Although newspapers, including the *National Police Gazette*, seemed to enjoy telling the nation about the newest fitness craze for women, female prizefighters remained firmly outside the realm of respectability. That did not stop numerous women from competing in both prizefighting and wrestling.

In the twentieth century, boxing would become codified under various sanctioning bodies, but the sport of wrestling had a more fascinating transition in the New World. Colonial Americans brought their wrestling traditions from all over the world and contested these styles in bouts that for American idealists were far less sensational or problematic than prizefighting. George Washington wrestled and even encouraged his troops to do so during the Revolutionary War. Future U.S. presidents Zachary Taylor and Abraham Lincoln both wrestled, with Lincoln's 1831 victory over Jack Armstrong solidifying his name as a fighter and his future as a leader. In the antebellum period, wrestlers in the Midwest eschewed the more violent free-for-all of the rough and tumble, and instead competed in a form of wrestling that allowed nearly everything but eye gouging, biting, and punching.

Greco-Roman style wrestling remained the most popular form in the United States, embodied by the first real hero of American wrestling, William Muldoon. Muldoon seemed the polar opposite of John L. Sullivan, prizefighting champion of the time. Muldoon was an adherent of the "muscular Christianity" movement, which prized godliness through physical fitness and strength while eschewing vices of the flesh, alcohol in particular. As a clean-living proponent, Muldoon was a mountain of a man at 250 pounds of muscle, making him an excellent Greco-Roman style fighter. He toured the country with a troupe of his protégés, performing their wrestling as sport and spectacle, offering competition for any locals who felt ready to take on the mighty Muldoon. Muldoon fought wrestlers practicing a variety of styles, from collar and elbow to back hold, and even sumo wrestling, as more Japanese fighters made their way to the United States. However, most of the matches were according to Greco-Roman rules, so Muldoon's expertise remained supreme.

When Muldoon retired in 1891, however, Greco-Roman style no longer maintained its ascendancy over American wrestling. Instead, catch wrestling rose to the top, defeating other approaches and initiating a new era in American wrestling. These wrestlers could use any takedown or throw, and once on the ground, they fought for submissions or for the pin. This "anything-goes" style of wrestling was a precursor to the new style of "catch-as-catch-can wrestling," which eventually would bifurcate into two types of fighting—theatrical and sport wrestling. When Muldoon retired in 1891, he seconded prizefighter Jake Kilrain when he fought George Godfrey, showing an interesting link between wrestling and boxing.

Before invasion by European conquistadors, many island communities had thriving cultural traditions that included sport. The original inhabitants of the various Hawaiian Islands practiced many activities that made use of the stellar weather and wide variety of terrains. From surfing to javelin throwing to martial arts, early Hawaiians, like many other cultures we have seen around the world, used sports as part of the performative aspect of ceremonial occasions. Before Hawaii was invaded and then annexed by the United States, history and storytelling were disseminated orally, and for that reason, we have no written accounts of the rules and particulars of their wrestling style. As part of that annexation of the islands, many of the original cultural traditions and practices were wiped out in order to better assimilate the inhabitants and make them more pliable under U.S. government rule.

Ancient Hawaiians marked Makahiki, a four-month celebration to honor Lono, the god of the harvest, of agriculture, and of rebirth. Makahiki runs from October/November through February/March, based on the lunar cycle. During this time, war was prohibited; and during their fighting abstention, warriors maintained their fighting prowess by engaging in ceremonial games, including foot races, wrestling, and boxing contests. One interesting contest was the haka moa, in which each contestant, man or woman, would grab his own left foot with his left hand, grab his opponent's free right arm, and try to throw each other to the ground. Another form of Hawaiian wrestling, hakoko, was fought inside a circle of people, and once the match ended, the winner would expend nearly as much time boasting as he (or she) did fighting. Hawaii's bare-fisted striking style, mokumoku, also took place during the Makahiki festival.

The Hawaiian martial art, *lua*, is a deadly style that originated from tribal warfare. Lua is a mixed martial art, comprising empty-hand and weaponed techniques designed to maim or kill enemy combatants. Throws and other wrestling maneuvers are done in conjunction with strikes in order to inflict more damage, and the striking includes eye gouges and grabs designed to rip flesh. Today, lua has been reintroduced as a cultural artifact, preserving the heritage of Hawaiian fighting by practicing the techniques of this deadly art in conjunction with music and dance.

As the nineteenth century came to a close in the newly formed United States, fighting sports were becoming more formalized and increasingly visible in the media. People living in widely disparate places could now follow fights all over the world. The increase in sports media led to an increase in sports practice, on the levels of both the amateur and the professional.

## ASIA

### Japan

The United States broke Japanese isolation in 1853, but by the end of the nineteenth century, Japan would engage in its own imperialistic quest, expanding its borders into China, Korea, and Okinawa. Jujitsu, the catchall term for empty-hand fighting, experienced a number of threats during this time, from internal powers that sought modernization and from foreign invaders looking to eliminate practices of Japan's indigenous culture. However, the demand for fighting sports inspired the Japanese government to control and regulate its martial arts, rather than to ban them outright.

In feudal Japan, numerous wrestling styles were delineated not only by their techniques, but also by their purpose. They included theatrical or performative wrestling, wrestling matches staged to raise money for shrines, wrestling that the aristocracy sponsored, village wrestling, and women's wrestling, and wrestling as a call for rain. By the 1600s, the government was tired of dealing with confrontations between the various styles and practitioners, especially when rivals would suddenly strip down to their underwear in a street alley to settle a score via wrestling. The Tokugawa government created laws to restrict unregulated wrestling, trying to eradicate these back-alley bouts and eliminate traveling bands of wrestlers who would declare themselves willing to take on all comers. However, Japanese citizens, from the peasants and the working class to the aristocracy and royalty, craved competition, so wrestling could not be banned outright. Instead, sumo was born.

In the late seventeenth century, government officials and wrestling promoters worked together to create a standardized, safe wrestling competition that entertained the citizenry and appealed to the government's sense of decorum. First, officials generated a firm set of rules and designated fighting arenas, called *dohyos*, made in sand pits. Fighters donned silk belts with a single strip extending from stomach to lower back to cover the backside. Combined with their hair styles, skimmed back from the crown and folded on top of the head, sumo wrestlers became some of the most highly recognizable athletes in the world and appealed to the government's desire for courtly decoration. Japanese officials also regulated sumo training, requiring licenses for training facilities as well as trainers and fighters. Under this very organized system, sumo wrestling flourished, operating in the 1790s under the patronage of Shogun Tokugawa Ienari and becoming popular in rural and urban communities. Over the next hundred years, sumo came to represent Japan as a formal, yet highly entertaining fighting sport, eventually making its way overseas and in 1993, into the first UFC octagon.

While Japanese wrestling became standardized through the formation of sumo, Japanese jujitsu flourished and proliferated in the 1600s and 1700s as numerous iterations of the empty-hand fighting style were taught in various schools and training academies. But during the Meiji Restoration of 1867–1868, the samurai were abolished and jujitsu threatened to become extinct. Some instructors attempted to keep the art alive, but they resorted to sordid means to do so. Jujitsu versus sumo matches created a popular spectacle, while some masters provided fighting instruction to the seedy underbelly of the Japanese streets.

In 1882, Kano Jigoro founded his modern system of jujitsu, *Kano ryu jujutsu*, commonly known today as judo. Jigoro publicly acknowledged the historic tradition of Japanese jujitsu as the foundation of his art and claimed it was a national heritage that needed to be preserved. Jigoro established his first "school for the study of the way," the Kodokan, in 1882 in Tokyo. Traditionally, Japanese martial arts were practiced using katas, or forms, in order to minimize the risk of injury; many matches included katas, where both partners knew the offensive and defensive techniques. This is an excellent way to avoid injury, but not necessarily conducive to the randomized reality of combat or competition.

Jigoro introduced the concept of controlled sparring, called randori, where practitioners would attempt to throw, pin, choke, or attack the limbs of an unwilling partner. As long as both fighters stayed within the confines of the rules and general etiquette, randori was an extremely helpful way to practice and learn. In fact, Jigoro's first students were so adept at mastering judo that they dominated in practical competitions with jujitsu schools practicing other iterations of Japanese martial arts.

Judo became celebrated and highly sought after as a means of self-defense. The Tokyo Metropolitan Police adopted judo and kenjutso to help in defense and arrests. In 1904, a Japanese practitioner named Higashi Katsukuma traveled to New York City to give a demonstration to the police department. The diminutive Katsukuma, who was five feet three and weighed 120 pounds, took on a 195-pound New York City cop and choked him unconscious within a minute. Jigoro's art of judo, therefore, had utility across demographics, from police officers to self-defense to sporting competition. Judo focuses on throwing techniques using the kimono, or gi, and grappling techniques on the ground. A striking component is practiced in the kata but not included in competition. In the twentieth century, judo competitions became formalized and spread across the world, a development addressed in chapter 4.

## China

Chinese martial arts continued to develop through the Ming and Ch'ing Dynasties, from approximately 1368 to 1911 CE, but it was during the latter's rule that boxing spread throughout the country and its borders. The Ch'ing (also called the Qing and the Manchu) Dynasty activated a spirit of unrest within its borders, in part due to China's burgeoning relationships with European powers. A number of secret societies emerged that centered around Chinese boxing and a fervent desire to return the Ming Dynasty back to power. These secret societies, known collectively as the "boxers," failed to overthrow the Manchu, but they did spread the art of Chinese boxing around the country and beyond, including Taiwan. In 1899, as the nineteenth century drew to a close, Chinese fighters rose en masse to expel all foreigners from their country, an attempt that ultimately failed despite the fierce fighting on the side of the boxers. Known as the Boxer Rebellion, this bloody encounter revealed that though the Chinese fighters were deadly in close-quarter fighting, they could not defeat the firepower of modern warfare. It is worth noting, however, that fighting forces from Britain, France, Italy, Russia, Germany, Japan, the Austro-Hungarian Empire, and the United States all had to be brought in to quell the Chinese Boxers in 1901.

During the Ch'ing Dynasty, a large number of Chinese people moved from the mainland to the neighboring island of Taiwan. Although little is known of Taiwan's indigenous martial arts prior to the arrival of the Dutch in the seventeenth century, archeological evidence suggests that they used knives as part of their native warfare. The Ch'ing Dynasty took over rule of the island in 1683, and an influx of Chinese citizens immigrated to Taiwan, bringing their customs and traditions to develop on the island. Over the following two hundred years, Chinese culture proliferated in Taiwan until the Japanese took control in 1895 and banned the practice of Chinese martial arts. Under Japanese rule, Taiwanese were indoctrinated in the practice of Japanese arts, especially judo and kendo.

In the aftermath of the Boxer Rebellion and the demise of the Ch'ing Dynasty, Chinese martial arts were brought into the new republic's government and made standard practice in schools and in military drill. Although martial arts may have been seen as backward during the Manchu Dynasty, in the Chinese Republic, martial arts were a symbol of national pride. In 1928, *wushu*—Chinese for martial "*wu*" and art "*shu*,"—was made the national sport. Competitive wushu is practiced as a form and as a fighting sport, known as *sanda* or *san shou*, a kickboxing style that includes takedowns and sweeps of all sorts, making it the ideal gateway to modern mixed martial arts.

At the same time that empires expanded and shifted all over the globe, sports became institutionalized, as a way to protect against

foreign influence and ensure the tradition of celebrated, national pastimes. Formalizing the boundaries of fighting sports clearly separated
boxing from kickboxing, Greco-Roman wrestling from catch-as-catch-
can, weapon-based war games from empty-hand styles. These rules also
dictated who could participate and who was barred from entry. In delineating these fighting sports, the rule makers of the 1800s created a
path for convergence to emerge in the 1900s and for fighters around
the world to pit their martial arts prowess against a completely different
style. By separating fighting sports into genres, the genre-breaking
MMA emerged.

**Kilted cartwheel by back-hold wrestler at Allan Highland Games 2019 in Scotland.** *Photograph courtesy of Richard Findlay.*

**Back-hold wrestling; Paul Craig and Greg Neilson at Inveraray Highland Games 2019.** *Photograph courtesy of Richard Findlay.*

Chinese wrestling (Shuaijiao) at the Taiwanese and Chinese American Athletic Tournament in the United States. *Photograph courtesy of Jumiana Weng.*

Chinese wrestling (Shuaijiao) at the Taiwanese and Chinese American Athletic Tournament in the United States. *Photograph courtesy of Jumiana Weng.*

Bokator (national tournament in Cambodia). *Photo courtesy of the Cambodia Kun Bokator Federation.*

Dambe fighter Danatibata Banka landing an overhand strike at an AWFC event in Nigeria. *Photo courtesy of the African Warriors Fighting Championships.*

Daugon Kudawa versus Isiya at an **AWFC** event in Nigeria. *Photo courtesy of the African Warriors Fighting Championships.*

Mgba wrestling competition (also known as gidigbo or kokowa) at an **AWFC** event in Nigeria. *Photo courtesy of the African Warriors Fighting Championships.*

Mgba wrestling competition (gidigbo or kokowa) at an **AWFC** event in Nigeria.
*Photo courtesy of the African Warriors Fighting Championships.*

Professional boxing match in the United States. *Photo courtesy of Kassandra Alonso.*

**Amateur kickboxing bout with protective gear in the United States.** *Photo courtesy of Kassandra Alonso.*

**Amateur kickboxing bout with protective gear in the United States.** *Photo courtesy of Trevor Bennion.*

Wrestling competition featuring Ross Ridpath and Simon Margelts in Cornwall, United Kingdom. *Photo courtesy of Richard Cawley.*

**Professional kickboxing bout in the United States.** *Photo courtesy of Kassandra Alonso.*

**World Sambo Championships in Cheongju, Republic of Korea, November 2019.** *Photo courtesy of the International Sambo Federation.*

International Sambo Tournament in Belarus, February 2020. *Photo courtesy of the International Sambo Federation.*

Submission wrestling tournament in the United States. *Photo courtesy of Kassandra Alonso.*

**Submission wrestling tournament in the United States.** *Photo courtesy of Kassandra Alonso.*

**Submission wrestling tournament in the United States.** *Photo courtesy of Antojo Photography.*

Muay Thai match between two young Thai fighters in Isaan, Thailand. *Photo courtesy of Tate Zandstra.*

Muay Thai match between Thai and Iranian fighters in the border town of Kelantan, Malaysia. *Photo courtesy of Tate Zandstra.*

**Burmese boxing match between a Thai fighter and a Burmese boxer in Mae Sot, Thailand.** *Photo courtesy of Tate Zandstra.*

NCAA wrestling featuring Jordan Burroughs and Ben Askren at Beat the Streets 2019 in the United States. *Photo courtesy of Victoria Diaz.*

NCAA wrestling featuring Becka Leathers and Diana Weicker at Beat the Streets 2019 in the United States. *Photo courtesy of Victoria Diaz.*

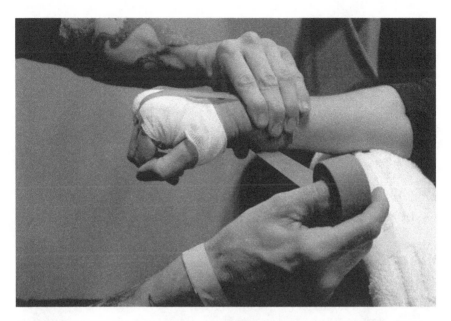

Athlete getting his hands taped prior to a fight. *Photo courtesy of Kassandra Alonso.*

Amateur **MMA** fight in the United States. *Photo courtesy of Franklin Photography.*

**Amateur MMA** fight in the United States. *Photo courtesy of Bryan Carr.*

# 4

# FIGHTING AROUND THE WORLD

In 1905, Georges DuBois was a well-established savate and fencing instructor, regularly contesting his French kickboxing against other fighting arts, including English boxing and karate. Fin-de-siecle France remained devoted to its national identity and culture, but the Japanese art of jujitsu was becoming a worldwide phenomenon, practiced by suffragettes in England, politicians in the United States, and families in Brazil. The French adored their national arts, and in October 1905, DuBois sought to prove that his home country's art of savate was the best fighting sport in the world. Fellow Frenchman Guy de Montgrilhard, known as Ré-nier, trained Japanese jujitsu and so loved this art that he published *Les secrets du jiu-jitsu* that same year. So, when DuBois and Ré-nier faced each other in a Parisian suburb in 1905, it was not merely a fight between two men—it was a battle between two cultures, with one man representing his native art and the other a foreign style. DuBois began the fight by throwing a *coup de pied bas*, a low leg kick, but Ré-nier avoided the strike and within seconds tossed the savate instructor to the ground and subjected him to an armlock. DuBois's loss was France's defeat, and in the aftermath of this mixed discipline fight, newspapers debated whether jujitsu was superior to savate and what that might mean for French martial arts. Soon after, Ré-nier lost to a Ukrainian wrestler, launching another media frenzy debating the efficacy of Japanese versus Ukrainian wrestling.

Although this might seem like an isolated test in France, it was, in fact, representative of the many struggles that would take place around the world in the twentieth century, as indigenous martial arts experts became exposed to differing styles from other cultures. Some fighters held tightly to their own traditional style, whereas others abandoned their cultural fighting sports in favor of foreign martial arts that seemed novel and exotic. And so, across the globe, fighters tested their disciplines, competing in bouts that matched boxers against wrestlers, kickboxers against sumo wrestlers, and any other combination that might prove interesting to fight fans. Initially, interdisciplinary fights clearly pitted one style against another, each fighter restricted to the techniques of his or her art. In most of these events, if a wrestler fought a boxer, the wrestler was not permitted to punch, nor the boxer to throw. Eventually every martial art would have to take on the techniques and attributes of other fighting sports in order to remain successful, but in those early days of mixed martial arts, fights were contested between styles rather than just between fighters. And as each fighter represented his style and, in turn, his nationality or ethnicity, those early bouts had meaning beyond a simple contest.

Twentieth-century developments in communication technologies would fundamentally change human interaction, and, with it, our sports. In addition, as transportation industries and technologies advanced, people began to travel more frequently than in any previous era. What were local events, sometimes shared by the newswire, suddenly became televised and visible to the world. Along with the advances in media communications technologies, tremendous efforts were made to regulate sports and unify athletes around the world. Boxing underwent a strict transition as governing bodies emerged worldwide, especially when the modern Olympics reconvened at the end of the nineteenth century. Wrestling experienced a similar streamlining process that clearly delineated two forms of competitive wrestling, Greco-Roman and freestyle. The organizations that oversaw both boxing and wrestling existed on the local level, as did international governing bodies, and the goals were similar: to protect athletes, eliminate cheating, and create a fair and equitable contest environment.

Both boxing and wrestling competitions were not just professional contests; both of these sports were practiced in schools and colleges, on military bases and in city programs. But as both sports grew in participation and in media coverage, new ways of contesting fights appeared, including interdisciplinary bouts. In the beginning, fights between boxers and wrestlers were not necessarily meant to be enjoyed for their displays of athleticism, but rather for the spectacle of seeing something novel. Early mixed bouts developed from rather silly curiosities to real contests, especially when fighters began to cross-train in order to be better equipped for battle.

Numerous books and articles reveal the histories of both boxing and wrestling in the twentieth century, providing thorough details on the figures and events that defined each discipline. For the rest of this book, we will look at how boxing and wrestling converged with other fighting sports and contributed to the development of interdisciplinary fighting, so some important events in the history of both sports will be omitted in order to focus on MMA.

In an increasingly globalized world, fighting sports expanded beyond the traditional geographical boundaries, and fighters became exposed to different modes of training and competition. This chapter will skip around in time and place, in conjunction with the development of technical communications such as the radio, television, and the internet, and the exhibition of fighting sports across the world. And nowhere was that convergence of culture, technique, and communications more apparent than at the inaugural Olympic Games held in Athens, Greece, in 1896.

## EUROPE

The modern Olympic Games, which evolved from the first modern event held in Athens in 1896, eventually included multiple fighting sports. Boxing and wrestling were early parts of the modern games, although pankration has yet to return. The Olympics have had a tremendous impact on the development of fighting sports, especially for fighters who went on to compete professionally in boxing, wrestling, and, eventually, MMA. But one of the most important evolutions was the distinction between professional and amateur athletes.

When in 1892 Pierre de Coubertin of France called for the revival of the Olympic Games, the primary discussion among the elite group of educators and public figures that formed the first version of the Olympic committee was to determine *who* would be allowed to compete. This may seem like a strange debate, but at the time, the concern was one of class, a concept that defined and organized life in Europe and in the United States. The late nineteenth century was still a time of imperialism, and the idea of reforming the Olympic Games to engender a feeling of international unity seems rather romantic and a bit tone deaf, especially when so many people in the world existed under the thumb of European nations. But Pierre de Coubertin truly believed that the new Olympics could unify people everywhere under the auspices of fair play, cooperation, and the appreciation of global cultural diversity.

The word amateur derives from the Latin word *amator*, or lover. In a sense, that is what it means to be an amateur—someone who dedicates himself or herself to a pursuit not for the money, but for love. Sports in the nineteenth century remained a luxury of the middle class, and lower-class athletes routinely were excluded from participation. The rules for the 1878 Henley Royal Regatta declared: "No person shall be considered an amateur oarsman or sculler . . . who is or has been by trade or employment for wages, a mechanic, artisan, or laborer."[1] Working in "trade," even working in general, was a mark of the lower and middle classes, and a distinction from those who had the time and money to pursue leisure activities. Historically, classism ruled the sports and athletic activities that the gentry practiced, not only to prevent the mingling of the higher echelons with the common masses, but because many of the elite insisted that the "plebeians" had no concept of sportsmanship and fair play.

At the end of the nineteenth century, it seemed to the inaugural Olympic congress discriminatory to prevent a day laborer from participating in a field event simply because he made his living by his hands. At the same time, it was unfair for a professional prizefighter to face off with a mechanic who boxed in his free time. Thus, the 1892 Olympic congress redefined amateurism so that it restricted those who profited by their participation in a sport. When the games began in 1896, participation was limited to athletes who did not receive any financial compensation for athletic endeavors. Interestingly, the ancient Olympic Games made no such restriction on how an athlete made his living. As long as one adhered to the other rules of participation, a boy or man could compete in the games and be compensated, with money or glory, based on his performance. In fact, the Olympic victor in the inaugural 776 BC Games, Coroebus of Elis, worked as a cook. But his culinary profession did not prohibit him from receiving remuneration as an athlete as well as a cook.

Although the Olympic definition of amateurism was seen as a way to not discriminate against the lower orders, it emphasized that those who did not have personal wealth or leisure time would not be able to support themselves with their sport. This continued the path of elitism, where athletes working a non-sport specific job still had to maintain a rigorous training regimen in order to be competitive. Over the century that followed the inauguration of the Olympic Games, rules changed: in 1988 the IOC made professional athletes eligible for participation in the Olympic Game complex, allowing the Dream Team to dominate basketball in 1992 with Michael Jordan at the helm. But for the vast majority of the twentieth century, only amateur fighters could participate in the Olympics, making it a highly visible entry point for fighters who later could make a living as professionals.

In the early twentieth century and in the aftermath of the first modern Olympics, it became important to establish an international set of guidelines and rules in order to ensure continuity in future international competitions. This way fighters around the world would know the rules of engagement prior to their bouts, which hopefully would diminish arguments about rules and protocols at the Olympic Games. In 1913, the first international congress met in Berlin, Germany, to establish the rules and regulations of boxing, wrestling, and weight lifting, known as the International Union of Heavy Athletics. However, in 1920, it seemed advisable for each sport to have its own governing body, and so the International Amateur Wrestling Federation and the International Amateur Boxing Federation were formed. That same year, South African bantamweight fighter Clarence Walker became the first African man to win an Olympic boxing title. Hungarian boxer Laszlo Papp became legendary when he won gold in 1948, 1952, and 1956. Takao Sakurai of Japan became the first boxing gold medalist from Asia in 1964, and Cuban fighter Teofilo Stevenson became another triple gold winning boxer.

The International Amateur Wrestling Federation established the statutes organizing both Greco-Roman and freestyle wrestling in 1920 and helped legitimize the sport of wrestling internationally. Over the next few decades, the number of weight classes increased, and so did global participation in the Olympic Games. Initially, European wrestlers dominated the competitions, in part because the vast majority of participating countries were from Europe and North America. The first African wrestler to win in the Olympics was Ibrahim Mustafa, of Egypt, in 1928. Shohachi Ishii was the first Asian wrestler to win a title, representing Japan in the Helsinki Games in 1952. That same year, Roger Coulon became president of the organization, renaming it the International Federation of Amateur Wrestling (FILA), and instituting several rules that would make Olympic wrestling one of the best organized and cogent sports in the games. He created a rigorous system for qualifying referees and reinforced continuing education in order to ensure that rules were enforced properly and comprehensively. Coulon also founded the General Association of International Sports Federations, which allowed sporting federations to better communicate with each other and improve the international sporting community.

Judo officially became an Olympic sport for men in 1972; in 1992, women were added to the program, making it the first Olympic fighting sport to include female practitioners. In 1988, tae kwon do was introduced as an exhibition sport in the summer Olympics, and in 2000 it became a full medal sport. When tae kwon do entered the Olympic Games, both men and women were included in the sport, a historic moment for women's equality in the fighting world. Each sport has its own governing body that determines eligibility and what is permissible compensation for an athlete.

Today, only wrestling continues to limit participation in the Olympic Games to amateurs only, as boxing, one of the last bastions of amateur-only athletics, now allows professional fighters to compete. It may be due to wrestling's vast history of functioning not only as a sport, but as a source of entertainment, particularly in twentieth-century traveling circuses. Fighting sports were a mainstay of the circus circuits for many years, and it was only in the middle of the century, after WWII and in conjunction with the development of television, that wrestling divided into "theatrical" and sport. This distinction, however, was not always very clear, and so establishment of governing bodies, such as the Boxing Commission and United World Wrestling, helped define how each sport operated, who was allowed to compete, and what rules constituted every event.

Europe was the epicenter of cultural development in the previous chapter, both through an internal artistic renaissance and by the process of imperialistic appropriation. But two world wars and social upheaval greatly impacted twentieth-century Europe, forever changing the economic, cultural, and natural landscape. During the twentieth century, many European countries and their fighters contributed to the organization of the newly reformed Olympics, and used their history of fighting arts to prepare for wars that, sadly, would go beyond the scope of hand-to-hand combat in the deadliness and efficacy of modern weaponry.

Much of Europe was deeply embroiled in war during a great deal of the twentieth century, which did not preclude sports competitions from occurring, although war, obviously, greatly disrupted athletic practice and competition for generations of athletes. Although this book cannot go deeply into European politics or history in order to remain focused on fighting sports, it is important to know just how deeply Europe was disrupted by war and political turmoil in the twentieth century. Nevertheless, fighting sports remained an important part of European culture, even as Europeans fought and died in battle, or left their home countries for a better life, typically heading to America. As immigration increased, so did the spread of various fighting sports, which would become amalgamated with the traditional sports in places such as America, Thailand, and other parts of Asia, to forge new martial arts, such as the famous Baritsu in England.

Japanese martial arts were some of the first fighting sports to be disseminated around the world, as wrestlers and boxers in Europe became fascinated with the elegance of jujitsu. In the early twentieth century, police officers in England began implementing jujitsu techniques to apprehend suspects. Meanwhile, women fighting for the right to vote often had to stave off verbal and physical attacks from men, including police officers, who detested this new form of female agency. Mrs. Edith Garrud became an expert in jujitsu and taught the art to her fellow suffragettes to protect themselves from male aggression. Although this is an example of a martial art used for self-defense, it does reveal the extent to which Japanese fighting arts became part of European combat culture. The famous fictional detective, Sherlock Holmes, was said to be an expert in jujitsu; and Hercule Poirot, Agatha Christie's fictional Belgian sleuth, used a throw to evade an angry murderer. That jujitsu entered Britain's popular culture in fiction, as well as in the police force and the new feminist movement, all within the first few decades of the twentieth century, demonstrates how globalization impacted Europe's social landscape.

While fighting styles from Asia began slowly trickling into the European fight scene, boxing remained the most popular combat sport in England, even if it often was vilified in parts of British culture. Boxing in the early twentieth century shifted from the bare-knuckle, free-for-all, and limited rule set of nineteenth-century prizefighting. With the adaptation of the Queensbury rules, and the new glove requirements, boxing became a more socially acceptable sport, and famous matches of the early twentieth century often were covered in nationwide radio broadcasts.

The addition of gloves, however, did not diminish the risks of bodily damage. Gloves were leather and only weighed four ounces, so fighters bolstered their chances by using thick tape underneath the gloves to make the punches exceptionally brutal. Mouthguards were not required, nor really used with regularity anywhere, and head injuries and permanent damage were commonplace. In addition, most places did not have strict guidelines regarding fighting frequency, so boxers might fight several times a week in order to generate a living.

Wrestling remained a popular fixture in England, especially in rural areas and the countryside. In the eighteenth and nineteenth centuries, Lancashire was home to a unique style of wrestling that would greatly influence the progression of wrestling tactics used in MMA in the twentieth and twenty-first centuries. Lancashire wrestling did not require special jackets or belts, no limits were placed on the kinds of holds or grips one could use, and the fights could end from a pin or a submission.

In the United States, Lancashire wrestling combined with parts of the rougher frontiersman style of fighting to create a new iteration, the American "catch-as-catch-can" wrestling. For Americans, part of catch wrestling's rise to prominence might have been an increasing sense of nationalism. Greco-Roman wrestling was not actually based on ancient Greece or Rome, but rather was an amalgam of French elbow-and-collar style wrestling that did not allow any holds below the waist. American and British wrestlers were not terribly keen on the Greco-Roman style even though it was part of the first modern Olympic Games in 1896. Catch wrestling was differentiated from this European art, and although some American wrestlers, including William Muldoon, discussed in the last chapter, excelled in Greco-Roman, catch seemed more exciting to Americans and the English. So embedded would catch wrestling become as an international alternative to Greco-Roman that the 1904 Olympics introduced the new sport of "freestyle wrestling." This new Olympic sport allowed fighters to attack the legs and provided many countries with a better line from their own indigenous styles to this new international sport.

Not only did Europeans export their fighting traditions to other parts of the world, they also imported fighters. India's long history of wrestling and physical fitness did not end during the English raj, although certain other sports were prohibited in order to diminish any threat of native revolt. In the twentieth century, an Indian wrestler, Mian Ghulam Muhammad, known as Gama, gained international recognition as one of the greatest fighters in the world. Gama's first victory came in a squat contest at the age of ten. Over the next few years, he dedicated himself to wrestling. Once a young man, he committed to a rigorous training and nutrition plan to maintain his highly muscular, five feet seven, two-hundred-pound frame.

In 1910, English wrestling promoter R. B. Benjamin took Gama and several other Indian wrestlers to compete in England. Gama was disappointed when he found only theatrical wrestling opportunities and no genuine competition. Finally, American wrestler Benjamin "Doc" Roller agreed to a match. "Doc" trained with Frank Gotch and was a highly skilled athlete as well as a real medical professional. But he was no match for Gama, who easily bested the American in a catch-style bout. Gama's next opponent was Polish wrestler Stanislaus Zbyszko, a mountain of a man who seemed to be a true challenge to the Indian champion. The men wrestled for two and a half hours, and in the end, time was called after Gama was unable to overcome Zybszko. It was not a terribly entertaining event—the press deemed the fight boring because Zybszko avoided all contact essentially by running away from Gama. When the men scheduled to meet again, Zybszko did not show up, and Gama won by default. Shortly after, Gama and his fellow Indian wrestlers returned home, disappointed by the lack of opportunities in Europe to showcase their superior wrestling skills.

English boxers and wrestlers embodied the idealized masculinity that British politicians and military officials believed necessary to the survival of their country during wartime. Indeed, militaries from around the world used combat sports to promote toughness and instill a work ethic that many older officers believed was lacking in that day's youth. The British used boxing to improve bayonet work, while the Germans focused on gymnastics and other strength-based activities to increase morale and focus on the idealized body so frequently referred to in Nazi propaganda. In the aftermath of WWII, Europeans began vacationing in Asia and Southeast Asia with renewed frequency, and numerous people became exposed to martial arts that differed wildly from the wrestling and boxing arts of Europe. In the Netherlands, an amalgam of Muay Thai and karate evolved, incorporating the heavy striking of English boxing with the devastating kicks and knees of Muay Thai. Since the 1970s, the sport of kickboxing has grown exponentially, and fighters such as Ramon Dekkers held titles in Europe and in Asia. In the twenty-first century, Dutch kickboxing and Muay Thai both have become popular worldwide and a fundamental part of the striking portion of MMA.

In Russia, an extraordinarily large country that contended with war, famine, and numerous other disasters in the twentieth century, politics reigned over the organization and practice of any activity, including sports. Under communist control, the idea of organized sports was contentious, in part because of ideals about the abuse of the worker body and consternation over the concept of bourgeois activities poisoning the Russian people. Although folk wrestling and other combat systems surely existed prior to the twentieth century, the vastness of the country and the political and social unrest led to a dearth of historical information about Russia's indigenous martial arts. Today, Russia produces some of the greatest wrestlers in the world, many of whom got their start training sambo.

Sambo is a Russian wrestling system said to have been created by Vasiliy Sergeevich Oshchepkov, a native of the Soviet Union who learned Japanese Kodokan judo while attending seminary in Japan in the early twentieth century. Oshchepkov received a second-degree black belt and when he returned to the Soviet Union during WWI, he taught a blend of Kodokan judo, savate, Greco-Roman wrestling, jujitsu, and English boxing to create a new style for training Russian youths. Oshchepkov would spend much of his life researching the fighting sports of other countries and perfecting his own system. The story of sambo's creation is long, winding, and fascinating, steeped in local and international politics. But in terms of MMA history, several major fighters out of Eastern Europe, including Fedor Emelianenko and Khabib Nurmagomedov, both of whom will feature prominently in chapter 5, got their start in sambo.

Europeans figured heavily in the formation of the rules, organization, and spread of martial arts as sports in the twentieth century. As fighters pitted their skills against other disciplines or in other parts of the world, martial arts separated from their countries of origins to become practiced and contested in other lands. In some places, however, fighting sports remained linked to the underworld, forcing the sports and the fighters to operate in the margins and outside of normalized social structures. Nowhere was this more apparent than in a former European outpost, where the white settlers and the indigenous people of Australia contended with issues of race, class, and freedom, deep in the outback.

## OCEANIA

Many islands make up Oceania, including Samoa, New Zealand, Hawaii, Guam, and Tahiti, as well as their largest close neighbor, Australia, which changed irrevocably with the influx of Europeans in the sixteenth and seventeenth centuries. These explorers brought their Western ideology to islands where individual tribal customs ruled for hundreds, if not thousands, of years. Generations after the influx of European settlers, many of these places have a culture where indigenous practices have been combined with European ones to generate a new, hybrid society. Fighting sports often are indicative of those cultural blendings, but we also see examples of fighting sports that remained constant to historical roots, even as they were contested in other places. English boxing, in particular, translated well around the world, but now included participants who never had set foot on British soil.

Australia was a British outpost on the other side of the globe, but much of the island's cultural practices were highly influenced by sports of the empire; cricket, "football," rugby, and sailing all were popular pastimes of Australia's inhabitants. Many of the British sports imparted to Australian citizens were designed to instill the mores of English society, especially in club sports such as cricket and rugby. It is important to remember that prior to Briain's annexation of the Australian continent, the indigenous aboriginal people cultivated their own social practices that included games and sporting activities. The English incursion marginalized the indigenous people, often violently, and threatened the native culture through forced assimilation, servitude, or threatened erasure. Many aboriginal groups moved away from the areas that Europeans occupied, inhabiting the harsher parts of Australia's landscape in order to ensure some type of protection from European invasion.

Meanwhile, boxing and wrestling increased in visibility as both traveling circuses and early films shared the sports around the world. In Australia, before protective rules were instituted, boxing was dangerous and, sometimes, deadly. Prizefighting took place surreptitiously behind racetracks or in circus tents, which led to the moniker "tent boxing" in that country. In the aftermath of WWI, amateur boxing associations formed internationally to encourage young boys to take part in healthy, rigorous exercise, but tent boxing in the outback remained the most popular venue for a fighter looking for fame, adventure, and a paycheck.

Tent boxers operated in troupes that traveled the Australian countryside. When the troupe arrived at a venue, they would stand up in a row in front of the crowd, willing to take on any and all who volunteered to fight. In some places, troupe members fought each other, often in prearranged matches where one member agreed to lose to the other. In the twentieth century, many aboriginal men joined these boxing troupes, which traveled around Australia to perform shows that at times featured wrestling as well as boxing matches. In a country highly divided among racial lines, it was one of the few places where white and black people mixed. Tent boxers worked in troupes of six to ten fighters on average, under the auspices of men who acted as promoters, showmen, trainers, managers, and controllers. The men who led troupes enforced grueling schedules, frequently underpaid their fighters, especially aboriginal men, and often did not provide enough food, water, or adequate lodging. Tent fighters fought daily, sometimes multiple times a day, and were held to a strict contract that required "good behavior." Drunkenness could get a fighter suspended, as could injuries, illness, or fatigue.

Tent boxing remains a part of Australian culture, operating as it did over the past century, and offering a chance for nearly anyone in the crowd to jump in the ring, much like American ToughMan competitions of the 1990s and early 2000s. Many professional troupes consist entirely of aboriginal Australians, who are tough, well-trained, and willing to get knocked around for the first round or two by an inept, but eager layperson (typically a white Australian), before coming back in later rounds to beat the challenger thoroughly.

For many professional troupes in Australia today, tent boxing is part of their heritage, but other Australians find the activity distasteful, especially when the motivation appears to be race-related. However, for many aboriginal men, tent boxing paved their way to successful professional boxing careers and gave them an opportunity to represent their culture in front of crowds that brought together Australians of every stripe. In the latter part of the twentieth century, Australia did see a shift from underground fistfights to sanctioned sport fighting, and numerous inhabitants would visit neighboring counties, looking to learn new fighting arts.

## AFRICA

The spread of Europeans throughout Africa in the colonial period increased the practice of organized sports. As previous chapters revealed, African cultures had their own rich sporting activities prior to European encroachment, but the British, French, Belgian, and Spanish colonists created institutions, governing bodies, and formal rules to govern sports all over Africa, a move of cultural sporting imperialism. Part of the colonial officials' encouragement of sport in Africa was to control the free time of Africans and to assimilate them into European sporting practices. Although many traditional arts, especially wrestling, remained fully ensconced in tribal celebrations, they frequently functioned as entertainment for white men and often were frowned upon by Christian missionaries.

During the twentieth century, many African nations achieved independence from their European overlords. Although these new nations were hindered by hundreds of years of violent European control and the sometimes-destructive force of capitalism, sports provided Africans with a source of pride and achievement. Indigenous wrestling remained part of ceremonial events, but many African wrestlers transitioned to the two primary Olympic styles of Greco-Roman and freestyle. The Nigerian striking art, dambe, returned to social prominence, and with the introduction of television, it became one of the most popular sports on the continent. The Canary Islands' wrestling system, Luca Canaria, became an official sport, and by 1985, it was televised throughout the country and the continent. Many Africans also focused on strict boxing, adhering to the various rules instituted by the IOC and other national and international governing bodies. In northern Africa and the Middle East, fighting sports contended with religious strictures, making it increasingly difficult for women to participate in competitions, although that would change in the twenty-first century.

The twentieth century would see the official end of European colonization in India, Africa, and other parts of the world, although cultural and economic imperialism persists to this day. Many people living in Africa, however, were seeing black fighters succeed as champions in boxing and wrestling, and in turn, many of those fighters looked to Africa as a way of reconnecting to their roots. Most of the world, however, did not look to Africa for martial arts. For the vast majority in the twentieth century, Asian countries became epicenters of martial arts instruction—places where Westerners could visit to expand their knowledge and, ultimately, take these ancient arts back to their own homelands.

## ASIA

### China

The twentieth century was a time of extreme nationalism worldwide, demonstrably revealed in the two major world wars that nearly tore the planet asunder. In addition, numerous countries threw off the mantle of their oppressors, whether that was a monarchy or an imperialistic nation. In China, the 1911 Revolution resulted in establishment of the Republic of China and the nationwide focus on China's great martial arts history. Some of the history China's newly established government spouted was mythical at best, and ignorant at worst, but all of it was designed to elevate the narrative of China's supremacy.

These historical narratives reinforced the government's decision to make martial arts training part of Chinese education, where swordsmanship and other weapons were taught alongside boxing and wrestling. The focus on Chinese physical education included a practical component for sparring, but an attempt to hold a freestyle fighting event in 1928 resulted in brutal injuries, most likely the result of a lack of rules and insufficient safety precautions. The Communist Revolution of 1949 furthered the emphasis on institutionalized martial arts training and maintaining the health of the Chinese citizenry. That same year, the Chinese government, under the leadership of Communist ruler Mao Zedong, advocated the practice of Chinese martial arts and other forms of exercise in order to make a more unified (and better trained) citizenry.

One of the most famous martial artists of the twentieth century was Hong Kong native Lee Jun-fan, known professionally as Bruce Lee, who immigrated to the United States in the 1960s. Before his early death in 1973, Lee revolutionized the depiction of martial arts in film, although he battled systemic racism that suffused Hollywood both on-screen and off. Lee studied numerous martial arts and taught an amalgamated style, known originally as Jun Fan Kung Fu, that included freestyle wrestling, traditional Chinese wushu and Wing Chun techniques, judo, boxing, and other fighting styles.

Lee's goal, it seems, was to eliminate the boundaries of traditional martial arts, find what was most effective for him as a fighter, and continue to add to his repertoire of techniques and tactics. His style, which might not appropriately be termed a system, because it was not meant to be a fixed discipline, was called Jeet Kune Do, and it was an ideal precursor to no-holds-barred fighting. Lee, along with his friend and student Dan Inosanto, taught Jeet Kune Do in the United States, and it has become a favorite for fighting sports enthusiasts around the world. Lee may never truly have entered the realm of MMA, but he was an inspiration to fighters who saw traditionalist martial arts as too limiting for a well-rounded fighter. His fame in the 1970s in Hollywood launched Chinese martial arts into an international phenomenon, and as a result, many of the traditional purveyors of kung fu were inundated with visitors from around the world. Westerners became obsessed with the Shaolin Temple, and that place of tradition opened its doors to allow the outside world inside the hallowed grounds.

While kung fu turned into an international obsession in the 1980s, many training academies in China sought to test their fighting skills in the real world, off the Hollywood screen. The fighting sport *sanshou* or *sanda* is similar to kickboxing, where fighters can punch, kick, and knee, but adds full clinch techniques as well as throws, shots, and slams. Once fighters hit the ground, they stand back up, making it similar to modern MMA without the ground work. Cung Le famously brought his sanda techniques to the UFC, but not until Zhang Weili won the women's strawweight belt in 2019 did the Chinese martial arts configure so strongly in the world's largest MMA venue. We will tell Zhang's story in due course, but other fighters also used sanda as part of their MMA style. In fact, because of their close geographical proximity, many Russian fighters also grew up training and competing in sanshou.

The Chinese art of wrestling, known as *shuaijiao*, developed in approximately 100 BCE, is an amalgam of Chinese and Han styles of fighting. In the twentieth century, it became the predominant wrestling style practiced in China, and remains a key complement to sanda. Fighters wear short jackets, like the Mongolian style of wrestling, and fights end once one opponent goes to the ground. The goal is for the fighter to remain standing after throwing his opponent. China did not fully join the MMA mania until the twenty-first century, but the fighting sports of shuaijiao and sanda made its athletes particularly prepared for rigors of the cage.

## Korea

The imperialism of the nineteenth century continued, albeit in different forms, into the twentieth century in many parts of Asia. In 1910, Japan annexed Korea, initiating a multi-decade period of cultural, political, and military subjugation. While under Japanese rule, Koreans continued to practice their traditional wrestling style, ssireum, and learned many of the Japanese arts, including judo, and the international sport of boxing. During the period of Japanese colonization, many Koreans trained karate, especially during the high points of WWII fighting, from 1944 to 1945, when all Japanese citizens, including ethnically Korean ones, learned armed and unarmed combat techniques. In the aftermath of WWII, Japan's control of Korea ended, but the country was split in two, with North Korea operating under the guidance of the Soviet Union and South Korea doing the same with the United States. As many of the Korean martial artists took karate back with them to their home countries, the style began to evolve. Karate's history will be explored later in this chapter.

It is difficult to trace one precise moment or just one person who generated the new art of tae kwon do, but suffice it to say that in Korea, the art of karate changed. This new style, tae kwon do (spelling differs according to style and place), was much more focused on sparring than on katas. The Korean emphasis on sparring might have been due to the forthcoming Korean War, whereas the Japanese focus on kata might reflect their unwillingness to seem combative in the wake of World War II. Initially, the Republic of Korea used tae kwon do for military combat, but it evolved in the following decades toward sport, cementing rules, and conducting contests all over the world, joining the Olympic Games in 1988. Many fighters began their fighting careers by training in tae kwon do as children, using it as a foundation for MMA.

## The Philippines

The Philippines span more than one thousand islands, nearly all of which have had their own languages, customs, and martial arts. Today, Filipino martial arts go by several names, including *escrima*, *arnis*, and *kali*, but for the purpose of this book, we will use the native Tagalog name kali rather than the Spanish names. In 1521 CE, famed Filipino chieftain Lapulapu used his superb fighting skills to kill Portuguese explorer Ferdinand Magellan when the latter demanded that the Filipinos pay tribute to the king of Spain. This did not prevent the Spanish from eventually occupying parts of the Philippines, and under Spanish occupation, indigenous martial arts were banned. Filipino martial arts primarily were weapon-based, although the wrestling system of dumog and the empty-hand panantukan were practiced in conjunction with stick and blade work. Panantukan included elbows and other strikes that were outside the realm of boxing regulations but could translate exceedingly well to modern-day MMA. Filipino martial arts did have unique footwork that would make the smaller fighters competitive against much larger, albeit slower, Americans and Europeans.

During the U.S. occupation from 1898 to 1946, boxing became a popular activity in Manila, the coastal capital of the Philippines, which had an active port where sailors from all over the world congregated. In this diverse setting, Filipino boxers competed with Americans, Australians, and fighters of other nationalities, many of whom were sailors or soldiers of mixed racial and ethnic heritage. Initially, Filipino fighters were consigned to the preliminary bouts in events that white promoters organized, but by the 1920s, indigenous fighters featured in main cards. In 1919, a group of American businessmen and boxing enthusiasts began hosting events in Manila, featuring fighters from around the world. The sport officially was legalized in 1921, and from there, the country fell in love with the sweet science.

The combination of speed, agility, footwork, and aggression made Filipino boxers some of the best in the world, as Manny Pacquiao would reveal in the twenty-first century. But Pac was preceded in his world domination by another Filipino boxer, the legendary Pancho Villa (originaly Francesco Guilledo), who became the first Asian fighter to become world boxing champion, as a flyweight, in 1923. Villa began boxing when he was sixteen, turned professional at nineteen, and died at the age of twenty-three of complications from a tooth infection. Villa stood barely over five feet tall and weighed a mere 110 pounds, but he was quick, aggressive, and charming, becoming fast friends with Jack Dempsey, among other celebrities. By the time of his death in 1925, he was beloved around the world, especially in America, due to his prodigious skill, diminutive size, and humorous, unaffected personality that made him a boxing sensation.

Filipino martial arts are the darling of fighting enthusiasts worldwide, in no small part thanks to Dan Inosanto, who in addition to being Bruce Lee's friend and student, has had a tremendous impact on fighting sports in the United States. Inosanto is Filipino American, born in the United States and tied closely to many Hollywood martial arts productions. In addition, he trained legendary MMA coach Greg Nelson as well as Erik Paulson, the first American Shooto champion, who would, like many of his cohort of MMA fighters in the 1980s and 1990s, go to Japan to contest his skills in the earliest professional contests of the modern sport.

## Japan

In the late nineteenth century, Japan's economic relationships with the United States and Europe led to cultural exchanges that included martial arts. Japan's primary fighting arts were sumo, judo, and jujitsu, all incredibly effective modes of throws and wrestling, while at the turn of the century, both England and the United States remained in the golden age of boxing. As Japanese citizens visited Europe or the United States and Westerners went to Asia, each became infatuated with the other. The English were enthralled with jujitsu, the Americans with judo, and the Japanese with boxing. In the aftermath of WWI, Western military personnel became obsessed with the culture of the many Asian countries they visited, and the feeling often was reciprocal. Japanese men in the United States and Europe who traditionally trained judo, sumo, or jujitsu saw boxing as something they could learn or a way to test their own fighting skills. Japanese military officers wanted to add boxing to training after seeing the British soldiers during WWI use pugilism as a unique supplement to rifle and bayonet practice.

It became popular for Western boxers in Japan to fight Japanese jujitsu practitioners in mixed-style bouts. One such match took place in Manila in 1908 between an American boxer who wore gloves and could only strike and a Japanese jujitsu fighter who wore a kimono and was only able to throw. This interdisciplinary approach, known as *merikan*, pitted strikers versus wrestlers, each only allowed to use his own style. The scoring benefited the wrestler more than the boxer, so most bouts ended with Japanese victories. According to some newspaper accounts, the boxers were easily tired by their continuous strikes, whereas the jujitsu players could reserve their strength and wait for an opening.

But many Japanese men looked to join the Western boxing phenomenon, and in 1909, Kano Kenji, a relative of judo founder Kano Jigoro, created Japan's first boxing club in Kobe. After boxing professionally in California for nearly twenty years, in 1921 Yujiro Watanabe opened the Japan Boxing Club. Watanabe was not only a boxing coach; he was a promoter who helped establish the sport of boxing in Japan. Watanabe, along with Kano and another contemporary boxing instructor, "Young Togo" Koriyama, created the Japan Boxing Association in 1922 to establish rules and regulate matches.

Early bouts were described as unscientific and a bit wild, with Japanese fighters employing the "piston attack" in which they punched as hard and fast as they could until they won the fight. Journalists described the Japanese fighters as crude and mechanical, unwilling to quit and fully able to withstand any amount of damage. Some journalists scoffed at the piston style, although it does seem to have been successful for Japanese fighters going against American and Filipino opponents. It is likely that denigrating the piston attack was a way for white journalists to put the Japanese fighters in their place in the boxing world by blaming their success on their willingness to endure extreme damage. Positioning Japanese fighters as "crude" ostracized them from the greater boxing world, and the "mechanical" description further separated them from the "sweet science" that Western fighters practiced. Of course, it behooved Western journalists and fighters to prize their own culture's version of boxing over the new Asian styles in order to try to retain their superiority in the boxing world. For the Japanese however, this aggressive style of fighting demonstrated the type of hypermasculinity their society valued. At the time, Korea was a Japanese colony, and it, too, joined the boxing craze. In fact, some of the best boxers representing Japan in the Olympics and other international tournaments were ethnically Korean.

Okinawa's indigenous tribes had their own practice of armed and unarmed warfare, which primarily was self-defense based, passed down both orally and physically from generation to generation. As other Asian cultures traded, visited, and occupied parts of the island, Okinawa's indigenous fighting arts expanded to include some of the foreign fighting styles exchanged both in combat and in the daily interactions between differing cultures. Chinese mainlanders frequently inhabited Okinawa, and in the seventeenth century the island was invaded by Japan and became part of the larger Japanese empire; when the indigenous people were banned from carrying weapons, empty-hand fighting increased. The resulting martial art, karate, is an amalgam of Japanese, Chinese, and indigenous Okinawan martial arts.

Numerous books, websites, and articles dedicated to karate examine the various origin stories and delightful narratives of early practitioners and heroes. For this book's exploration of MMA history, the most salient point is that karate evolved from years of cultural exchanges, morphing the fighting styles of the Chinese and Japanese and adapting those techniques to fit the ever-evolving martial arts of Okinawa. In the early 1900s, karate forms were introduced in Okinawan schools, providing physical training along with a martial arts education. Not until after WWII did karate add a sport component, the kumite, to upper-level practice. Also in the aftermath of the war, karate began to spread around the world, arriving in the United States and in Europe.

Edmund Kealoha Parker is credited with bringing karate to the United States in 1954, where he became a fixture in Hollywood. Eventually, in 1974, *Black Belt Magazine* named him "The Father of American Karate." Parker trained Gary Cooper and Warren Beatty, and he introduced Chuck Norris and Bruce Lee to Hollywood. Parker even trained Elvis Presley and once punched Tom Jones in the stomach after Jones asked Elvis, in Parker's presence, to demonstrate his art. Jones apparently kept interrupting Parker's demo, asking asinine "what if" questions, so Parker punched him in the solar plexus, reportedly saying, "To hear is to doubt, to see is to be deceived, but to feel is to believe."[2] Parker maintained his relationship with Hollywood, training stars, while many of his students turned to sport fighting. Over the next few decades, karate became one of the most widely practiced martial arts in the world, and fighters contested their skills in light-sparring and full-contact matches.

The end of World War II also was the end of certain types of martial arts training in Japan. Judo and the Kodokan school that Kano Jigoro founded were deemed "too militaristic" by the Americans operating in Japan after the end of the war. Because Japan had so thoroughly embraced martial arts in its military's practice, judo instructors, nearly all of whom served in the military, found themselves unable to teach their art in the postwar years. As a result, judo moved even further away from its practical roots, focusing instead on the sport version. By the early 1950s, judo competitions were springing up around the world, and for the first time, weight-class divisions were introduced to the sport. The emphasis on sport, the addition of weight classes, which was antithetical to the idea of a martial art not dependent on size or strength, and the general popularity of competitions created a rift in the judo community. Then, in the 1964 Olympics held in Tokyo, a judo demonstration further disrupted its traditionalists roots when Anton Geesink of the Netherlands defeated all of his opponents to become the Olympic champion.

The success of an outsider in the Japanese art was an early indicator of how martial arts might change in a more globally connected world. It also revealed that the transition from traditional martial arts to sport fundamentally changed the trajectory of judo, as well as other martial arts that would become competitive. Many techniques and theories foundational to Kano's art were altered or sometimes eliminated in the sportive iteration. Less emphasis on katas and more practice in randori, or freestyle practice, changed not only how judo looked but how the schools approached training and advancement. Despite the success of the 1964 demonstration in Tokyo, the next games held in the summer of 1968 did not include judo. Judo officially was made an Olympic sport for men in 1972, although not until 1988 was a women's division added to the games. Judo remained one of Japan's most highly regarded martial arts and part of the foundation of performance wrestling, which included techniques from judo, jujitsu, sumo, and other arts.

Before accepting his legendary 1976 proto-MMA fight with Muhammad Ali, in 1972 Japanese wrestler Antonio Inoki founded the New Japan Pro Wrestling venue. Professional wrestling was a popular form of entertainment in Japan, although these "worked" matches were highly choreographed and the outcome predetermined. Inoki believed there was a market for more realistic matches that used legitimate tactics, known as "strong" wrestling. Originally, even these "strong-style" matches had predetermined outcomes, but as Inoki began signing a higher caliber of fighters, and with the help of Belgian wrestling coach Karl Gotch, the "God of Pro Wrestling," his venue transitioned from "worked" to genuine sport wrestling. Eventually, Inoki's venue began including striking, further morphing his venue into a novel, innovative style of no-holds-barred fighting.

This new mixed martial arts venue attracted fighters from around the world, and the demand to practice professional wrestling inspired retired wrestler Satoru Sayama to open his own training academy in the early 1980s. Sayama taught submission wrestling and eventually began his own fighting venue, Shooto, in the mid-1980s. Shooto was unique in that it began as a sporting event with no predetermined results, so that fighting truly became a contest rather than just a performance. In Shooto, fighters, known as "shooters," could punch, kick, knee, wrestle, throw, and do submissions, the crowning glory for shoot fighters. Originally, no ground striking was allowed, but the venue eventually added those strikes to reflect the larger MMA movement. Over the next few years, other mixed-discipline fighting venues emerged in Japan, including RINGS, which initially had shoot-style matches but with predetermined outcomes. Even in the 1980s and 1990s, confusion remained about whether certain shoots were "worked" or "strong," and it frequently depended on the fighters as well as the venue. In the late 1990s, RINGS eliminated "worked" matches and switched to legitimately contested MMA fights.

The year 1993 was a banner one for inaugural MMA venues: the UFC held its first event in the United States, and professional wrestling venue Pancrase launched in Japan. Pancrase used the rules of professional wrestling but allowed open-hand strikes to the head and closed-fist strikes to the rest of the body. Some of Pancrase's early bouts were fixed, but it quickly moved to legitimate sport fighting and ultimately paved the way for Japan's largest homegrown fight venue, Pride Fighting Championships, which we will discuss in due course.

In the last few decades of the twentieth century, Japanese sport fighting venues created innovative fighting events that predated and eventually inspired the UFC. Japanese fans also were highly tuned to the nuances of MMA, politely clapping for intricate ground techniques and defensive positions that would incite boos from most American audiences. In this way, Japan was much better positioned to accept MMA as a sport, rather than just a spectacle, in no small part due to its own history and appreciation of fighting as an art form.

## SOUTH AMERICA

Although Mexico and other parts of Central and South America have become strongholds of boxing talent, the sport did not truly become a popular pastime until the late 1920s. Prior to that, most indigenous sports revolved around ball games and some forms of wrestling, but striking was not practiced greatly. When famed U.S. boxer Jack Johnson went to Mexico while avoiding extradition for a Mann Act conviction, he trained boxing with police officials and taught local teenagers. He went to Cuba in 1915 to fight Jess Willard and spent a good deal of time in Mexico before finally surrendering to U.S. authorities in 1920. But Johnson engendered a love of boxing in many young Mexican men and helped cultivate generations of Mexican fighters. Since the 1960s, Mexico has produced some of the best boxers in the world, including Julio César Chávez, who remains one of the greatest boxers of all time.

Segments of Cuba's population also adopted boxing, making it one of the most popular sports in the country next to baseball. Boxing was part of physical fitness in schools, and amateur fights were highly successful as entertainment and in reinforcing Cuban nationalism. However, in the twentieth century, Cuba only allowed amateur boxing, so some skilled boxers defected to other countries where they could pursue the sport professionally. Nicaragua produced some of the best boxers in Central America, including Alexis Argüello; *The Ring* magazine considered his legendary 1982 super lightweight match against Aaron Pryor the fight of the decade.

Mexico's *lucha libre* is one of the most popular forms of entertainment, from tremendous organized televised events to small, local productions. Lucha libre matches are carefully orchestrated, fixed bouts, and fighters famously cover their faces with colorful, highly recognizable masks. Similar to Japan's wrestling events, the crowd knows that lucha libre matches are fixed, but it revels in the narratives and theatrical production. Other parts of Central and South America feature theatrical wrestling, although many of the smaller, indigenous cultures continue to practice traditional wrestling styles. But the most influential fighting art to come out of the Americas was from Brazil; and although some confusion continued between choreographed matches and sport fighting, what emerged from Brazil would be the definition of a "strong" wrestling style.

## Brazil

Brazilian jujitsu (BJJ) arguably is the most famous fighting style contributor to modern MMA. As the name suggests, the style evolved from Japanese jujitsu, a grappling style based on small circles (i.e., small joint manipulation), but became something incredibly unique and utterly modern in the coastal city of Rio de Janeiro. Only in the twentieth century, with an increase in travel and corporate branding, could this new fighting style emerge and, ultimately, come to dominate fighting sports in a way that never had been seen previously. Brazil and Japan have a fascinating history based on similar goals: to succeed as newly industrial powerhouses in the twentieth century. In the early 1900s, a number of Japanese men immigrated to Brazil looking for work in a variety of growing industries, including the rubber and latex trades. Newly flush Brazilians began indulging in leisure activities, including attending circus performances, where strongmen and professional wrestlers from around the world performed for the crowd. What started as a Brazilian boy learning wrestling from a Japanese professional wrestler would grow into one of the largest sporting franchises in martial arts history and the equivocation of a new martial art with one family, whose name would become a byword for MMA.

Mitsuyo Maeda was a diminutive Japanese wrestler who hankered after a career in sumo but found himself practicing Kodokan judo instead. In 1904, Maeda accompanied Tomita Tsunejirō to New York, then traveled to West Point to demonstrate the art of judo. Tomita demonstrated techniques on Maeda, and when several cadets demanded to wrestle Tomita, he agreed. After successfully throwing one cadet, Tomita failed to throw a varsity football player, which the American and Japanese press considered a humiliating moment for Japanese wrestling.

Tomita and Maeda began a judo club in New York, but just a few years later, Maeda horrified the Kodokan by becoming a professional wrestler, demeaning himself in the eyes of his former colleagues by competing for money. Maeda traveled the world, facing wrestlers of all sizes from a variety of backgrounds, in matches that were sometimes fixed and sometimes legitimate competitions. At 155 pounds, Maeda was small compared to many of his English and American opponents, but wrestling matches at that time were not always fair contests. The twentieth century saw a break in the wrestling world between sport and performance, and sometimes that line was not terribly clear. Maeda impressed fighters and fans wherever he went, and after competing in Scotland, Spain, Mexico, and Cuba, he finally landed in Brazil in 1914.

Maeda performed there as a professional wrestler with the Queirolo Brothers Circus. One of the circus's investors, Gastão Gracie, brought his fifteen-year-old son, Carlos, to train with Maeda, hoping to funnel his son's aggression into a more acceptable platform. Carlos devoted himself to training jujitsu with Maeda and taught his younger brothers everything he learned. The Gracie family, which had gone bankrupt in 1921, then moved from the beautiful Belém do Para to the rougher Rio de Janeiro. In 1925, Carlos realized his dream and opened a jujitsu school in Rio, the first "Brazilian jujitsu" gym. He brought his younger brothers, Oswaldo, George, Gastão Jr., and Hélio, as assistant instructors. The school was a tremendous success, due to the high-caliber wrestling skills that the Gracies demonstrated, as well as their familial connections, business savvy, and political support from the unsavory yet burgeoning fascist party in Brazil.

The Gracie brothers were highly skilled grapplers, although Carlos would not allow Hélio to participate in sparring at the gym. The move from Belém do Para to Rio disrupted young Hélio's life, and he suffered health problems, including chronic dizziness. In addition, he was a very tall, lanky youth who looked vastly different than his shorter, stockier, and more muscular brothers. Carlos remained protective of his youngest brother, and so while Oswaldo, George, Gastão, and other fighters trained and sparred aggressively, Hélio focused on his technique and sparred with his brothers only when Carlos was out of the gym. However, when Carlos discovered Hélio sparring and realized his youngest brother's skill and aptitude, he forgave Hélio and eventually took him on as the top Gracie student. Hélio trained boxing in addition to jujitsu, and when opportunities arose for the Gracie family to test their skills against other martial artists in vale tudo challenge matches, Hélio represented the family. Vale tudo, or "anything goes," became a popular entertainment that traveling circuses provided in Brazil in the early twentieth century. These matches often pitted different fighting styles against each other with few rules or limitations on the types of attacks allowed.

Hélio Gracie developed his own streamlined version of the style Carlos taught him, useful for a smaller fighter. At this time, wrestling matches frequently walked the line between sport and theatrics, but Hélio regularly fought in legitimate matches. It is purported that his older brother, George, left the original Gracie academy because he wanted to fight Hélio and prove who was the best fighter in Brazil, but Carlos refused the match. In 1932, Hélio defeated boxer Antonio Portugal with a choke less than one minute into the fight. Hélio did fight other challenge matches over the years, then took time off until 1950, when he returned to help Carlos organize the first jujitsu tournament in Rio, the Campeonato Carioca. When, in 1951, the Gracies discovered that the legendary fighter Masahiko Kimura was traveling in Brazil, they issued a challenge to him, but the judoka (one who participates in judo) demurred. Although the Gracies might have established a name for themselves in Rio, they were not yet famous, and Masahiko saw no reason to fight these seemingly random dilletantes.

Masahiko Kimura is still considered the most famous judoka of all time, reportedly only ever losing four matches in his very long fighting career. Masahiko became a fourth-degree black belt at fifteen, and in 1935, at the age of eighteen, achieved his fifth degree. That same year, Masahiko sustained his four losses and after a brief moment when he considered quitting the art, Masahiko began training more intensely than ever. He did a thousand push-ups and trained nine hours every day, focusing in particular on his osoto gari throw, which he practiced against a tree. His deployment of osoto gari, an outside leg throw, was so proficient and devastating that he regularly knocked his opponents unconscious. Some future opponents even asked him to refrain from using it lest they, too, end up with a concussion. Masahiko Kimura's rigorous training regimen, coupled with his technical skill and aggression in the ring, make him, along with Gene LeBell, one of the fathers of modern MMA fighting.

Masahiko may not have known who the Gracies were, but they were determined to test their skills against the legendary fighter. Competing against Masahiko was a necessity for the Gracie family, who sought to establish their credibility in the martial arts world, particularly as Brazilians, people not known for martial arts in the same way as Japanese or even English fighters. So, when Masahiko refused the fight, the Gracies turned to one of his fellow Japanese judokas, Yukio Kato, a twenty-two-year-old who at 154 pounds was much closer in size to the 139-pound Hélio Gracie. Hélio and Kato met in a ring, adhering to rules that Gracie himself dictated: the match would go to submission or unconsciousness rather than rely on scoring. After moving a bit stiffly at first, Kato managed to throw Gracie, but once on the ground, Hélio choked Kato unconscious, although there was some debate as to whether Hélio illegally deployed a shoke hold durin ga break imposed by the referee. Regardless, after this defeat, Masahiko agreed to fight Hélio, and on October 23, 1951, the two faced off in front of twenty thousand fans.

According to Masahiko, an empty coffin was waiting, provided by the Gracie family for Masahiko's eventual demise at the hands of their champion. The judoka claims that he laughed, and after being pelted with eggs on his way to the ring, defeated Hélio with a reverse armlock in the second of their ten-minute rounds. When Hélio refused to stop, Masahiko broke his arm, and Carlos threw in the towel. It was a devastating defeat for Hélio, but Masahiko was so impressed with the Brazilian's fighting that he awarded Hélio a rank in judo. The reverse-arm submission that broke Hélio's arm has, henceforth, been called the "kimura," in honor of the great Masahiko Kimura.

Five years later, Hélio had his last vale tudo match against Waldemar Santana, who might be called the first of the "Gracie killers," with Sakuraba following in his footsteps many years later. Santana was a former Gracie protégé who left the fold after a disagreement with Hélio, perhaps exacerbated by Santana's friend, future manager, and Brazilian journalist, Carlos Renato. Santana trained in BJJ, along with boxing and capoeira, connecting him to his country's roots as opposed to the Gracies, who sometimes were portrayed in the Brazilian media as elitist. With the help of his manager-cum-journalist hype man, Renato, Santana challenged his former teacher, and Hélio agreed, even though he had been out of vale tudo for a number of years.

In Brazil, capoeira was primarily associated with those of African descent, such as Santana, and thus a rift existed, not only between the fighting approaches of wrestling versus striking, but also the practitioner's skin tone. The Gracie family occupied an economic, social, and ethnic class that gave their wrestling style gravitas as well as some form of elitism in the country. At the time, jujitsu seemed exotic and elicited a level of respect from the media that capoeira had yet to achieve. And for many Brazilians, capoeira, with its ties to slavery and African history, was inextricably linked to poverty and violence.

In fact, headlines of intra-style fights in the 1930s and 1940s often noted the racial difference in the fighters. A 1928 *New York Times* headline covering a bout between a Japanese fighter and a Brazilian fighter of African descent read, "Jiu jitsu beats Brazilian Capoeira: Diminutive Japanese Conquers Huge Negro."[3] Although this *Times* headline is blatant in framing a racial distinction between the Japanese and Brazilian fighters, the coverage of the Santana and Gracie fight still was framed in terms of ethnicity, race, class, and social position.

Some news media outlets promoted it as a grudge match between the hard-working local hero, Waldemar Santana, and the established symbol of patriarchal, elitist power, Hélio Gracie. Others, however, depicted an elegant Gracie contending with the uncouth Santana and, ideally, putting the upstart in his place. However, when the fight finally took place, nothing about it was elegant. The men battled for nearly three hours, and in the end, twenty-six-year-old Santana defeated the forty-two-year-old Hélio with a kick to the head. In the aftermath of the fight, Carlos Gracie called out Santana, demanding that the man fight his son, Carlson, an accomplished vale tudo fighter who trained with both his father and his uncle Hélio. When Carlson and Santana met the first time, the fight ended in a draw, but a rematch gave Carlson the opportunity to avenge his family and show off his striking when he TKO'd Santana with punches from mount. The two men fought again, but some of the interest in this particular rivalry had waned.

As the Gracie family's notoriety spread, and the sport of Brazilian jujitsu grew, media promotion and coverage of vale tudo matches entered a new phase. The exploits and dramas of the emerging BJJ scene, coupled with the often-tempestuous relationships between Gracie family members, their protégés, and rival gyms, made fascinating copy, and newspapers hustled to cover every match. In the 1950s, filmed bouts became a popular addition to television programming, with several early Gracie matches caught on film. Between newspapers, film, and eventually television, the media coverage helped turn the Gracie family into stalwart figureheads of Brazilian fight sports.

The Gracie family undoubtedly helped launch the art of jujitsu in Brazil, sharing not only the techniques that Carlos learned from Maeda, but expanding them to include more groundwork and submissions. But as often is the case in fighting sports, many of their instructors and students left the fold to start their own training facilities, frequently igniting rivalries that still exist. The Gracie family was the ultimate signifier of power in the burgeoning BJJ community. They had credibility in the martial arts world, funding from their academy and other business ventures, and support from political connections, and they were the darlings of the Brazilian media—even if the coverage was not always positive, they were always present in news stories about vale tudo and BJJ. Although this was an ideal situation for Carlos, Hélio, and their growing families and stable of fighters, those outside the Carlos Gracie cohort looked at the family as the ultimate dragon to slay.

If the Gracies represented the elite establishment, then their challengers seemed to represent the people. The early to mid-twentieth century saw tremendous development in the sport of wrestling in Brazil, as the Gracies rose to prominence as an elite family of martial artists, and other fighters challenged their throne. Euclydes Hatem, known as "Tatu," developed the luta livre, a style of wrestling that seems to be based on Japanese sumo and the English/American version of catch-as-catch-can. Tatu's students sneered at the traditional gi worn by the Gracies and instead, practiced a heavy and aggressive form of wrestling perfect for vale tudo. Tatu defeated George Gracie in 1929 with a bent-arm lock, which would be called "the Kimura" after Masahiko Kimura used it in 1951 to break Hélio Gracie's arm.

Stories seemingly are endless about the development of wrestling and vale tudo in Brazil in the twentieth century, which have been outlined in other books and article series devoted to Brazilian jujitsu. For the purpose of this book, it is significant to see how the influx of Japanese culture in Brazil aided in the explosion of martial arts out of South America, and how the media used the rivalries of different schools and families to spread the sport. In addition, we can see how the Gracie founders, Carlos and Hélio, became portrayed as elitist because of their desire to protect their family's legacy and only teach their art to the most "deserving" students. Meanwhile, other martial artists in Brazil seemed to share their knowledge willingly, further setting up a dichotomy between the Gracie family as the "establishment" and other schools as freedom fighters. This may not be fair to the Gracies, who did seem to fear that their art could become bastardized or that they would lose power if they shared it, but ultimately, wanted primarily to protect their family's legacy.

However, one of the biggest challenges to Carlos and Hélio's desire to contain their fighting techniques in the family came from within. Carlson Gracie, son of Carlos and nephew to Hélio, competed under the Gracie jujitsu banner in his childhood and early adulthood, then left the fold to open his own school. Carlson believed that anyone should have the opportunity to train, opening his doors to anyone who wanted to learn and even allowing lower-income students to train for free. Carlson taught group classes, further differentiating himself from the one-on-one training by his father and uncle. Finally, Carlson was adamant that the only way to improve was to challenge oneself constantly, and, famously, he would troll beaches, asking anyone he came across to fight him. This may have been bombast or a bit of insanity, but Carlson's insistence on the importance of competition helped him create one of the most dominant fight teams in the world. He did not fear losing; instead, he seemed to object to complacency and what he believed was the misguided idea that only victories matter. When he died in 2006, he wrote a list of official black belts under his name, thereby formalizing his lineage and reinforcing his own legacy.

Like his father and brothers, Hélio produced a slew of sons who would become BJJ legends and ambassadors. His oldest son, Rorion Gracie, would become one of the greatest of the family, earning a ninth degree as a red belt and formally aligning his family with Hollywood when he worked on the 1987 film *Lethal Weapon*. Rorion was born in Brazil and moved to California in 1978, where he worked in films as an extra and taught Brazilian jujitsu in a garage. He convinced his younger brother, Royce, to join him in 1985; together, the two Gracie brothers introduced the United States to their family's martial art tradition and, eventually, helped create the largest MMA venue in the world. But their story resides in the United States, which by the late twentieth century already had a deeply entrenched fighting sport culture that was eager to see the birth of anything new.

## THE UNITED STATES

The United States embraced the idea of sports and physical activity as important aspects of an ideal American lifestyle, with the leisure time dedicated to pursuing these activities a signifier of wealth and success. Golf, tennis, sailing, swimming, and rowing were all aristocratic sports, practiced by people who had the time and money to enjoy physical activity. Boxing and wrestling still were viewed as activities that those who occupied lower rungs of the social ladder practiced, but the introduction of foreign martial arts helped fighting sports to become more socially acceptable.

The twenty-sixth American president, Theodore Roosevelt, practiced judo in the White House basement with his family, his private secretary, future president and then secretary of war William Howard Taft, and secretary of the interior Gifford Pinchot, all under the tutelage of Yamashita Yoshiaki. Yamashita arrived in the United States in 1903 at the behest of Sam Hill, a wealthy businessman who wanted his nine-year-old son to train judo lest the boy become "soft." The judo master and his assistant provided Hill and his cronies with an exhibition of their skill, and so dynamic was the performance that the audience believed it to have been staged. Concerned, Hill wanted to ensure that his investment was genuine and put Yamashita against a 210-pound English boxer in a mixed-discipline fight. The diminutive Yamashita evaded the boxer's blows repeatedly and threw the larger man numerous times.

Delighted now by Yamashita's obvious skill, Hill sent him to Washington, D.C., to train his young son. Yamashita and his wife, Fude, taught judo to the children of numerous Washington socialites, and eventually, President Roosevelt hired him to train him three days a week at the White House. Roosevelt was considered an earnest and enthusiastic student, although he apparently did not have tremendous control and often ended up injured. His primary goal was to lose weight rather than become an expert, and perhaps this is why he eventually stopped training and sent Yamashita to teach in the U.S. Naval Academy.

The United States participated in several major wars, primarily on their own soil prior to the twentieth century and internationally in the twentieth and twenty-first centuries. Each war, from the Revolutionary War, to the American Civil War, to World Wars I and II, to Vietnam, Korea, and Desert Storm, would fundamentally change American culture, including sports practice and sporting competitions. During WWI, the United States focused on sports for military preparedness, something the young(ish) country had yet to do compared to older nations such as Japan, China, or England. Part of this emphasis on sports in the military operated as a way of cultivating an idealized form of masculinity as a representative of American nationalism. A young American male should be healthy, active, strong, and thus ready to fight for America. As athletic training and sport became part of military preparedness, so did many of the "champions" around the country leave their jobs as professional wrestlers or boxers when they enlisted or were drafted into service.

After the war, many states instituted governing bodies to control sporting activities. Former fighter William Muldoon became part of the New York State Athletic Commission, which dictated boxing and wrestling rules, and required promoters to carry licenses for events. Wrestling promoters sought to entertain the American public, which flocked to an ever-increasing number of movie theaters, by staging extravaganzas of live sporting events to rival the cinema. In the past, wrestling matches had few rules and often no time limits, and fights could be long, often tedious affairs that bored some spectators. In these new shows, wrestling had clear time limits and rules, and in order to truly captivate a crowd now hungry for highly visceral action, fights were predetermined, "fixed" matches. These fights were designed to look realistic, but they were carefully choreographed to include spectacular throws and painful-looking submissions. Today it is easy to discern campy, theatrical wrestling from sport wrestling, but the delineation was not as clear in the early twentieth century, and many fans were angry when they discovered that the matches they enjoyed were rigged.

However, the rigged matches were greatly entertaining and translated easily to the screen. Depression-era films frequently included wrestling and allowed for the expansion of role playing, in particular solidifying the characters of the hero and the heel. The choreographed techniques grew more carnivalesque, with helicopter spins and slams that would become standard gimmicks in theatrical wrestling. As theatrical wrestling grew further away from sport wrestling, so did the media coverage. Theatrical wrestling was incredibly popular in film and television, while sport wrestling became more deeply entrenched in high school and on college campuses, giving rise to the name "scholastic wrestling" to separate it from the insanity happening on-screen.

In the early twentieth century, circuses and traveling shows made their way across the United States, performing in towns large and small and including acts such as strongmen, boxing, and wrestling. Carnivals would arrive in a city and invite local heroes to test their skills against the traveling wrestlers. Greco-Roman bouts, which could go on for an exhausting period of time, were not terribly exciting to an undiscerning audience; but catch-as-catch-can wrestling, which was fast and dynamic, entertained the crowds and made for more efficient matches. When traveling wrestlers fought each other, the matches were often fixed in order to create a more exciting performance. Sometimes professional wrestlers operated as dupes in the audience, pretending to be challengers and either beating the circus champion definitively, or lasting until time ran out and the champ looked diminished. Then legitimate audience members would think they had a chance to beat the circus champion and gladly pay for the opportunity, only to be dispatched quickly. These locals might be incredibly strong and athletic, but the techniques seen in catch wrestling were brutal, seemingly convoluted, and notoriously difficult to escape if one did not train in the art. Locals rarely won, and, sometimes, wrestling troupes had to quit villages quickly in order to escape the crowd's ire.

But catch wrestling grew in popularity outside the circus circuit. One of the first American heroes of catch wrestling was Martin "Farmer" Burns, a man with a bizarrely thick neck who regularly would challenge entire college football teams to matches. Burns developed a thorough curriculum of catch-as-catch-can style and sold his guidebooks to young men around the country. These books included wrestling techniques as well as guides for physical conditioning.

One of his most famous students was Frank Gotch, whose notorious "stepover toehold" made him a rough fighter in a field that consistently added newer, more brutal submissions to the sport. In 1908, Gotch faced George Hackenschmidt, a Russian strongman who declared himself to be the world's greatest wrestler. Hackenschmidt had avoided Gotch in his previous visit in 1905, but when offered $10,000, he agreed to face the American. Much of the press played up the distinction between Gotch, a rough farmboy from Iowa, and Hackenschmidt, the elegant Russian émigré. After two hours of fighting, Hackenschmidt conceded the match to Gotch, although he later complained that he was unable to defeat the American due to dirty tactics. Gotch apparently did target Hackenschimdt's eyes and might have greased himself prefight, but the American press gleefully reported the supremacy of a wrestler from Iowa over a European champion.

When the two met for a rematch several years later, it was a rather embarrassing return for Hackenschmidt. He had sustained a knee injury during training and tried to forfeit before the match, but Gotch refused. He threw the Russian easily, and, in fact, it appeared that Hackenschmidt offered no defense. The match was a letdown, but it sustained Gotch's reputation as an American hero while continuing Hackenschmidt's legacy in Europe as an excellent fighter who had been bested only by a crafty and unscrupulous American. When a Belgian wrestler named Karl Istaz came to the United States in 1959, he took on the name of one of his heroes, Frank Gotch, to make his transition as an international wrestling hero, Karl Gotch, complete.

In the early twentieth century, playing sports began to signify wealth, because one would have to have time to dedicate to a nonessential activity. Golf, rowing, and tennis were leisure activities associated with upper-class aesthetics, and for many middle-class Americans, engaging in sports demonstrated their place in the cultural hierarchy. Fighting sports, however, were not typically practiced by the social elites, and so most practitioners were firmly ensconced in what would be considered the lower echelons of society, specifically the working class.

Of course, there were exceptions. Several American presidents, including George Washington and Abraham Lincoln, competed as wrestlers, but that was long before conspicuous consumption ruled American aesthetics. Boxing for fitness, however, became a very popular activity at the turn of the century, as young women and matrons of New York City flocked to gyms to box away their excess pounds.

Some American women trained in fighting sports in earnest, including the celebrated female athlete Babe Didrikson, who was a professional golfer, tennis player, and amateur boxing enthusiast. Didrikson trained at Artie McGovern's renowned gym in New York City along with many others of that city's elite. McGovern's workouts consisted of stretching, weight training, and cardio training that included jumping rope or using the rowing machine or treadmill. But McGovern also specialized in training athletes using sport-specific exercises while simultaneously targeting muscles that are not developed through the sport alone. McGovern's training preceded today's "functional training" obsession, emphasizing a well-rounded approach to gaining strength and flexibility.

McGovern was a former professional boxer, and because of his extensive fighting sports background, everyone at his gym, from professional golfers and baseball players, to wealthy lawyers and millionaires' wives, to a famous opera soprano, trained in both boxing and wrestling. He boasted that his trainers had keys to their clients' homes in order to let themselves in first thing in the morning and, if necessary, rip the blankets off of those titans of finance in order to start their training.

McGovern's inclusion of boxing and wrestling may have been for the purpose of fitness for the majority of his clientele, but the training was not relegated to bag work alone. All of the clients sparred, which sometimes led to bizarre matchups between athletes, celebrities, and businessmen. A photo from the time shows Babe Ruth wrestling with J. G. Hall, the youngest member of the New York Stock Exchange; in another, McGovern wrestles and boxes with opera star Nanette Guilford in 1933. Babe Ruth famously came to McGovern to help him shave off pounds after years of binge eating and excess drinking and discovered a love for boxing. So much did the Great Bambino enjoy his boxing training that he claimed he would compete professionally, a declaration that never came to fruition. Babe Ruth continued to be a boxing fan for the rest of his life, visiting his friend Joe Louis while the great boxer trained for a fight in 1937. His personal dream of competing as a heavyweight boxer never arrived, but he was able to train in the sport he loved while dominating as one of the greatest professional baseball players of all time.

The golden age of prizefighting in the United States neared a close in the early twentieth century, and the title of heavyweight champion became boxers' new goal. In 1908, Jack Johnson became the first black champion, inspiring a search for the "great white hope" in an example of the racism and nationalism endemic to sports at the time. Boxing went from the margins of respectability to a high-class event when master promoter Text Rickard featured Jack Dempsey fighting Georges Carpentier in 1921, the audience populated by New York society members in black tie and evening gowns.

Boxing remained a popular sport during WWII, and in the late 1940s, as televisions proliferated in American homes, networks created regular programs featuring fights. Boxing was an easy sport to film and show on home televisions, and Americans tuned in to Friday Night Fights, one of the most watched programs in the country. Sport wrestling did not have nearly as much appeal as boxing, but its theatrical sibling was perfectly primed for a successful translation to television. But the family most famous for bringing pro wrestling to American households got its start not in wrestling, but in legitimate boxing matches.

One early boxing matchmaker was Jess McMahon, a fighting enthusiast who offended numerous fans by setting up cards featuring fighters of all races at a time when many white Americans felt disenfranchised by the loss of the great white hope against the original G.O.A.T. (greatest of all time), Jack Johnson, in 1910. Jess did not just set up matches; he sought out the best fighters, regardless of their race, convincing managers and fighters alike to compete in his events. Jess frequently moved as the promoter of one arena or another, and in 1932 he promoted his first professional wrestling event at the Municipal Stadium in Freeport, New York. His most successful wrestling contact was with wrestling great Joseph Raymond "Toots" Mondt, with whom Jess would create the Capitol Wrestling Corporation in 1952. By that time, Jess's son, Vincent J. McMahon Sr. (who eventually would become father of Vince McMahon Jr., the current scion of the WWE), had become an integral part of his father's business endeavors. Jess was getting older, and in 1953 Vince's passion for wrestling catapulted their business from the Capitol Wrestling Corporation into joining with the National Wrestling Alliance.

Like his father, Vincent had a gift for fight promotion, and in the burgeoning television phenomenon of the 1950s, he saw a space for his father's events to thrive. In 1952, Vince purchased Turner's Arena, a wrestling venue William "Joe" Turner ran, for $60,000 from Joe's widow, Florence, and her new husband, matchmaker Gabe Menendez. Vince inherited Menendez's stable of wrestlers and the fighters of his business partner, Toots Mondt. He eventually lured big-name talent to his venue, including Gorgeous George and Killer Kowalski.

In the early 1950s, several other wrestling promoters experimented with televised wrestling matches. Most of these shows were small, locally produced fights, but Vince foresaw the potential explosion of promoting wrestling on the silver screen. In December 1955, just as his father was building Capitol Wrestling with Toots Mondt, Vince revamped the Capitol Arena, installing cameras at his own expense and paying DuMont, one of the first television networks, to show his events for the first few weeks. The first televised event took place on January 5, 1956, and two weeks later, DuMont and McMahon signed a contract to show his events regularly. Vince Sr.'s foray into televised wrestling events was a longshot, one at which many of his contemporaries sneered. They even expressed resentment, because it might impact in-person ticket sales. Yet as Vince Sr.'s television shows launched in early 1956, his local events continued to sell out, despite predictions that television would destroy ticket sales.

Pay-per-view began in fits and starts, first in 1951 using telephone lines, although satellite technology quickly outpaced it. In 1975, HBO transmitted the Muhammad Ali versus Joe Frazier "Thrilla in Manila" fight via pay-per-view and thus established the technology as the preeminent method of viewing live sporting events worldwide. On March 31, 1985, Vince McMahon promoted the WWF's Wrestlemania I, at New York's Madison Square Garden. Always seeking to tie his wrestling events to other forms of celebrity, Vince McMahon managed to wrangle some of the biggest names in sports and music to attend. Muhammad Ali refereed, Liberace acted as timekeeper and danced with the Rockettes, and Mr. T headlined the event with Hulk Hogan. Wrestlemania I dwarfed previous wrestling events, generating more than $10 million in pay-per-view subscriptions alone.

Although McMahon's televised events were highly theatrical stage performances rather than legitimate fights, they revealed the public zeal for fighting sports and catalyzed media production venues to feature boxing and wrestling cards. Television fundamentally changed sports worldwide, firmly entrenching sports in the capitalist machine. This is not necessarily a critique; the rise of television allowed sports teams to better support players and individual athletes access to wealth that could not have been possible in previous times. But television made sports go corporate, generating the many problems that accompany privatization in the media. Twenty-four-hour networks, cable broadcasts, and pay-per-view provided more sports coverage than ever, and money poured in from advertising and promotions, especially in the 1980s and 1990s. MMA as a sport proliferated rapidly in the early 2000s because of the commercial media machine. But before the UFC ever dared to air a fight, mixed-match bouts evolved from the globalizing effects of immigration, communication, travel, war, and the demand for entertainment.

What would become known as "mixed-match" fights started in the early 1900s in the United States, typically added to a fight card as a gimmick designed to test which style, wrestling or boxing, could defeat the other, much like Japan's *Merikan*. Journalists and fight pundits loved debating striking versus wrestling, and matchmakers responded by adding mixed-match fights to cards. In these contests, the boxers could punch standing, but not once they were on the ground, whereas the wrestlers could only do takedowns, submissions, and pins. Mixed-match bouts were truly about two separate styles contesting their skills rather than the interdisciplinary matches seen in the late twentieth century. Although the fights were gimmicks designed to allow fighters, coaches, and fans to argue over the supremacy of boxing or wrestling, they typically ended in a wrestling victory. Ultimately, these were victories for the media, who loved sparking controversy in fight fans, especially when well-known names entered the fray.

In 1922, catch wrestling champion Ed "Strangler" Lewis challenged Jack Dempsey, one of the greatest boxers of all time, to a mixed-match fight, and Dempsey agreed with alacrity. Dempsey was a brawler, and in addition to his devastating left hook, which he regularly used to knock out opponents, he practiced wrestling and believed he could defeat the Strangler with his boxing skills or his wrestling experience. Lewis scoffed at such a notion, claiming that Dempsey would break his hands if he tried to hit him. Besides, Lewis was incredibly fast, and he firmly believed that by the time Dempsey tried to punch him, the boxer already would be on the ground. Interestingly, although both men were the undisputed best in their respective arts, they both cross-trained as young men, moving through the American countryside and learning boxing and grappling in various gyms and backyard training sessions. Both Lewis and Dempsey's camps made extraordinary claims about which side would win, and continuously raised the financial stakes. Lewis personally offered to bet $50,000 on his own victory, and Dempsey's manager claimed that the boxer would knock Lewis unconscious in twenty minutes. But the fight was entirely verbal, and sadly, these two fighting giants never actually met for a mixed contest.

Wrestlers monopolized victories in these mixed-match bouts. In 1923, catch wrestler Vernon Breedlove defeated champion boxer "Tex" Walker less than one minute into the first round in a Davenport school auditorium; and in Tampa in 1929, William Demetral defeated three boxers in one evening. A 1935 bout between boxer Kingfish Levinsky and catch wrestler Ray Steele also ended with a win for the wrestler only thirty-five highly active seconds into the fight.

With perhaps one of the best fight monikers of all time, Art "Whataman" Shires competed as the boxer in several mixed matches in 1936, although he also moonlighted as a professional baseball player and sometime wrestler. Shires was highly strategic in using his striking to keep the wrestlers from closing in on him, perhaps because of his own experience as a wrestler, but they always managed to close the gap and pin him in the end. In a bout against 240-pound Greek wrestler George "Crybaby" Zaharias, the 209-pound Shires used this approach to knock down the larger man six times. In the end, however, Zaharias tackled and pinned Shires in the second round. Eventually, Shires desired to be on the winning team and transitioned to professional wrestling. Wrestlers were nearly always victorious because once the fighters clinched, the boxers could only defend the takedown, and, as many sparring sessions around the world reveal, it is nearly impossible to stop a determined, skilled wrestler.

One of the most famous mixed-match fights took place in 1963 when "Judo" Gene LeBell defeated boxer Milo Savage in Salt Lake City. Gene LeBell cross-trained in a truly modern fashion, training catch wrestling with "Strangler" Lewis, boxing at the Main Street Gym, becoming a champion judo player, and learning kenpo, karate, and tae kwon do. After an article claimed that a boxer could beat any "judo bum," karate phenom Ed Parker asked LeBell to take on the challenge. Savage was a professional boxer and the hometown hero in Salt Lake City, a man with a tough reputation who also had some wrestling experience. LeBell agreed to the mixed-discipline bout, and in the media appearances prior to the fight LeBell was a natural humorist, making jokes about how he would beat his future opponent and even choking a radio host unconscious when demonstrating his grappling skills. Gene LeBell may have been asked to represent karate in this fight, but LeBell thought of himself as an everyman, a fighter who trained in all of the arts and therefore, the mixing of styles rather than a single martial art.

The rules of this fight were based on the earlier mixed-match bouts rather than a modern MMA contest. Savage was allowed to box, both standing and on the ground; LeBell was restricted to grappling only. Kicking was not allowed, and both men had to wear judo tops, although Savage showed up well-oiled and wearing a much tighter-fitting karate gi instead. Savage avoided several of LeBell's takedown attempts and was saved from a submission by the bell in the second round. The match ended in the fourth round when LeBell choked Savage unconscious in front of fifteen hundred of his hometown fans. LeBell later worked in Hollywood and trained some of the greatest fighters of all time, including master catch wrestler Gokor Chivichyan and Ronda Rousey, the first UFC female MMA champion. And when Muhammad Ali set up his own mixed-match fight, LeBell was the official referee.

Perhaps the most infamous mixed-match bout was the 1976 exhibition match between boxing legend Muhammad Ali and judoku Antonio

Inoki. Both at the time and in the intervening years, this fight has been described as both a farce and as the origin of modern MMA. The truth is somewhere in between. This fight is significant because it pitted two major names in the fighting world from very different cultures and traditions against each other. Although it may not have been an exhibition of superlative MMA skill, both men did represent their particular style and tradition well in the ring.

Most of the criticism of the bout was based on the hefty purses that both men received. Ali's willingness to fight beyond the confines of the boxing world earned him nearly $6 million, but it cost him in reputation and prestige. The World Boxing Council stripped Ali of the 1975 boxer of year title, declaring that he had "brought boxing into disrepute."[4] The WBC head explained: "We realize that Muhammad Ali has done great things for contemporary boxing but we feel he is presently showing no respect for the sport to which he owes absolutely everything."[5] But Ali already had proven, time and again, that he was a man of incredible integrity. He had previously refused to fight in the Vietnam War, was subsequently stripped of his title, and lost a great deal of his personal wealth.

It would be reductive to claim that Inoki, a successful businessman and fighter, or Ali took the bout for the money alone. In fact, it seems like the novelty of the bout, which challenged their own fighting skills, interested both men and drew them to the match. And it is that element of challenging oneself beyond the limits of one sport, such as boxing or jujitsu, that makes this fight an important moment in the history of mixed martial arts.

Antonio Inoki was a professional wrestler who trained under the famous catch wrestler Karl Gotch and Rikidōzan, who is considered the father of Japanese professional wrestling. Muhammad Ali, meanwhile, was not faring as well as he had previously. Although he was still the champion, he had just endured the embarrassing matchup against Jimmy Young, who Ali could only outpoint despite being twenty-one pounds heavier. Ali, the champion in bravado as well as in boxing, reiterated his claim that he could beat anybody, any place. Inoki took exception to Ali's assertion and challenged the boxer. Ali accepted. This was not a fixed match, but a highly publicized, legitimate mixed-match bout between two extraordinary athletes.

Both Ali and Inoki were adept at using the media to generate public-ity for their previous fights, and this bout was no exception. They both trash-talked through the press and leaked details on their fight prepara-tion, which included rather bizarre techniques that may have been more hype than reality. Ali declared that the bout would be the last fight of Inoki's career. Inoki promised to beat the boxer so badly that Ali should bring crutches with him to the fight. Inoki prepared for the event by practicing boxing and karate, and included some rather bizarre methods of preparation against Ali's heavy fists by having people stand on his chin and jump up and down. While Inoki trained in his striking, Ali boxed with several wrestlers in preparation for the June 26 match. In one particularly bloody training session, Ali split the eyebrow of wrestler Buddy Wolff after Wolff charged the boxer in anger after being declared the loser of a three-round bout. The ring reportedly filled with spectators, all of whom, including Ali and his handlers, were covered with Wolff's blood.

On the day of the exhibition, Ali donned four-ounce gloves; Inoki fought bare handed. The fifteen-round contest allowed rabbit and kid-ney punches as well as kicks and could be ended by a knockout or a pin. When asked if he wanted to allow for submissions, Ali responded, "To hell with that. Let him break it, I'm not going to quit."[6] The match did not end up including much wrestling, but Inoki kicked Ali's legs so savagely that the boxing champion never had another knockout win after this fight, although it is unclear whether his decline was due to the debilitating leg strikes. Inoki spent most of his time on the ground, waiting for Ali to get close enough for him to sweep, while the boxer called for him to stand up and fight. Both men clowned in the ring; Ali stuck out his tongue and windmilled his legs on the ropes while Inoki crawled around the ring on his back. The fight was a spectacle, but when it was over, fans and journalists were disgruntled rather than clamoring for more mixed-discipline fighting events. In fact, some fans reportedly threw objects into the ring in disgust when the fight ended in a draw. The fighters were also disappointed with the outcome, express-ing their discontent litigiously rather than just vocally. Ali sued for breach of contract, claiming that he earned less than the agreed upon $6 million. Inoki, meanwhile, sued for damages to his reputation.

The press described the fight as inactive, but it may be that they simply were not accustomed to the pace of a mixed-match bout. Ali was the greatest boxer in the world; Inoki, one of the best wrestlers. So the men moved warily around each other, trying to be strategic when they got in range. Between his head movement, footwork, and punches, Ali's boxing matches were suffused with action, but never before had he worried about kicks or takedowns. And Inoki rightly was concerned about receiving one of Ali's knockout punches. So, in this contest, the two fighters look like a number of other bouts between top contenders—warier of making mistakes than of initiating the action.

The day after his fight with Inoki, Ali visited the U.S. 2nd Infantry Division in Seoul and fought two exhibition matches against American soldiers. The two contenders, Specialist Fourth-Class Gerald Noble, 202 pounds, and Private First-Class Larry D. Rice, 149 pounds, both put in serious effort to best Ali, who was rewarded at this event not with cash, but with a 2nd Infantry Division sweater. Ali took it easy on both the soldiers, slipping punches and throwing light strikes, but he later revealed that his leg had been severely injured in the fight with Inoki. In fact, he had two blood clots in his leg, which nearly led to an amputation. The press continued to excoriate Ali and Inoki in the aftermath of the 1976 bout, and Ali never again engaged in a mixed-match fight, although his contribution to the fighting world, including the new sport of MMA, is unquestioned. Inoki, meanwhile, would help launch the sport of MMA in Japan, where fighters from all over the world would go to test their skills in mixed matches that were becoming increasingly interdisciplinary.

In the twentieth century, numerous mixed-match fights took place throughout the United States and in other parts of the world. The rising trend among martial artists seemed to take two primary paths: devotion to a single martial art or dedication to learning any and every fighting style. The latter version was the future of MMA, perhaps best embodied by Gene LeBell as a well-rounded, cross-trained, interdisciplinary fighter who would use any technique to win a fight. But most of the early iterations of mixed martial arts were a test of styles. The mixed-match fights of the early and middle twentieth century pitted fighters of two different styles against each other, confining each to the techniques of his own art.

A newer version of interdisciplinary fighting began to emerge that eliminated these restrictions, going back to the catch-as-catch-can fights of the turn of the century but adding the striking that preceded the

Queensberry rules. These new fights, known as vale tudo in Brazil, Shooto in Japan, and no-holds-barred in the United States, had very few rules. Fighters were not supposed to eye gouge or fish hook, but nearly every other attack was legal, including all kicks, knees, elbows, stomps, submissions, punches, and even hair pulling. Many of the early successful stars of MMA threaded the needle, learning numerous fighting arts, such as boxing, karate, tae kwon do, freestyle wrestling, judo, kickboxing, Muay Thai, Japanese jujitsu, or Brazilian jujitsu. And it was this last art, newly arrived in California and eager to test the fighting world, that helped launch what would become the largest fight venue in the world.

In the 1980s, Rorion Gracie taught Brazilian jujitsu out of a garage in California, offering free lessons to anyone and everyone he met. Rorion did whatever work he could to survive, and began acting as an extra in television. More important, he forged relationships in the film industry that he would eventually use to help solidify the Gracie dynasty. Soon, his classes outgrew his garage, and he opened the first dedicated BJJ gym in the United States. Rickson, Royler, and Royce Gracie joined Rorion, and together they began to prove that their style, combined with some stand-up, made them deadly adversaries to every fighter. Some of the Gracie family's students left their previous martial arts instructors to train BJJ, and many of those former instructors felt disgruntled by these upstart Brazilians. Sensing an opportunity to take a firm hold on the martial arts market, the Gracie family offered cash prizes and a willingness to fight anyone as long as their opponents agreed for fights to be videotaped.

The Gracies used this footage to promote their schools and to fully assert their stated position as undefeated fighters. Their renown grew, but the Gracie name still was isolated in Southern California. Eventually, they ran out of other martial artists to fight. Rather than sending his brothers and cousins to live in other parts of the country to start their own gyms, Rorion realized that the best way to spread the Gracie revolution was through the media.

Using the network forged during his early days in California, Rorion connected with promoter Art Davie and filmmaker John Milius to pitch his modern vale tudo concept. After HBO and Showtime declined, the team found SEG, a small production company that agreed to produce the event. The concept was relatively simple: eight fighters from various martial arts backgrounds would compete in a tournament to determine who would be the ultimate fighting champion (thus the name). It had no weight-class restrictions and ostensibly no rules, although fighters could be fined for eye gouging, biting, or striking the groin. Rather than a traditional ring, the fighters would be ensconced in an eight-sided chain-link cage, which became the trademark of the UFC.

The first Ultimate Fighting Championship took place in Denver, Colorado, on November 12, 1995, in front of a mere seventy-eight hundred people, shown live on pay-per-view and later sold on videotape. The fighters were a mixed bag of martial artists, representing judo, boxing, savate, kickboxing, Shooto, and, of course, Gracie jujitsu. Rorion initially set his brother Rickson to be the family champion, but when he was discovered teaching students outside of Rorion's official academy, Rickson was replaced with Royce Gracie.

While UFC 1 can seem terribly dated with the childish graphics and random assortment of experts chiming in throughout the event, the fighters themselves were legitimate representations of their various styles and lineages. It is fascinating to see the bodies of many of these men, especially compared to the chiseled specimens that populate many of the UFC's cards in later years, wearing ill-fitting shorts and without the requisite media training that many professional athletes undertake in the twenty-first century. Each fight is preceded by a short video introducing the fighter, giving him a chance to tell the audience about his background and why he is the best fighter in the world.

The night opened spectacularly with Gerard Gordeau of the Netherlands kicking Hawaiian sumo champion Teila Tuli in the face and knocking out the larger man's tooth, all within the first twenty-six seconds of the fight. The match ended so quickly that the audience and the fighters seemed stunned. It was a brutal moment, captured in perpetuity and communicating to the audience and fighters that the UFC was something completely, utterly new.

The second fight between super heavyweight ISKA champion kickboxer Kevin Rosier and karate champion Zane Frazier ended in a technical knockout by Rosier, who seemed surprised and a bit shell-shocked himself in the post-fight interview. There is something rather endearing about Rosier's timidity in front of the camera and his overall demeanor after the fight. It seems incongruous with the man who just stomped his opponent's head multiple times before a towel soared through the air, ending their bout.

The third fight featured Royce Gracie, who is cast as the obvious favorite to win the tournament by the editing and the commentators' chatter. Royce entered the ring in the famous Gracie chain, each man jogging in a line with his hands on the shoulders of the man in front. Hélio himself helped corner his son, who quickly defeated boxer Art Jimmerson in the first round with a smothering technique from the mount. The crowd erupted in booing and jeers, apparently because they could not understand why Jimmerson was down. But the boos became louder in the next match when Denver's hometown hero, boxer Pat Smith, lost to Ken Shamrock.

Ken Shamrock, next to Royce Gracie, was the best situated in the group to participate in the inaugural UFC event and would become one of the men who established the foundation of modern MMA. In his short introduction video, Shamrock appears in medias res, finishing a set of lat pull-downs before he begins speaking to the camera. In the cage, wearing vale tudo shorts that the commentators described as "swimming trunks," Shamrock defeated Pat Smith by a solid heel hook, but both the crowd and Pat were angry, as though Shamrock used some illegal technique. Although Shamrock lost to Royce Gracie in the next round of the tournament, he would go on to become the UFC's first Superfight champion when he defeated Dan Severn in 1995.

Gerard Gordeau easily defeated the much larger Kevin Rosier in his second match of the tournament, and so all attention turned to the final bout between Gordeau and Gracie. Although UFC 1 primarily is re-membered as the launching ground for Brazilian jujitsu via Royce Gra-cie, Gordeau is a fascinating man to watch in the cage. He is deliberate and efficient, moving purposefully to land strikes and defend take-downs. Although unable to withstand Royce Gracie's superior grappling skills, Gordeau exemplifies the early generation of fighters who could successfully translate their individual martial arts experience in the cage. But Royce Gracie, the clear winner of the evening with quick submissions of all of his opponents, did exactly what Rorion wanted him to do: he made the name Gracie synonymous with the rising sport of MMA.

The next few years of UFC events maintained the tournament for-mat, with Gracie, Shamrock, and a few new top fighters, such as Dan Severn and "The Russian Bear," Oleg Taktarov, routinely clobbering the men who agreed to enter the octagon. In 1994, Royce Gracie and

Ken Shamrock faced off in the UFC's first Superfight, hailed as a grudge match. Shamrock had lost only once in the octagon, and that was to Royce Gracie, and he was ready to avenge his loss. Unfortunately, this was the first UFC event to include time limits, and after more than thirty minutes of fighting with a five-minute extension, the fight ended in a draw.

UFC 5 also ended Rorion Gracie's relationship with the venue, and Royce, the reigning undefeated champion did not return until UFC 60 in 2006, although he fought several times in Japan in the intervening years. We will get to those fights, and the infamous "Gracie Killer," Kazushi Sakuraba, in chapter 5. Because UFC 5's Superfight ended without a winner, it continued into the next event, when Ken Shamrock defeated Dan Severn for the title. UFC 6 also introduced David Lee "Tank" Abbott, one of the UFC's most notorious fighters, who seemed to take sadistic enjoyment in inflicting pain on his opponents.

In 1997, two of the sport's most famous fighters, Randy "The Natural" Couture and Tito Ortiz, known as "The Huntington Beach Bad Boy," joined the UFC roster. Couture is one of the most beloved MMA fighters in history, despite his later arguments with future UFC figurehead Dana White, and even though his contribution has been downplayed as a result, Randy Couture was instrumental in making the UFC a legitimate sports venue.

Part of the UFC's struggle for that legitimacy came from criticisms across the board, from liberal to conservative political ideologies, that the venue was a purveyor of violence. Of course, MMA does have a visceral quality that can make uninitiated viewers feel queasy, but the UFC struggled from its very first fight, when Gerard Gordeau kicked Teila Tuli's tooth out of his mouth in the first thirty seconds of the fight. Republican senator John McCain became one of the strongest and best-known opponents of the young fight venue, sending letters to all fifty state governors requesting that they ban "human cockfighting" in their respective jurisdictions.

McCain was a boxing enthusiast, but the new sport of MMA was so very different from the sweet science or Olympic wrestling. In fact, the new stars of MMA, such as Frank Shamrock, Tank Abbott, and Royce Gracie, regularly knocked out or choked out their opponents who were champions in their own singular disciplines of professional boxing or freestyle wrestling. Some of the videos capturing these knockouts included truly terrifying footage of downed fighters receiving head stomps, or being choked until they were unconscious and appearing to succumb to seizures. Not surprising, then, that a large group of people attempted to boycott MMA, given the long, troubled history of prize-fighting in the United States.

Although it is easy to see McCain as the villain, it is important to remember that the early UFC shows had few rules, which meant that fighters did not receive the same level of protection as in other sports such as boxing or professional football. McCain and other opponents of MMA took umbrage at the lack of safety protocols, and the fact that the UFC and its owners seemed to delight in not offering fighters protection. Indeed, within a decade of its inception, the UFC would begin shifting away from the original image of boorish backyard brawling to a more sophisticated, well-defined professional sports venue.

Before ZUFFA took charge of the floundering promotion, the UFC managed to continue producing shows in states such as Alabama, Colorado, and Wyoming and generating viewership from its target audience of 18–35-year-old males. In 1999, *Slate* ran an article claiming that the UFC would devolve into underground, tough man-style fighting due to the pressure from McCain and his cohort. What the senator and fellow activists did not realize, and what *Slate* magazine missed, was the future earning potential of mixed martial arts, embodied in the Ultimate Fighting Championship venue.

The UFC lacked the support of a sophisticated media conglomerate that could elevate it into the realm of other professional sports outlets. With proper backing and strategized rebranding, the UFC had the potential to generate an enormous amount of money and with that financial success, to align itself with the type of political power that could remove the bans put in place to hamstring the sport of MMA. With financial success and lobbying, the UFC could become a legitimized professional sports outlet. But first, it needed help reaching that next rung in the ladder. Luckily, a group of men had been eyeing the venue and saw a potential to share this new sport and to make an enormous amount of money.

After the departure of the Gracie family as owners in the venue, the UFC limped along for a few years under SEG's ownership. They made several structural changes, such as implementing weight classes and time limits, and enforcing several rules to improve safety, such as eliminating head stomps, hair pulling, and small joint manipulations. UFC 14 introduced official MMA gloves in 1997, and later that year they set up the first event outside the United States, UFC Japan 1, which featured two more legends—Frank Shamrock, the brother of veteran Ken Shamrock, and Kazushi Sakuraba, who we will get to in chapter 5.

In 1998, the UFC held the first event in Brazil, and Pat Miletich, Chuck Liddell, Pedro Rizzo, and Wanderlei Silva, to name a few future stars, joined the roster. Bas Rutten and Evan Tanner fought in 1999, with Rutten quickly fighting for top-dog status, and Matt Hughes made his first appearance in the octagon, as did Jens Pulver, who would become the first UFC lightweight champion. Most of these fighters had the most significant moments of their careers in the twenty-first century, so we will continue their stories in chapter 5, but their addition to the UFC roster in the late 1990s shows the venue's appeal to a wider variety of fighters who were training specifically for a mixed martial arts fight.

It seems like a quick transition from the mismatched competitions in the UFC's inaugural event in 1993 to the focused, well-rounded athletes competing in 1999. Fighters such as the U.S.'s Tito Ortiz, the Netherlands's Bas Rutten, and Brazil's Wanderlei Silva demonstrated the growth and refinement of a sport that was not just an American phenomenon. Instead, the twentieth century closed with a hint at the globalizing effect that MMA would have on martial arts worldwide. In just one hundred years, the world had gone from telegraphs to the internet, and from fighting styles that were isolated and fixed in a specific region to those being practiced, translated, and contested around the world.

# 5

# GLOBALIZATION, MEDIA, AND MMA

**W**hen Liz Carmouche walked into the cage to wait for her opponent, Ronda Rousey, on February 23, 2013, she made double history; not only was she the first woman to enter the UFC octagon, she was also the first openly gay fighter in that promotion's history. After years of UFC president Dana White claiming that his venue would "never" allow women to compete, the dynamic and wildly popular Ronda Rousey was given the UFC bantamweight women's title, and Liz Carmouche became her first challenger. Wearing her signature rainbow mouthguard, Carmouche faced the champion, who at the tail end of the first round of the championship fight, defeated the challenger with her signature arm bar. Carmouche and Rousey, in less than five minutes, put on a show that was exciting, filled with action, and gave audiences exactly what they expected in that ferocious arm bar. But more than that, Liz Carmouche and Ronda Rousey showed that despite its economic success and huge media reach, even the UFC could change its corporate policy to embrace these women who just wanted to compete in the sport they loved.

The UFC is the most visible example of MMA around the world, but the vast majority of mixed martial arts fights take place in smaller venues that can range from local shows in small cities to huge events featuring fighters from around the world. However, the latter still tend to be dwarfed by the power of the UFC. This chapter examines how the sport of MMA became globalized, due in large part to the power of media and capitalism. We will also consider how various indigenous martial arts both have embraced MMA and purposefully remained independent from the engulfing forces of this interdisciplinary art. The sport of MMA has had an almost colonizing impact on martial arts around the world. In an effort to improve performance in a context where any tool could be useful, and with the diverse backgrounds of so many fighters, nearly every martial art on the planet has had elements of itself translated into application in the cage. That is both interesting and exciting, because the streamlined version of MMA today does not have one single lineage. Instead, modern MMA is an amalgam of numerous fighting sports and traditions from around the world.

However, the homogenizing power of MMA has been detrimental to some individual martial arts. In an effort to both retain their old practitioners and generate new athletes, some traditional fighting sports have shifted their practices to look more like MMA. It is heartbreaking for some traditional martial artists to see the individual style they love assimilate in order to better reflect the popular passion for MMA. For many indigenous arts though, the traditions remain alive in their original place, even if they look completely different when translated to other parts of the world.

Muay Thai is an excellent example of this phenomenon. The Thai art is wildly popular and one of the most respected fighting sports in the world, but a Muay Thai fight in Thailand looks completely different from a Muay Thai fight in other countries. In Thailand, where Muay Thai originated, fights are not limited by the conventions of other countries and their attempts to import the sport. Most venues in the United States and Europe have stringent rules that might require protective gear, such as shin guards, or do not allow certain movements, such as knees to the head, in order to protect participants, and more likely, to get the appropriate insurance for their events.

In Thailand, not only are all of the elements and techniques of Muay Thai present, but the atmosphere and the environment are original. Therefore, no Muay Thai fight in any other part of the world will be as original or traditional as in Thailand. The same goes for every other indigenous sport. It could be translated into other places and into other cultures and communities, but it will always be most fully itself in its country of origin. These differences in translation do not mean that people cannot love and enjoy Muay Thai in other parts of the world, but simply that they will love and enjoy an American or Dutch or Mexican version of the sport.

Places are important. Even in an increasingly globalized society, cultural translation of a practice from one place to another produces a new iteration rather than an exact replica, which is rather thrilling. But it remains important to understand and remember that context matters. What makes MMA exciting is that it is, in a way, context free. It evolved from so many global traditions and emerged as a sport on camera. Because that emergence was captured in the media, even if the audience was relatively small in the beginning, people from all over the world saw the sport and emulated it while adding their own personal preferences and traditions. MMA as a sport is both singular in its rules and action, yet as unique and diverse as every fighter who practices it. Every fighter brings his or her own martial arts history and tradition to the sport, which makes MMA simultaneously steeped in tradition and completely without tradition.

In the late twentieth century, interdisciplinary fights took place all over the world under various headers such as Shooto, vale tudo, and ultimate fighting. Some of the monikers, such as anything goes, no-holds-barred, and cage fighting, implied a type of uncontrolled and unregulated brawl that upset many of the sport's opponents. Some detractors even referred to the UFC as human cockfighting. The rather clean name of mixed martial arts, first used in the late twentieth century, went a long way toward helping the sport gain legitimacy by tying it to martial arts instead of just fighting. The abbreviated MMA, meanwhile, provides brevity and is much easier to translate to languages other than English.

In the 1980s and 1990s, MMA primarily was contested in the United States and Japan, and in the twenty-first century the sport rocketed around the globe. By 2020, nearly every country had an established MMA scene that boxing commissions oversaw. The establishment of official sanctioning throughout the world marks a difference from backyard or street fights that some people less familiar with fighting sports might consider part of the MMA umbrella. Officially sanctioned MMA events are as streamlined and tightly controlled as any other sport, with rules that tend to have a universal standard, especially as various institutions such as the International MMA Federation and ordinances such as the Unified Rules of MMA became standardized.

Establishing the norms of MMA was an important part of promoting mixed martial arts as a reputable sport. The International MMA Federation (IMMAF) emerged in 2012 as the official international governing body. IMMAF works to make mixed martial arts an internationally recognized sport by hosting tournaments; generating recommendations on rules, rankings, and safety protocols; and advocating for admitting the sport to the Olympic Games. Specifically supporting amateur fighters, the IMMAF hosts huge tournaments all over the world, from regional events to an international final. This international organization created a stable governing body that helped constitute credibility in the sport. Far from the free-for-all tournaments of the past, IMMAF carefully organizes safe fights with clear rules that are consistent throughout the world. By cultivating young fighters backed by their individually recognized national MMA federation, the IMMAF forged a pipeline from amateur to professional athletes around the world. Because of this careful organization, MMA has the potential to be even more diverse in the future and may perhaps move away from the monolith that is the UFC to a plethora of high-profile, well-funded venues around the world.

In the twenty-first century, thus far MMA has proved that it was not a flash in the pan, as some traditionalists contended. Instead, the first two decades saw the meteoric rise of the UFC as a business and elevation of some of its fighters to superstardom. This final chapter looks at the convergence of media and sport, focusing on the UFC as well as other professional MMA venues. In addition, this chapter considers how gender, race, ethnicity, religion, sexuality, and economic status have impacted the development of MMA from a highly contentious spectacle to a legitimate, highly regarded sport. We will travel back in time in order to understand what happened in the twentieth century, but for the most part, we will examine how MMA survived and thrived, and how indigenous cultures retained their own unique, individual fighting arts.

## THE UNITED STATES

Martial arts training expanded greatly in the twenty-first century as both youth and adult programs flourished in a variety of disciplines. Brazilian jujitsu, made popular by its prevalence in the UFC, became one of the most practiced fighting arts around the world, especially in the United States, where many black belts emigrated from Brazil in hopes of generating wealth and prestige in an open market. Muay Thai training, seen as the ultimate striking foundation for MMA, spread throughout the United States, although tae kwon do, karate, and judo remained the three most widely disseminated Asian martial arts. Boxing and wrestling continue to be two of the most prolific fighting sports, both growing significantly in the twenty-first century as more women and girls began to practice and compete.

But the biggest growth in the twenty-first century in the martial arts world—and probably in the entire international sports industry—was in the UFC as it went from a malingering, somewhat farcical spectacle to one of the most powerful, economically viable sporting companies on the planet.

Throughout the 2000s, fighters would enter the UFC octagon and become superstars in their field—Georges St-Pierre, Chuck Liddell, Andrei Arlovski, Rashad Evans, Rich Franklin, BJ Penn, and so many others that it would be impossible to list them all. Instead, this chapter will highlight moments that significantly impacted development of the sport and the various industries that developed in conjunction with martial arts around the world.

The final few years of the twentieth century saw the introduction of well-rounded, highly conditioned athletes—a far cry from the barroom brawlers that Tank Abbott represented. When Brazil's "Phenom" Vitor Belfort fought the United States' Randy Couture in 1997, it was a prescient moment—a glimpse into the future of MMA. These two men, both champions in their respective sports of Brazilian jujitsu and collegiate wrestling, demonstrated how top athletes would perform in this seemingly marginal sports venture. Both men trained specifically for the rigors of a mixed martial arts fight and prepared to counteract each other's style. This may seem obvious now, but at the time Couture and Belfort's combined athleticism, technical prowess, and strategies revealed the potential for MMA to provide skillful action that was far from the UFC's original fights. Couture defeated Belfort via TKO in their first meeting in 1997, but Belfort won their second scrape in January 2004. Later that year, Couture won again, further solidifying his place as one of the world's greatest MMA fighters.

In 2000, Dana White, then manager of Tito Ortiz and Chuck Liddell, an interesting combination given the two men's later rivalry, heard that SEG looked to unload the UFC, its young, not terribly successful fight venue. White reached out to his childhood friends Lorenzo and Frank Fertitta, sons of Las Vegas entrepreneur Frank Fertitta Sr., to see if they would be interested in purchasing the UFC. Frank Sr. discouraged his sons, but they decided to go against their father's wishes and in January 2001, they acquired the UFC for $2 million. The Fertitta brothers created ZUFFA, LLC, as the official parent company of the new UFC and made their friend Dana White president and unofficial figurehead of the venue. White saw the potential that SEG missed in its floundering last years in control of the UFC. By the time ZUFFA purchased the UFC and White took the helm, the promotion was bankrupt (SEG had liquidated nearly all of its assets), and the sport was banned in many states around the country after political pressure from numerous lobbying groups and politicians to bar what Senator John McCain had called "human cockfighting."[1] White, however, had a plan to radically change the trajectory of the UFC.

White assiduously sought out politicians, commissioners, and other groups with the power to lobby for the UFC, working with them to legalize the sport of mixed martial arts around the United States. One of the Fertitta's most important hires was Marc Ratner, executive director of the Nevada State Athletic Commission and a nonparticipatory inductee into the Boxing Hall of Fame for his work as a highly regarded boxing inspector. Ratner left the NSAC to join the UFC as vice president of regulatory affairs. Ratner's reputation for integrity, competence, and respectability helped the venue establish credibility with boxing commissions around the country, and during his tenure, MMA became legalized in all fifty states and in Canada.

The UFC already had a strong roster of talent at the time of the ZUFFA acquisition, but viewing its events was cumbersome and not conducive to wider distribution and promotion. White improved pay-per-view events by increasing marketing, all the while working to make MMA a more widely acceptable sport. More rules were put in place to protect fighters and make MMA more palatable to the audience. Fans who had watched the UFC from the beginning may have been inured to the blood and damage often seen in the first decade of events, but in order to acquire new fans and thus increase financial earnings, the UFC needed a bit of a makeover. It took several years, and, at one point, because the Fertitta brothers were losing so much money, they asked White to find a buyer for the struggling venue. But White persisted doggedly, facilitating rule changes and, more important, creating marketing that elevated the UFC from its DIY graphics to a more sophisticated professional sports venue. White also hired comedian Joe Rogan to act as a commentator, which eventually would result in Rogan, like White, becoming a noncombatant star of the UFC.

In 2005, the UFC made its way onto cable broadcast when it joined Spike TV in presenting *The Ultimate Fighter* (TUF), which pitted upcoming fighters against each other for a highly coveted six-figure contract with the UFC. At a time when reality programming was in high demand, particularly the genre that forced people to live in a single house à la MTV's *Real World*, the UFC made an excellent call both in meeting the market demand for "real" competitions and in using cable broadcasting rather than pay-per-view.

Even in the early days of ZUFFA's ownership, White and his colleagues recognized that the UFC easily could be bundled into various commodities, from video games to DVD sales, in addition to the pay-per-view streaming. Adding a reality show contest provided the brand with a new audience who might not otherwise fork out money for pay-per-view fights but eventually would need to do so in order to follow the sport. TUF introduced cable viewers to MMA, generating a new audience with tremendous advertising potential. The final event for the first season, with Randy Couture and Chuck Liddell acting as coaches, saw Forrest Griffin defeat Stephen Bonnar, although both men ended up receiving contracts with the UFC. Griffin and Bonnar were ideal finalists, both likable men with personality and charm who put on an incredible fight that delighted audiences. That fight catapulted the UFC to a new realm, shifting it from a marginal venue that only fans who already knew about MMA watched, to the signifier of a mainstream sport. *The Ultimate Fighter* would continue for dozens of seasons, hosted in the United States, China, Brazil, Latin America, and a season that pitted Australian fighters against fighters from Canada. But that first season truly changed the trajectory of the UFC and of MMA, to the point where some less informed fans began referring to the sport itself as the UFC, as in "Do you train UFC?"

In the early days of the UFC, fighters were highly stratified based on their martial arts background. Wrestlers, boxers, kickboxers, and grapplers had a general understanding of well-rounded training, but few were able to truly bring together all of the tools necessary for success in the octagon. Fighters with a background in high school and collegiate wrestling had an advantage in takedowns and ground control, but they often stuck their head, arms, and legs in the perfect spot for BJJ and catch wrestling submissions.

The fighters who were able to bridge that gap, such as Pat Miletich and his future protégé, Matt Hughes, immediately became dominant. Not only could these men successfully take down their opponents, but they could avoid sweeps and submissions, rain down punches, and set up their own chokes and joint locks to finish the fight. In order to meet the requirements for successful competition, and even before *The Ultimate Fighter* launched the UFC into mainstream culture in 2005, MMA training was beginning to undergo a systemic shift. Young, up-and-coming fighters trained in a combination of striking, typically Muay Thai or American kickboxing, along with freestyle wrestling and submission grappling, usually BJJ or catch wrestling.

Under ZUFFA's ownership, the UFC acquired new fighters who would diversify their roster and initiate some of the most exciting rivalries in the sport's history. The light heavyweight division saw Randy Couture, Chuck Liddell, Vitor Belfort, Quinton Jackson, Rashad Evans, Lyoto Machida, Jon Jones, and Daniel Cormier compete for the title. Anderson Silva, Georges St-Pierre, Luke Rockhold, Robert Whittaker, Michael Bisping, and Israel Adesanya all became middleweight champions. Rivalries between Urijah Faber and Dominick Cruz made the already dynamic bantamweight division even more exciting. The arrival of Henry Cejudo, Triple C, whose bizarre trash talk could not rival the intelligence of Cruz, certainly generated a great deal of press. Many modern UFC fighters have used the media in a way similar to their fighting ancestors; the greatest (or at least, the loudest) modern self-aggrandizer in the MMA world, Conor McGregor, will be discussed later in this chapter.

Suffice it to say that ZUFFA's sixteen-year tenure as the owners of the UFC forever changed the venue and the sport in general. The UFC moved from the margins of respectability and the edge of financial ruin to becoming one of the most successful sports productions in the world.

MMA emerged as a respected and elite form of combat sport that is highly entertaining and has a tremendous audience reach, nationally and internationally.

ZUFFA sold the UFC for $4 billion in 2016 to talent agency WME-IMG, which has changed its name to Endeavor. In addition to stakeholders such as Dana White, Endeavor performed a unique move in acquiring a group of celebrity investors, including Mark Wahlberg, Food Network star Guy Fieri, and supermodel Gisele Bündchen among others. Early in 2020, the celebrity investors were awarded more than $300 million in dividends, and the executives and other large stakeholders also received tremendous payouts. It may be this particular information that has infuriated numerous UFC fighters who have been fighting for compensation increases for years. The UFC reportedly pays a mere 16 percent of its overall income in salaries, whereas other large sports venues, such as the NFL and NBA, allocate nearly 50 percent of their revenue to players. Although the UFC might be able to claim that it pays its athletes the highest in the sport, that does not necessarily make their pay fair. Former UFC and Strikeforce contender Cung Le long has spoken out against the UFC's pay scale for fighters, arguing that with the exception of a select few, most fighters receive a pittance in exchange for the risk of competing in the octagon. Most UFC fighters generate the vast majority of their income from sponsorships rather than fight purses.

Some fighters abandon the UFC to compete in other venues. Bellator Fighting Championships was established in 2009 as a return, of sorts, to the eight-man fight brackets that earlier promotions, such as the UFC, used. For Bellator, single-elimination brackets from bantamweight to heavyweight took place over the course of several months, culminating in a tournament winner for each bracket, each of whom would receive a $100,000 purse and an opportunity for a title fight against the current Bellator champion. Bellator was successful immediately as an entertainment venue among fight fans, with a focus on the fighting rather than on generating drama between athletes. Bellator featured some of the best athletes, including Michael Chandler, "Rampage" Jackson, Lyoto Machida, Cris "Cyborg" Justino, and many others. Several MMA fighters joined Bellator after leaving the UFC, including Russia's Fedor Emelianenko and America's Quinton "Rampage" Jackson, Chael Sonnen, and Frank Mir. Bellator cannot truly compete with the UFC in terms of money or viewership, but it has provided exciting events around the world by having continent-specific versions of its promotion.

As every media entity eagerly sought to form its own streaming platform, the UFC created its own version, the UFC Fight Pass, which would allow subscribers to watch every fight in its own historical catalog, as well as events from Invicta FC, an all-women's MMA venue, and UFC's acquisitions such as PRIDE and WEC. In addition, some UFC cards air on ESPN, a sign that the sport has truly entered the mainstream. The UFC Fight Night cards, which typically take place on Friday evenings on ESPN+, rather than the Saturday shows available on pay-per-view, are ways for the promotion to hold events in cities in other parts of the world that won't interfere with pay-per-view sales. For many fighters, UFC Fight Nights are undercards compared to the much larger UFC events held on pay-per-view. Even as the company looks to expand, the American market is still the primary target; therefore, large pay-per-view shows have to take place with American audiences in mind. A show in Las Vegas might run live on pay-per-view at 4 a.m. in Europe or Asia, but it must be in prime time for Americans.

For that reason, most shows that take place overseas will not contain the major star power of a stateside production because the UFC will not let its biggest stars fight at times that might hinder pay-per-view sales. However, most overseas shows feature fighters from that country, so when the UFC strawweight champion, Brazil's Jéssica Andrade, faced China's Zhang Weili in 2019 in Shenzhen, it made sense to have a title match at local China time. It was odd to have a title match on a UFC Fight Night card, but it seems that UFC executives thought the presence of a Chinese challenger made it appropriate. In addition, not a great deal of buzz preceded the fight, in part because the women's divisions do not typically generate the type of media frenzy that certain men's divisions do, and because Zhang was a relative newcomer to American audiences. But that night Zhang TKO'd the champion in the first round and revealed to the UFC and the world that she was the most dominant strawweight on the planet. A few months later, Zhang fought Joanna Jędrzejczyk in what was considered by many to be the best women's MMA fight of all time, if not one of the best of all time, full stop.

The UFC's women's divisions are relatively new to the venue, arriving when Liz Carmouche and Ronda Rousey fought, as mentioned previously, in 2013. Prior to the UFC's including women, they were competing in MMA in Japan in the late 1990s; in the early 2000s, Strikeforce FC included women in its rosters, including Julie Kedzie, Gina Carano, Cris "Cyborg" Justino, Miesha Tate, and Ronda Rousey. In 2011, Dana White staunchly claimed that women would "never" fight in the UFC, but two years later he reversed that decision when Ronda Rousey began to make headlines.

Rousey, an Olympic judo medalist, was the UFC's first female champion and one of the most important figures in MMA history. Her performance in and out of the cage introduced the sport to the masses, and the largest media outlets took notice of female fighters. In 2014, the overall coverage of women in American sports media was dismal at 3.2 percent.[2] Social media, however, was just emerging as a powerful tool for businesses and individuals. Rousey used both traditional media and social media to bring attention to herself, demanding that Strikeforce give her a title fight against the current champion, Miesha Tate.

Tate and other women in the Strikeforce roster were critical of Ronda's self-promotion because other women were in line to take on the champion. But Ronda recognized that Strikeforce and women's MMA needed media attention, and using a combination of trash talk and bravado, she certainly was generating press. In 2012, Ronda broke Miesha Tate's arm in the Strikeforce cage and, six months later, defeated Sarah Kaufman with her signature submission. Despite his previous insistence that women would "never" compete in the UFC, Dana White changed his stance on women's fighting, creating the first UFC bantamweight women's division and naming Ronda Rousey its champion. The inaugural fight was made doubly progressive with Liz Carmouche, the UFC's first openly gay fighter. Rousey seemed unstoppable in her first six UFC fights, until Holly Holm famously knocked her out with a brutal head kick on November 14, 2015.

For many critics, Rousey's defeat signified the end of WMMA's prominence, especially as the belt changed hands several times before Amanda Nunes secured and defended it in 2016. In the immediate aftermath of Ronda's defeat and retirement, as she left the UFC to join the WWE, MMA pundits argued that women's MMA was over. Part of the problem was that the UFC based the entire division on Ronda, naming her champion before the first fight, and continually positioning her as the single embodiment of a champion female fighter. Ronda's absence did not ruin the division, nor did it sound the death knell for women's MMA as a whole. Amanda Nunes, Valentina Shevchenko, Julianna Peña, Cris "Cyborg" Justino, and Holly Holm, among others, kept the division dynamic while Jéssica Andrade, Joanna Jędrzejczyk, Claudia Gadelha, Rose Namajunas, and others excelled in the strawweight division. Women's fighting continued after Ronda's defeat, just as it existed before her entrance.

The opening of the women's bantamweight league in the UFC started with Ronda, and in her wake, a group of highly qualified, fantastic athletes finally were given the opportunity to fight in the top echelon of their sport. Again, the UFC probably would have allowed women to compete in their venue at some point, although it seemed content to have them remain in the smaller venues of Strikeforce and Invicta FC—sidelines to the "real" fighters in the UFC. But with Ronda, Dana found himself unable to hold out. When he retracted his famous "women will never compete in the UFC" stance not just Ronda benefited, but all women—from first-class MMA fighters such as Liz Carmouche, Cat Zingano, and Holly Holm, to the women and girls who, at gyms in their local towns, could finally point to the UFC, the most elite platform in the MMA world, and see themselves.

MMA probably is the fastest growing sport in the world, both in its practice by individuals in gyms around the world and in viewership. The UFC's distribution agreements with DAZN and ESPN+ created more pathways for viewership and opportunities for advertising across a diverse swath of platforms. Although the UFC does operate internationally, the United States remains its home country with what might be its most important demographic of fans. The UFC arguably would not have been able to succeed to the same degree if it had originated anywhere other than the United States, because the United States loves its sports, especially the tremendously large and commercially successful professional sports venues and the multibillion-dollar media machine that serves them.

## ASIA

It is nearly impossible to find a country that has not joined the international MMA community, even if indigenous martial arts remain far more popular. In Thailand, Muay Thai far outranks MMA, and in other places, boxing or wrestling easily eclipses MMA. Some countries just beginning to promote MMA have the potential to be important training grounds for fighters. The UFC ended 2019 with a December show in South Korea featuring that country's most famous fighter, Chan Sung Jung, who goes by the moniker the Korean Zombie. Jung lost that fight against Frankie Edgar, but he still is the first fighter to pull off a twister submission in the UFC cage.

South Korea has its own MMA venue, the Road Fighting Championships, and many fighters also compete in ONE Championships out of China. In other parts of Asia, such as the Philippines, boxing is the far more popular fighting sport, although MMA fighters in the thousand islands typically travel to compete in ONE or other venues closer to home. Vietnamese-American fighter Cung Le, who retired with an undefeated career in kickboxing and Chinese sanda and competed in both Strikeforce and the UFC, paid homage to his home country in his fights, but the sport of MMA has only just begun to become popular in Vietnam. The two biggest players in the Asian MMA scene undoubtedly are China and Japan, the latter for having helped establish and grow the sport in the early days, the former for producing the UFC's biggest competitor, ONE Championships.

### China

In the twenty-first century, MMA's popularity entered Chinese culture, although traditional martial artists offered some resistance. The relationship between China and the United States became increasingly tenuous during Donald Trump's presidency, yet the UFC and other professional American entertainment industries eagerly sought to tap the wealth and breadth of the Chinese market. Many Chinese citizens worried over the growing encroachment of American and other international corporations taking root in the mainland and perhaps subsuming the native culture. MMA created a rift in some Chinese communities between the modern sport and the tradition of some Chinese martial arts.

In 2017, a video emerged on social media in which Xu Xiaodong, a Chinese MMA fighter, easily defeated tai chi master Wei Lei just twenty seconds into their underground grudge match. Xu spent much of his time online calling out the men who claimed that their martial arts skill gave them magical powers. Wei Lei had long claimed that he could capture a dove in flight using his mind and other seemingly bizarre side effects of his tai chi prowess. Xu took umbrage at these men, some of whom falsely aligned themselves with the Shaolin Temple, sullying the name of Chinese martial arts. In the aftermath of his victory, however, Xu was accused of disparaging Chinese culture, maligning Chinese martial arts, and, even worse, putting Western arts above Chinese ones. He and his family received death threats; he was banned from social media, and tai chi practitioners from all over the country camped outside his gym, eager to avenge their art.

Xu claimed that his intention was not to disparage Chinese martial arts, but the damage already had been done. As in many other places around the world, the power of MMA felt like a threat to Chinese history, tradition, and culture. The backlash that Xu received by defeating Wei Lei was not just cultural, of course; it was political. The Shaolin Temple and many other parts of kung fu have become emblems of the Chinese government, and ridicule of them has severe political and social costs. Xu's mission may have been to reveal charlatans who claim to have magical powers, or those men and women who claim to be Shaolin monks, yet have absolutely no true tie to the temple. But by defeating Wei Lei, and calling some tai chi claims into question, Xu brought down the approbation of the government and his culture. Xu Xiaodong's mistake in ridiculing what were seen as traditional Chinese arts was a lesson for other martial artists who sought to expand MMA in China. Instead of antagonizing Chinese culture and, in turn, the Chinese government, new MMA venues would need to work within the social, economic, and political conventions of the country.

Multiple MMA venues exist in and around China. The Art of War Fighting Championship, which Chinese-American Brazilian jujitsu teacher Andrew Pi started in 2005, ran through 2016. Several Gracie family members fought in the venue in an attempt to spread BJJ in the giant country. In 2009, Hong Kong-based promotion Legend FC worked to spread interdisciplinary fighting in the region, although it was sold later and relaunched as a Chinese fighting promotion. Two of Legend FC's most popular fighters, Li Jingliang and Jumabieke Tuerxun, were signed to the UFC in 2014. At the time, the UFC already had begun to infiltrate the Chinese MMA scene, hosting the *The Ultimate Fighter: China* show featuring Vietnamese-American MMA fighter and sanda champion Cung Le as the head coach and mentor. The UFC's initial forays into China were successful, but its biggest competitor was in the process of creating its own empire.

In 2011, ONE Championship launched in Singapore, which offered MMA, kickboxing, and Muay Thai fights featuring athletes from around the world, including several UFC champions. Some fighters competed in ONE before going to the UFC, such as Ben Askren, and Demetrious Johnson left the UFC after becoming its first flyweight champion. Some debate surfaced about how competitive ONE is with the UFC due to confusion in the financial reporting, but ONE certainly features the most Asian fighters. Chatri Sityodtong, ONE's founder and CEO, claims that his promotion has created a refined, sport-focused venue that does not allow for some of the poor behavior certain UFC athletes demonstrate. Sityodtong argues that ONE promotes fighters as superheroes, as opposed to the UFC's use of drama and "bad blood" to generate media attention. Citing China's long appreciation of fighting sports as an art that Buddhist monks practiced and perfected, Sityodtong repeatedly has argued that the East appreciates MMA far more than the West, especially Americans, who he claimed are far more interested in drama than professionalism. Sityodtong's vision for ONE carefully aligns with the government's mission: presenting a unified, positive image of Chinese business ventures.

Demetrious Johnson, the inaugural UFC flyweight champion, never reached superstardom because he didn't "play the game" by trash-talking or otherwise generating controversy and drama. But he was one of its most successful fighters in the cage and is one of Sityodton's greatest acquisitions from the UFC. Sityodtong believes that ONE's approach to MMA could appeal to Americans who are tired of the extreme drama and trash-talking of the UFC, which Conor McGregor exemplified.

The coronavirus pandemic of 2020 forced ONE, like every other international sports venue, to pull back from its expansion goals. Indeed, ONE laid off 20 percent of its workforce, although it also received $70 million dollars in support from its investors to keep the company financially solvent.[3] Sityodtong announced in June 2020 that the venue would return in late summer or early fall of 2020 to host shows in China, Singapore, and Thailand. Although expanding into the United States must be delayed, it remains to be seen if the venue will be able to transition to the United States, where the UFC dominates the market. Despite the economic turmoil the novel coronavirus brought about, ONE continued to sign top fighters from around the world, in particular focusing on strikers from GLORY and Rizin.

Interestingly, because ONE includes not only MMA fights but also Muay Thai, it has been able to diversify its audience and, in theory, create a through line for fighters to consider transitioning from one sport to another without having to leave the venue. In addition, ONE's relationships with telecommunications giants from around the world, including a deal with Turner Broadcasting, provides ONE with increased distribution and reach worldwide. ONE also established sponsorships with TUMI, JBL, and RedBull, to name a few. As ONE Championships secures funding, media convergence, high-profile sponsorships, and top athletes from all over the globe, it has situated itself to become a rival to the UFC. ONE may claim that its primary mission is to change the narrative of fighting sports from amplified rivalries to battles between superheroes, but the underlying goal is still the same as the UFC: to secure as much of the global MMA market as possible.

However, the UFC, perhaps seeing the potential of the tremendous Asian market and the breadth of talent numerous Asian countries offer, began hosting events in China in 2017. In 2018, Zhang Weili joined the UFC's strawweight division with a record of 16-1, her only loss at the very beginning of her career. Zhang went on to secure five straight victories, culminating in taking the division title from Jéssica Andrade on August 31, 2019. Zhang's victory made her the first Chinese fighter to become a UFC belt holder. On March 7, 2020, Zhang's fight with Joanna Jędrzejczyk of Poland was widely considered one of the greatest fights of all time, let alone the greatest women's MMA bout.

The UFC generally allocates a decent amount of financial and promotional resources to its Fight Nights, even if it doesn't pay similar dividends to its pay-per-view fights. However, in the case of Zhang Weili fighting in China, the August 2019 Fight Night in Shenzhen probably did more to increase the UFC's bottom line than any prior event.

In the aftermath of the fight, the UFC used Zhang's popularity as a bargaining chip when renegotiating its contract with Chinese media distributor PPTV, which resulted in a deal from which the UFC will rake in $100 million over five years.[4] Zhang's victory as the first Chinese UFC champion generated fervor in her home country and tapped into a market that is astronomical in its potential buying power.

## Japan

At the very end of the twentieth century, while the UFC struggled amid controversy and exhibition restrictions in the United States, Japan organized its own MMA promotion, Pride Fighting Championships. Pride FC eventually would be acquired by the UFC in 2007, but in the early 2000s, it was a direct competitor to the American venue. The first show, held October 11, 1997, in Tokyo, featured Rickson Gracie against Nobuhiko Takada, a famous professional wrestler who was ill-prepared for the Gracie family jujitsu style. Rickson was the target of several Japanese wrestlers who looked to diminish Rickson's seeming dominance in the fight world. Royce Gracie also fought in the inaugural Pride FC show, although his match ended in a draw, and UFC alums Dan Severn and Oleg Taktarov both defeated their opponents. At the time, Pride offered better purses than the UFC, so MMA fighters from around the world went to Japan to test their skills in the ring. In particular, the Gracie family primarily fought in Pride for a period after leaving the UFC, no doubt as a consequence of disagreements on rule sets and fighter compensation. Pride held eight events in the 1990s, which included the introduction of Kazushi Sakuraba, who defeated his first Gracie opponent, Royler, via arm bar in 1999.

Royler's defeat roused Royce Gracie, who returned to the sport after six years of retirement to avenge his family. Gracie demanded unlimited fifteen-minute rounds, to be won by knockout, submission, or throwing in the towel. Sakuraba eventually acquiesced, even though the rest of the tournament did not use the same Gracie rules. On May 1, 2000, Sakuraba met Royce Gracie, where the two men battled for ninety minutes filled with multiple submission attempts, takedowns, and Sakuraba's brutal leg kicks. By the sixth round, Royce no longer was able to walk, so Rorion Gracie threw in the towel.

Sakuraba, meanwhile, continued in the tournament, fighting an additional fifteen minutes against heavyweight fighter Igor Vovchanchyn from Ukraine. His corner threw in the towel after the first round, citing exhaustion, but the fans and MMA community at large were astonished that Sakuraba had attempted to fight Vovchanchyn, who was sixty pounds heavier, just moments after his ninety-minute battle with Royce Gracie. Royce and Sakuraba had a rematch in a 2007 K-1 event called Dynamite USA!!!, where the Gracie fighter won by decision. However, shortly after the fight it was revealed that Royce had tested positive, before and after the bout, for the anabolic steroid nandrolone metabolite. Brock Lesner tested negative for performance-enhancing drugs at that same event along with Sakuraba and the rest of the Dynamite!!! USA fighters with the exception of former NFL player Johnnie Morton. It was a tremendous scandal, although it has been forgotten in large part because Gracie was able to retain the victory due to a loophole in the promotion's rules. Back in 2000, just a few months after Sakuraba defeated Royce Gracie, the Gracies had another opportunity to take on Sakuraba, but this time it was Renzo Gracie whose elbow was destroyed when he refused to tap to Sakuraba's kimura submission. That same year, Sakuraba defeated his fourth Gracie, Ryan, and officially became known as the Gracie Killer. In just one year, Sakuraba destroyed the worldwide assumption that the Gracies were unbeatable and demonstrated the type of dynamic fights that Pride could offer.

Pride FC gloried in presenting action-packed bouts; in fact, fighters could lose a portion of their purse for being inactive or passive in a fight. In 2007, ZUFFA acquired Pride FC, ostensibly bringing together the talents of East and West. However, ZUFFA did little with Pride, other than feature its backlog of fights on UFC Fight Pass, and seemingly remove one of their oldest and most successful competitors. Although ZUFFA claimed that the UFC/Pride merger would be similar to that of the NFL and AFL, this did not materialize. MMA news outlets and fans drooled over the potential matchups, but instead, Pride ended with a whimper as its staff were let go and the fighters either brought into the UFC fold or left to find other outlets for their talents.

After Pride shuttered, several other Japanese MMA promotions attempted to combat the power of the UFC and launch new venues. As we have seen in previous chapters, Japan inaugurated many of the original mixed-match and professional wrestling events, and the demise of

Pride seemed to impact the country's own sense of honor. The UFC continued to hold events in Japan in the twenty-first century, but the loss of Pride left a void that many venues attempted to fill. Several executives, managers, promoters, and matchmakers from the defunct venue banded together to create DREAM, which ran from 2008 to 2012. Then, in 2015, the former parent company of DREAM, which included the one-time president of Pride, founded Rizin Fighting Federation, a new MMA outlet that hosts tournaments in Japan. Rather than competing with the UFC, as ONE Championships expressly has pursued, Rizin claims its goal is to showcase fighters around the world who can represent their unique customs and traditions.

## Southeast Asia

In chapter 2, we looked at the origins of Muay Thai, along with Kun Khmer of Cambodia and Burmese boxing, whose art remained intertwined even as they developed into decidedly different arts. Of the three, Muay Thai clearly is the most popular globally and certainly one of the most respected fighting arts in the world. Thai fighters compete on a much more regular basis than many Western athletes; some fight every few days. Therefore, training focused on increasing stamina through running and swimming, and using the large Thai training pads, attached to the holder's forearms, to practice kicks, knees, elbows, and punches. Sparring is well-controlled in order to diminish the risk of injury and maintain fighter health, but the frequency of fighting and the commitment to their art make Thai fighters pound-for-pound some of the most dynamic martial artists in the world.

Thailand became a popular vacation destination in the 1970s, and Europeans who watched Muay Thai fights in one of the country's many stadiums began training with local instructors and, eventually, exporting the sport to their home countries. Muay Thai associations began to spring up across Europe, and fighters from other disciplines, such as karate and savate, began to test their skills against Thailand's fighters. The dominance of Muay Thai fighters above so many other kickboxing styles further increased Western obsession with the sport, and Thailand became a training mecca for sport fighters around the world. Meanwhile, Thai fighters and coaches who immigrated to Europe and the United States opened their own training academies, spreading the art across the world. In Europe, Dutch kickboxing, a new version of Muay Thai, evolved, emphasizing leg kicks and powerful punches.

However, the tradition of Muay Thai is the focus of a great deal of concern as it is disseminated outside its home country. Many Muay Thai enthusiasts are concerned by the watering-down effect of Western translations and the fact that the sport has become conflated with other martial arts, in particular MMA. In fact, Muay Thai is one of the most popular training protocols for mixed martial artists looking to land devastating kicks, elbows, and knees. But it has to be adjusted to translate successfully to a sport where the threat of takedowns ever looms. The translation of Muay Thai techniques into an MMA format does, indeed, deviate from the Thai tradition, and it is important not to conflate the two different sports. But it does make sense that MMA fighters around the world would want to train in this particularly brutal and efficient fighting art.

Muay Thai martial artists seek to preserve the legacy of the sport and keep it safe from the homogenizing tendencies of Western capitalism. However, many Muay Thai gyms in Thailand are not immune to the pecuniary benefits of MMA training. Some traditional Muay Thai training camps have expanded to include MMA in their titles and in their offerings, especially as American and European fighters travel to Thailand to hone their skills. The country has remained a martial arts destination for many Westerners, creating a demand for training that has expanded to include beginners as well as experienced fighters. Many gyms offer special classes for Westerners who want to try out a Muay Thai class between visits to the beach or elephant sanctuaries. This commodification of the art, however, has its benefits: catering to vacationers has created better financial stability for indigenous fighters and coaches. Serious martial artists, including fighters in the top echelon of Muay Thai and MMA professional venues, also can visit the country to train with some of the greatest teachers and fighters in combat sports. The relationship, then, between visitors and camps, seems to be mutually beneficial and perhaps a way to preserve the art of Muay Thai in a highly capitalistic, homogenized, and globalized twenty-first century.

When ONE Championships held its first event in Bangkok in 2016, it spared no effort or expense to entice an audience who might otherwise have been indifferent to MMA. For most Thai people, fighters train in Muay Thai; MMA still is a foreign conceit. ONE's inaugural show included two of Thailand's most popular bands; and the famous Muay Thai champion Dejdamrong Sor Amnuaysirichoke, known as "Kru Rong," headlined the event. Although the Thai Sports Authority declared the sport of MMA a threat to Thai culture, MMA has not dampened the passion for traditional Muay Thai, both in Thailand and abroad. Instead, MMA seems to have introduced many people around the world to Muay Thai. MMA fighters flock to Thailand to train and pay homage to the ancient and brutal art of Muay Thai. Muay Thai has become so intrinsic to the sport of MMA that it is difficult to think of a UFC fighter who has not trained in it in some capacity.

While the fight continues between Cambodia, Burma, and Thailand as to who originated Southeast Asia's kickboxing style, Muay Thai certainly has become the most widely known of the three. In the early twentieth century, rules were instituted to specify round times, allowable techniques, and to require the use of gloves. Before gloves were instituted, Muay Thai fighters used sections of cloth to wrap their hands, a tradition that continued in Burmese boxing. In 1929, Muay Thai rules required the use of gloves. Lethwei continued to be a bare-knuckle sport, and it included head butts as an attack, making it the art of nine weapons as opposed to Muay Thai's eight. On the border of Burma and Thailand, fights take place in highly charged events that pit country against country, style against style.

Burmese boxing has become increasingly popular, especially as one of the most famous Lethwei fighters, David LeDuc, a Canadian, brought the sport to wider media focus. LeDuc does not shy away from claiming that Lethwei is superior to Muay Thai, although one of his more interesting arguments is that Lethwei can improve Myanmar's economy, much as Muay Thai did for Thailand. Although MMA does not allow head butts, the fingerless gloves worn in the cage have more in common with the simple tape and gauze that Burmese boxers use than the larger gloves worn in boxing, kickboxing, and Muay Thai.

Cambodia's fighting arts, again conflated with Thailand and Burma's histories, have made a fascinating transition in the twenty-first century with the creation of a new, yet historically based fighting art known as bokator. Bokator is a modern amalgam of traditional Cambodian fighting arts that combines indigenous wrestling and the striking art of Kun Khmer, also known as Pradal Serey.

When the Khmer Rouge controlled Cambodia in the 1970s, many people escaped to evade imprisonment, torture, and execution. Among those was San Kim Sean, who sought refuge in the United States but returned to Cambodia in 2004, intent on resurrecting traditional Cambodian martial arts to practice. He sought out other Cambodian martial arts teachers and formed the first federation designed to promote a new fighting art. This new art would be interdisciplinary and include many of the ancient features of Cambodian fighting arts, including traditional costume. For San Kim Sean, bokator was a way for modern Cambodians to reconnect to their ancient roots after decades of atrocities and attempted cultural erasures.

Like many martial artists seeking to preserve their country's tradition in the face of mass globalization and homogenization, San's organization of bokator sometimes leans heavily on anecdotes to prove its legitimacy. San might be better served to allow the beauty and brutality of the sport to speak for itself. Cambodia's bokator often is called into question, particularly by pedantic internet "experts" who look to disprove every martial art but their own. Bokator may not have a perfect through line from ancient to modern times, but this new art form is a fantastic sport that martial arts enthusiasts can, or at least should, appreciate. Bokator is an amalgam of Cambodian kickboxing and wrestling in a thoroughly modern context, making it simultaneously both new and old.

Most modern fighting arts that are based on ancient traditions have undergone these types of systemic shifts, for many reasons. Frequently, the political history of the area meant that various conquerors and leaders prohibited indigenous fighting arts and forced them underground. In addition, imperialization typically required cultural assimilation, so many ancient civilizations were stripped of their cultural practices and forced, instead, to take on the traditions of their overlords. In 2006, Cambodia launched its first international bokator tournament, which now includes hundreds of participants from around the country. As the sport continues to grow, bokator could prove an excellent analogue to MMA and provide Cambodia with the type of sports tourism industry that Thailand enjoys and to which Myanmar and Cambodia may aspire.

Although not located in Asia, nearby neighbors Australia and New Zealand have worked more with Asian fight promotions than with American ones. Australia banned the cage for mixed martial arts events for several years, holding fights in a ring instead of the octagon. Government officials and some members of the public felt that the cage projected an image of violence that could be reinterpreted in the streets. However, fighters and fight officials argued that the cage made it safer for fighters, and the UFC refused to hold events that would not use its trademark octagon. Once the rules changed and cages were permitted, the UFC started holding events in Australia in 2010.

Australia's closest neighbor, the tiny island of New Zealand, regularly provides some of the most exciting fighters in the world to both ONE and the UFC, as well as other area MMA events. Mark "The Super Samoan" Hunt fought in Pride, the UFC, and K-1 as a heavyweight, typically walking out while performing the traditional haka of the Maori. Hunt retired in 2018, but an up-and-coming group of champions represents New Zealand in the cage. Israel Adesanya, Alexander Volkanovski, Dan Hooker, and Kai Kara-France all train in Auckland, New Zealand, and compete in the UFC.

## Central, Southern, and Western Asia

Martial arts may have originated in the Fertile Crescent, like humanity itself, but war and turmoil have disrupted the rise of MMA in that area and in its near neighbors. Some fighters who were born in parts of Central and Western Asia, which includes Iraq, Saudi Arabia, the United Arab Emirates, Iran, India, Afghanistan, and Pakistan, train and compete in their home countries, while others immigrated to other parts of the world in order to find fight opportunities. Alan Omer was born in Iraq but immigrated to Germany, where he trained with Stallion Cage, an MMA facility in Stuttgart. Omar eventually fought in the UFC, becoming the first Iraqi to join the world's largest fight venue. Iraq also has its own MMA venue, the Iraqi Combat Fighting Championships, which has held six events since 2011. But most fighters in Central and Western Asia, as well as Africa, Eastern and Southeast Asia, Oceania, and Central Europe look to other promotions to compete at a professional level.

Several large MMA promotions evolved to include fighters in closer proximity to each other than the UFC. Phoenix Fighting Championships is a dual MMA and Muay Thai promotion that has hosted events in Beirut, London, Dubai, Phuket and Bangkok in Thailand, and Abu

Dhabi. Khalid bin Hamad Al Khalifa Mixed Martial Arts (KHKMMA) was founded in 2015 and supported by His Highness Khalid bin Hamad Al Khalifa in Bahrain. The organization was designed to bring MMA to the Middle East and to break up the monopoly that the UFC and the United States have over the sport worldwide. In 2016, KHKMMA established Brave Combat Federation (Brave CF), which holds professional events in Africa, Asia, Europe, South America, and the Middle East. Brave CF hosted twelve MMA shows in as many different countries in both 2018 and 2019, an incredible feat for a new venue. Although its stars are not as famous in the United States as those in the UFC, Brave CF has the potential to be an international powerhouse in the MMA world due to its royal backing, its roster of fighters with fan bases beyond the United States, and its access to extraordinary amounts of wealth.

In the summer of 2020, KHK looked to increase its presence in the professional boxing world and hired boxing broker Daniel Kinahan to help facilitate matches. Kinahan apparently assisted in negotiating a two-fight deal between boxing superstars Tyson Fury and Anthony Joshua for 2021. After Kinahan's name appeared in the press as a "boxing promoter," the Irish government reached out to KHK and the UAE to reveal Kinahan's insalubrious past as a crime boss. Although Kinahan was not prosecuted for any crimes, he had long been a nefarious figure under investigation by the Irish Gardai and specifically was named in an Irish court document in 2018 as head of a gang that trafficked guns and drugs and was responsible for dozens of deaths. KHK immediately ended its relationship with Kinahan, and the future of a Tyson Fury and Anthony Joshua superfight again was in limbo. These kinds of international fights, especially those that require extensive brokerage, often run into problems due to the many laws, regulations, and restrictions that govern trade relations. However, the passion of fighters, fans, and supporters with very deep pockets indicates that the sport of MMA will continue to grow in Central and Western Asia.

As MMA develops as a professional sport, wrestling has maintained a stronghold in Central, Southern, and Western Asia, especially for countries such as India, Turkey, Turkmenistan, Uzbekistan, and Iran. Iran's wrestling program excelled in the twenty-first century, demonstrating that their prowess at the sport dates to their ancient roots. The Iranian government began investing resources into rebuilding the country's wrestling program in the 1920s and eventually introduced the rules of Olympic freestyle wrestling. Once Iran began to compete in international venues, the country vaulted to the top tier of world champions. Iran is well situated to produce incredible MMA fighters because the country excels in wrestling and tae kwon do competition. However, most Iranian wrestlers stick to their own sport, and considering their ascendancy over nearly the rest of the world, it is understandable. Although wrestling can translate well into an MMA career, it can be difficult to return from MMA to the rules, structure, and energy of wrestling.

Iranian fighters who have competed successfully in the UFC, the largest world stage for MMA, include Gegard Mousasi, who was born in Tehran to Armenian parents and moved to the Netherlands at age four; and Beneil Dariush, who moved from Iran to the United States when he was nine years old. Neither man currently resides in Iran, which makes their participation in international competition run much smoother than their counterparts still living in the country. In 2019, Iranian heavyweight fighter Amir Aliakbari was forced out of his contract with the UFC when U.S. sanctions prohibited the transfer of his earnings. After six months of troubleshooting with the UFC, Aliakbari could find no means of routing the law, so he went back to competing in other venues. At this writing, it seems that fighters residing in places that the United States or other international powers deem problematic only will be able to compete in the UFC if they abandon their home countries. But for many of these athletes, remaining in place, with their families and histories, far outweighs the money, power, and fame that perhaps could be afforded to them if they left for the United States or Europe.

As MMA and other fight sports continued to grow in the Arab world, the UFC looked to solidify its relationship with the United Arab Emirates by hosting a series of events in the capital city, Abu Dhabi. The country has long had a passion for martial arts, hosting one of the biggest Brazilian jujitsu invitational events every year. In July 2020, the UFC launched a series of fights in an effort to create a safe, semi-isolated environment for fighters during the coronavirus pandemic. UFC's "Fight Island" included a number of its most famous stars, all of whom participated in advocating for Abu Dhabi as an ideal vacation spot.

The vast majority of Central and Western Asian people practice Islam as their primary religion. Islam in these countries dictates nearly every facet of life, which requires interesting accommodations for both training and competition. During Ramadan, a holy month in which Muslims focus on prayer and reflection, fasting from dawn until dusk, the entire community shifts its normal practices. For fighters, Ramadan means training while fasting, or training in the middle of the night in order to eat before and after practice. In countless interviews with Muslim athletes around the world, Ramadan presents difficulties, but athletes seem to revel in them, using Ramadan as an opportunity to further challenge themselves while celebrating their religion.

Women have been competing in martial arts more in the twenty-first century, despite some extremist groups' threats of violence or social ostracization in places such as Iran, Pakistan, and Afghanistan. Through repressive religious or political practices, historically women have been constrained culturally, socially, religiously, and spatially through systematic marginalization, but a growing shift in the culture means that many girls and women are empowered through practicing and participating in sports.

As more families are invested in letting their girls play sports, and adult women are pursuing their education and careers before marriage, female participation in sports is rising. However, female athletes remain a contentious subject, especially when the sport completely defies the established cultural and religious codes. Yet boxing, judo, tae kwon do, kickboxing, BJJ, wrestling, and MMA are becoming more popular, even in traditionally conservative cultures. Although men have few boundaries to prohibit them from training in martial arts, it is far different for potential female fighters. Most Muslim women must be accompanied by a male family member, so many women training in martial arts do so with their fathers, brothers, or husbands.

In Pakistan, the first woman to become a professional MMA fighter, Anita Karim, trains with her brother, Ali Sultan, fighter and coach at The Fight Fortress in Islamabad. Anita is the first woman in Pakistan to train in MMA at a level that would allow her to fight—and she was the only one, which made it difficult for her to find an opponent. In order for her to find a fight, she signed with ONE Championships Warrior Series, going straight to professional because she had no opportunities to fight as an amateur. And this is a problem that women in certain isolated or highly conservative places have to contend with: how can they begin their career as a fighter if they have no one to fight? In the end, Anita found a solution, even if she had to contend with threats of violence from some religious extremists. Her coaches and teammates, however, have stood by her side, helping to sustain an environment where it is safe for women to train in MMA. Anita Karim, just a few years younger than activist Malala Yousafzai, who was shot in 2012 for speaking out against the Taliban in Pakistan, has found her own way to fight oppression and pursue her dream.

MMA continues to evolve in Central, Southern, and Western Asia, taking into its practice, training, exhibition, and competition all of the nuances and richness of the traditional culture and communities. Many of these fighters have to leave the region in order to compete at a professional level, but they take with them their religions—Islam, Hinduism, Judaism, and Christianity, among others—to give them strength in the cage. Fighters with strong religious backgrounds are not necessarily better morally, of course, but devout religiosity does impact the fighters as well as the venues that exhibit in those places.

The UFC's relationship with Abu Dhabi developed a potentially lucrative market that other entertainment venues are eager to explore. Other Gulf countries are looking to expand their international sports empire, including Saudi Arabia, which partnered with the WWE in 2014 to host events that might contribute to opening up the country and creating an environment that might entice foreign travelers. Those travelers, however, will have to adapt to the social mores of the place, which are evolving but nevertheless remain deeply rooted in a long history and tradition of art, beauty, and religious practices.

## AFRICA

The twenty-first century brought tremendous change throughout the world, and the many regions, cultures, and communities of the African continent were no exception. With the end of apartheid in South Africa in the 1990s, and an expansion in technology and communications, African culture became increasingly commodified even as Western corporations encroached further into the continent. Africa is seen as a largely untapped and potentially lucrative market by many corporations, including the largest MMA venue on the planet. But even as the UFC made plans to expand into northern and sub-Saharan Africa, the many indigenous martial arts flourished as their own media moguls began featuring African fighting sports in large-scale events and broadcast media. The UFC may have potential to generate enormous revenues from streaming and broadcasting in Africa, but it will have competition from that continent's own fighting sports and traditions.

The African Boxing Union, the official sanctioning body of the continent, formed in 1974. While many people around Africa took to training and competing in boxing, indigenous fighting sports also saw a resurgence in the twenty-first century. As we discussed in chapter 2, Africa generated a wide variety of fighting arts, highly dependent on region and topography. The striking art of dambe draws huge crowds in Nigeria, and even larger viewer demographics through broadcast and streaming platforms. Young men across Nigeria and in other parts of Africa grew up training in the art, which has been passed down from generation to generation for thousands of years. Those who did not learn from their fathers, uncles, and grandfathers can now learn the ancient art from coaches and training facilities that produce some of the toughest fighters in the world. Dambe fighters, with their right hands heavily roped and taped, strike each other primarily with overhand punches and have mastered the art of moving their heads while they punch. To the untrained eye, dambe seems slipshod because the fighters punch wildly and duck their heads while striking. But this technique of simultaneous striking and evading is far more sophisticated and elegant to a true master of martial arts. By loading the rear hand, stepping off-line with the lead foot, and turning the rear shoulder, the fighter's head ducks far out of range, even while his punch comes down with tremendous force.

In 2019, Maxwell Kalu, a public relations executive born in England to Nigerian parents, began African Warriors Fighting Championships, a fascinating venue that features indigenous African fighting arts. Rather than try to import MMA, AWFC instead promotes dambe and mgba, a form of Nigerian wrestling, also known as kokowa, which we discussed in chapter 2. Even as MMA becomes known all over the world, many traditional fighting sports have thrived, rather than suffered, from the homogenizing power of mixed martial arts. Many young men who compete in AWFC might matriculate into the UFC's rosters, but for most of them, the pleasure of competing in sports such as dambe and mgba has such tremendous cultural significance that they eschew the larger venues. Even so, UFC fighters such as Kamaru Usman and Israel Adesanya, both Nigerian-born fighters, provide a source of pride to the country, and their personal investment in their heritage has made both men advocates for traditional Nigerian fighting sports.

In Senegal, the wrestling art of laamb is the most popular sport; tens of thousands of fans fill stadiums, and athletes' faces cover newspapers, magazines, billboards, and television media. Laamb is deeply rooted in Senegal's history, passed down through generations from ancient ancestors who wrestled for pride, glory, and, of course, self-protection. The name, laamb, derives from the indigenous language of Senegal before colonialism forced adoption of French. The traditional Senegalese wrestling has two forms: *lutte traditionnelle sans frappe* (traditional wrestling without punches) and *avec frappe*, a newer form established in the 1920s that includes bare-knuckle punches. Prior to the French invasion and subsequent colonization, laamb was a communal and celebratory activity, featured in marriage and coming-of-age ceremonies as well as harvest celebrations. But in the nineteenth century the French found Senegalese wrestling entertaining and began to create events with small monetary prizes for winners, effectively turning laamb from art to commercial sport. In 1924, Maurice Jacquin, French filmmaker and entrepreneur, opened a movie theater in Dakar, where he began to train locals in boxing, Jacquin's other passion. As Jacquin became more deeply entrenched in Senegalese culture, he ingeniously thought of combining boxing and native wrestling to create the wrestling avec frappe. In the 1970s, an official governing body was created to organize the sport, clearly demarcating the two different types of wrestling for competition.

The history of tribal warfare and the version of Islam practiced in the country are deeply entwined with Senegal's indigenous religion and mysticism. Athletes anoint themselves with oil, pray to Allah, and wear small scrolls containing excerpts from the Quran in small bags around their necks. This combination of traditional mysticism and Islamic influences makes Sengalese wrestling a spiritual and physical endeavor. Even as fighters outfit themselves in traditional loincloths in competitions, they frequently are sponsored by media corporations and other big businesses, a sign that Senegal's sports have become capitalist ven-

tures as in every other part of the world. The wrestlers are exceedingly
well-trained, muscular, lean, and strong, putting as much energy into
their cross-training as they do into the technical drills of wrestling. The
size, skill, athleticism, and dedication to wrestling have situated Senegal's wrestlers to excel in MMA, perhaps better than many other indigenous fighting arts in the twenty-first century.

Although laamb remains Senegal's most popular fight sport, MMA is
making inroads, especially as the stars of wrestling transition to the
cage. ARES Fighting Championship, an MMA venue based in Dakar,
features fighters from around Africa and Europe. Senegalese wrestling
champion Oumar Kane, known as Reug Reug, competed in his first
MMA fight in December 2019, going straight to professional competition against French fighter Sofiane Boukichou, who already had ten
professional fights under his belt when they met in the cage. Oumar
may have been the less experienced fighter in the cage, but he demonstrated superb wrestling technique and finished off the Frenchman in
the second round with punches. Other African wrestlers from a variety
of indigenous traditions, as well as the Olympic Games, have begun to
populate the ARES fight roster, and in 2020 Cameroonian-French professional boxer Hassan N'Dam N'Jikam signed with the venue.

The UFC is the largest MMA venue in the world, with a tremendous
fan base and viewership worldwide, yet its roster of fighters is largely
Western. On the African continent, Extreme Fighting Championship,
or EFC, is the largest purveyor of African MMA fighting. Founded in
2009, the EFC features fighters from around the world, including Africa, Europe, Asia, and the United States. As of 2020, the UFC has yet to
host an event on the African continent, and for many African MMA
fans, watching UFC events remains difficult due to exhibition limits.
The EFC, meanwhile, hosts approximately ten professional events every year and features a roster of talent that often feeds into the UFC. In
2019, Dana White mentioned that the UFC is likely to hold an event
somewhere in Africa in the future, and considering that several of its
champions at the time hailed from parts of Africa, the move seems
highly warranted and necessary for its continued success.

In 2019, the UFC partnered with SuperSport, Africa's largest sports
broadcasting network, which serves more than fifty countries in sub-
Saharan Africa. Yet even as the UFC expands its commercial relationships, additional MMA venues have launched in Africa and around the

world, not necessarily as a counter to the UFC, but rather to showcase talent outside the UFC's typical reach. The UFC has signed fighters from Africa, although they are such rarities as to make headlines when it does. EFC, ARES, ONE, and other fight venues provide a more diverse and realistic representation of fighters and fans. ARES held its inaugural event in December 2019 in Senegal, but due to the global Covid-19 pandemic, the 2020 shows scheduled for Belgium and Africa were put on hold. Extreme Fighting Championships (EFC) has held more than eighty events at the time of this writing and broadcasts to millions around Africa.

Nearly every country or region has its own indigenous fighting arts, but laamb and dambe are excellent examples of how traditional fighting arts can maintain their autonomy and thrive in the modern world. The UFC and other MMA venues are making headway in the African continent, accumulating talented fighters and enthusiastic fans, but the traditional fighting sports have been able to harness the sports media industry to thrive in the digital age.

## LATIN AMERICA AND THE CARIBBEAN

The UFC sought to increase its reach into Central and South America by hosting *The Ultimate Fighter* series in 2014, hoping to encourage young Latin-American athletes to cross-train in boxing, kickboxing, and wrestling so that they would be prepared for the rigors of interdisciplinary fighting. The UFC lagged, however, in truly expanding its efforts in Central and South America, but the continent's own Combate Americas took ascendancy in the UFC's place, scouting countries such as Chile, Argentina, Peru, Uruguay, and, of course, Brazil, for the next top talent. One of the UFC's early cofounders, Campbell McLaren, an entrepreneur and marketing expert, was part of the cohort to sell the UFC to the Fertitta brothers in 2001 for $2 million.

In 2014, McLaren returned to his television promotion and MMA roots to help create Combate Americas, first as a reality show competition for a contract to fight for the brand-new MMA venue of the same name. Combate Americas (CAMMA) specifically sought to capture the Hispanic market and to generate new fans who might not otherwise watch UFC events. Expanding into the Latin American MMA market was not just about generating more distribution rights or pay-per-view purchases; it also meant cultivating a lively interest in the sport—a somewhat grassroots effort to create an audience. McLaren's gamble was successful; since then, Combate Americas has provided a platform for MMA fighters across Latin America to advance their careers. Offering pay comparable to the UFC, CAMMA CEO McLaren asserted that his promotion is not a launching ground to the UFC, but instead, is a secure, profitable venue where fighters could start and end their careers, as big a star in the Spanish-speaking world as any UFC fighter.

As the venue grew, so did its reach, signing fighters from Puerto Rico, Mexico, and the United States and broadcasting its shows throughout South, Central, and North America. In 2017, CAMMA hosted an eight-man tournament, mirroring the UFC 1, in Cancun, Mexico, that included a live broadcast in English on NBC Sports as well as in Spanish on Telemundo Desportes. This English-language broadcast in North America marked a seminal event for Combate Americas, which was formed, according to McLaren, not so much for Hispanic fighters, but for Spanish-speaking MMA fans. McLaren stipulates that in the vast collection of twenty-one countries throughout Latin America, fans were much more likely to become invested in a sport covered in their own language, an elegant and obvious conceit. McLaren also stated that CAMMA's fighters have their own styles, more aligned with Mexican boxing than the UFC. Dynamic, fast-paced, aggressive, and driven to end fights with TKOs or submissions, CAMMA fighters seem to disdain even the idea of winning on points.

In 2016, Combate Americas signed a deal with the UFC to allow its shows to stream on UFC's Fight Pass, but that ended just one year later. Instead, CAMMA joined Bellator and other MMA venues in granting North American distribution rights to the streaming service DAZN. That relationship ended when, in 2019, Combate Americas signed a new deal with AXS TV that would include ESPN commentator Max Bretos and UFC fighter Julianna Peña to provide the English-speaking commentary. The inaugural pay-per-view Combate Americas event featured UFC veteran Tito Ortiz defeating WWE fighter Alberto Del Rio, a somewhat bizarre matchup. Although the fight card was not necessarily a stellar representation of CAMMA's talent, the event's success created a foundation for the venue to continue its rise in the English-speaking market.

Fighters from Brazil represent some of the best talent in the world, including Anderson Silva, Lyoto Machida, Cris "Cyborg" Justino, José Aldo, Amanda Nunes, Vitor Belfort, Jéssica Andrade, and many other phenomenal athletes. Although there have been difficulties in establishing MMA venues in the country, Brazilian fighters compete in CAMMA, along with Bellator and, of course, the UFC, which regularly holds events in the country. As the fan base in Central and South America expands, fighters across the continent have more opportunities to fight in front of an audience without the need for translation.

## EUROPE

The official sport of MMA affronted many European countries that saw the cage and the action within to be unnecessarily violent. Most countries, however, allowed official amateur and professional MMA bouts, especially with the possibility that large, highly lucrative venues such as the UFC might choose to hold international events in their respective lands. Europe has provided the UFC with some of its greatest fighters, including Andrei Arlovski of Belarus, Poland's Joanna Jędrzejczyk, Alexander Gustafsson of Sweden, the United Kingdom's Alistair Overeem, and Valentina Shevchenko of Kyrgyzstan. Three of the most famous names in UFC's history are all Europeans as well: Michael Bisping, Conor McGregor, and Khabib Nurmagomedov. Bisping, who won *The Ultimate Fighter* Season 3, is the only fighter from England to hold a UFC belt.

The UFC held its first event in England in 2002, but it was poorly attended and had a low pay-per-view buy rate. Despite an exhibition agreement with Sky Sports, the UFC did not return to England until 2007. Since then, however, MMA fandom has skyrocketed, rivaling professional boxing fandom, an incredible feat for a country that long celebrated pugilism as an English art.

Fighting arts are popular throughout the United Kingdom, especially boxing and wrestling. Both sports have long histories in the United Kingdom, and the programming for children, teenagers, and adults has ensured that martial arts are not just enjoyed on television, but lived in everyday activity. MMA, BJJ, and Muay Thai gyms have sprung up throughout the United Kingdom alongside wrestling and boxing programs, creating a pipeline from amateur practitioners of martial arts to fans of MMA. The growing number of top-ranked European fighters in major MMA venues indicates that European athletes can compete on a level with American fighters, who have been the primary nationality represented in the UFC. Of course, it makes sense that an American company primarily would sign fighters in closest proximity, especially in the beginning. The UFC largely has expanded its roster, continuing to bring in athletes from South America, Asia, Africa, and Europe, but a dedicated European venue can do far more to promote the sport in that area by featuring local fighters.

Bellator created a European-focused branch of its promotion in 2019, called Bellator Europe, in an effort to grow the sport's fan base and change the misconceptions of the sport. Bellator Europe's purpose was to hold events regularly around the United Kingdom and mainland Europe. Shows in Dublin, London, and Milan appealed to each country's nationalism, featuring Irish, British, and Italian fighters along with talent from other parts of Europe and the world. In 2020, Bellator finalized a distribution deal with Sky Sports in the United Kingdom, making it easier for fight fans to stream live action happening in closer proximity than the overseas UFC shows. In an effort to generate even more interest in the sport, Bellator Europe signed retired professional rugby player James Haskell to its heavyweight division, which might assist in bringing in a new fan base of rugby enthusiasts. Haskell's May 2020 debut was postponed due to the coronavirus pandemic, and time will reveal whether his transition from rugby to MMA might inspire other European athletes.

Although the forced halt of sporting events during the coronavirus pandemic stopped Bellator's projected growth, the goal is for Bellator Europe to be a successful, stand-alone entity to serve the fighters and fans in Europe. If it succeeds, Bellator could become the dominant MMA promotion in Europe with regular content, a localized roster of talent, and a regional fan base that does not have to wait for one or two shows a year from the UFC. Bellator also committed to signing more local athletes, diversifying its roster of fighters in Europe, Asia, Africa, Oceania, and the United States.

France has a long history of fighting arts, but MMA was banned as an official sport in 2016. The decree officially banned ground striking, as well as the use of a cage, limiting all fighting sports to a ring with three or four ropes. As we mentioned in the previous chapter, France hosted many early mixed-match fights, with savate fighters competing against other disciplines, but for some French martial artists, MMA seemed a tremendous threat to their own existence. In 2015, the French Judo Federation (la Fédération française de judo) announced that any judo instructor found teaching MMA would officially be expelled from the organization. The decision seemed to be based on the fear of the growing power of MMA, which might, in hindsight, have done more to promote the art of judo than to destroy it. But the power of the FJF, combined with other bureaucratic efforts to eliminate what was seen as a violent American import, caused the sport officially to be outlawed.

MMA enthusiasts around France revolted at the ban, which they believed to be disrespectful. Some venues offered a change in nomenclature, calling their fighting sport "Pancrase" in reference to the ancient Greek sport of pankration. Pancrase permits strikes while standing and only submissions on the ground, but the proffered middle ground did not suffice for many French MMA fighters, who were forced to look outside their home country for competition. Cheick Guillaume Ouedraogo, known as Cheick Kongo, is a French heavyweight MMA fighter who has competed in both Bellator and the UFC. Francis Ngannou, born in Cameroon, immigrated to France as a young man to pursue professional boxing and eventually joined the UFC's heavyweight division. Both men trained in France and in the United States but competed internationally due to France's MMA ban.

Although France officially may have banned the sport of MMA from exhibition, people all over France actively have been training in MMA and competing in the many other fighting sports that are legal, including boxing, kickboxing, savate, Muay Thai, judo, karate, and wrestling. In September 2019, the sports minister announced that the French Boxing Federation would oversee development of professional MMA as an official sport, and the UFC eagerly awaited the finalization in order to book its first Parisian show. That event should have taken place in 2020, but Covid-19 stymied the UFC.

Germany also has had a tumultuous relationship with MMA. The UFC held a show in Cologne in 2009, but by the next year, German officials prohibited airing mixed martial arts on televised events, effectively curtailing the relationship with the UFC and other MMA venues.

The UFC filed a lawsuit against the Bavarian State Media Authority, and in 2015 the courts overturned the ban, and MMA again could be broadcast on German television.

Norway banned any sport that could be won via a knockout, which essentially made true MMA competition impossible. Norwegian fighters traveled to compete in boxing, Muay Thai, kickboxing, and MMA, although the Norwegian king did sanction a local competition called "Merkekamper." Merkekamper, similar to an unsanctioned "smoker" in the United States, allows gyms to host their own internal events in which MMA fights can take place, although there are restrictions as to how hard one can hit an opponent. In 2016, the ban on knockouts was lifted for professional boxing, and in 2019, the Norwegian Sports Federation agreed to allow the Norwegian Combat Federation to oversee MMA and Muay Thai, which in essence, allows the country to enter the International MMA Federation (IMMAF) and host its own amateur and professional MMA events.

Michael Bisping did a great deal to generate interest in the UFC, but it was Ireland's Conor "Notorious" McGregor who truly brought Ireland, the United Kingdom, and many other European fan bases to the sport of MMA. Ireland's long fighting history continues in the twenty-first century, with Katie Taylor as the two-weight world champion in boxing, but even as the country celebrates its famous boxing daughter, Ireland has a turbulent relationship with MMA. As of 2020, the sport has yet to be recognized by Sport Ireland, the country's official governing body, and without official state sanctioning, MMA regulates itself.

Conor McGregor's coach, John Kavanagh, has led the way in creating a path to legalize the sport in Ireland, citing as an example France's success. McGregor himself has brought both glory and infamy to the sport in Ireland between his victories in the octagon, his cult of personality, and the many instances of behavior that have polarized the MMA community in Ireland and the rest of the world. McGregor is a phenomenal success story, as a man who rose from plumber's apprentice to becoming one of the wealthiest athletes in the world. McGregor fought in several UK venues, including Cage Warriors, where he began to craft his image and develop a reputation as an unorthodox but effective and exciting fighter. In 2013, he signed with the UFC, delighting hardcore MMA fans who had watched his performances in Europe. He racked up accolades, earning Knockout of the Night and Performance of the

Night at multiple events before he defeated Chad Mendes to secure the Interim UFC featherweight title in 2015.

McGregor next fought Nate Diaz in one of the most publicized fights in UFC history. Diaz, along with his brother Nick, is another example of the UFC superstar who created a brand around his brash, unapologetic personality. The Diaz brothers do not adhere to many of the policies that the tightly controlled marketing machine of the UFC set in place, but instead abandon press conferences, smoke marijuana at public UFC press events, and flout any efforts to corporatize their image.

Nate Diaz defeated McGregor after months of some of the greatest smack talk in UFC history, ending McGregor's run of victories. When the men met again just a few months later, McGregor won by decision. Just a few months after defeating Diaz, McGregor fought Eddie Alvarez for the lightweight championship, which he won in the second round, becoming the first UFC fighter to hold simultaneous titles in two divisions (a feat that Daniel Cormier, Amanda Nunes, and Henry Cejudo later accomplished as well, becoming "Champ-Champs"). After this win, McGregor took a few years off from MMA, wanting to attend to his girlfriend, Dee Devlin, for the birth of his first son.

In 2017, sports media outlets around the world exploded with the news that UFC lightweight champion Conor McGregor would abandon the octagon to meet five-time world boxing champion Floyd Mayweather Jr. in an exhibition boxing match. The media fervor for this fight was unprecedented, as were the prospective purses both men negotiated pre-fight. In the days leading up to the fight, every news media outlet in the world was talking about it, and people everywhere who never cared a bit for fighting previously suddenly were experts on the nuances of boxing. McGregor and Mayweather, both champion self-aggrandizers in addition to being champions in their respective realms, outdid themselves in generating press.

Some media pundits described the fight and its leadup as a spectacle, others as a circus. Many fight enthusiasts believed it was a farce, an insult to the fighting world. The fact that Conor essentially would vacate his title to fight a match he could not win was an insult to the sport of MMA. By the time McGregor did lose to Mayweather after ten rounds, fans of MMA and boxing were jaded, irritated most, it seemed, by the trash-talking and concerned for the future of both sports, an echo of the public's reaction to the 1976 Ali–Inoki fight. McGregor, however, looked to regain his lightweight championship belt from one of the most determined men in UFC history: Khabib Nurmagomedov.

Russia's MMA fan base expanded significantly when Nurmagomedov became the first champion representing that country, although the fighter is ethnically and culturally a member of the Dagestani community. A devout Muslim, Khabib has been vocal in supporting his fellow Russian fighters and in encouraging the UFC to promote them as well as himself. Before joining the UFC, Khabib had three of his professional fights in Russia's largest internal MMA venue, M-1 Global, which holds events all over the world but is based in St. Petersburg, Russia. In 2018, the UFC announced that it would partner with M-1 for its return to Moscow, a surprising move given the UFC's history of working against rival venues. But in this case, the UFC invested in promoting its brand in Russia, signing a deal to install its subsidiary UFC gyms across the country and allow M-1 fighters to compete in both venues.

That same year, the UFC secured a title fight that would become one of the most discussed events in the venue's history. Conor McGregor proved himself a master self-aggrandizer, but when he faced off against Khabib Nurmagomedov at UFC 229 on October 6, 2018, the fight ended not only in his defeat, but with the infamous cage-side brawl that disgusted and infuriated many fans. McGregor had used the time prior to the fight to generate massive press, constantly insulting Khabib in the media and frequently devolving past bravado and into ethnically charged insults. Perhaps it was the language barrier, but Khabib did not see McGregor's tactics as mere bombast; it went much deeper than mere pre-fight banter. McGregor insulted Khabib's father, his country, and his religion, all sacred to a very serious fighter and man such as Khabib. In addition, McGregor already had proven himself to be volatile when he threw a hand trolley through the window of a bus carrying Khabib, along with other UFC fighters, after the media day for UFC 223 on April 5, 2018, which resulted in a significant eye injury for fighter Ray Borg.

The drama between McGregor and Khabib seems too convoluted to detail here, but the bus incident, the deeply antagonistic pre-fight press, the fight itself, and the post-fight brawl all resulted from a deep disconnect between two very different worldviews. Conor McGregor's brand always has been built on bombast and excess, and his media antics increase his visibility and, thus, his cultural cachet. Whether his statements reflect his true beliefs or are simply part of the performance of being Conor "Notorious" McGregor is not clear. Khabib, meanwhile, is a deeply introspective fighter whose priorities are his training, his family, and his religion. He uses media as his managers, agents, and the UFC promoters instruct, but it is obvious that he does not really care about "creating a brand." Khabib believes in respect, which has not always translated well.

The UFC norm of having fighters touch their foreheads together aggressively after weighing in either was not communicated to Khabib, or he simply saw any sign of aggression from an opponent outside the cage as disrespectful. Either way, when Abel Trujillo pushed his forehead against Khabib's before their 2013 fight, Khabib shoved Trujillo hard, generating cheers from the crowd and a swift response from Dana White. Khabib, at the time, was an undercard fighter, but he was rising quickly to the top of the UFC's contenders as one of the most aggressive and relentless in the cage. Khabib's signature papakha headdress, signifying a warrior in Dagestan, his faith in Islam, even the footage of him wrestling a bear cub as a child, make Nurmagomedov a unique UFC champion.

Tensions between McGregor and Nurmagomedov were exacerbated by the press, the fans, and even the UFC. Instead of attempting to control McGregor, especially in the aftermath of the bus incident, the UFC allowed him to continue to antagonize Khabib in a way that was highly offensive to the Dagestani fighter as well as numerous fans who found Conor's insults ethnically and religiously charged. It is not surprising that Khabib and his team retaliated, and for the UFC's representatives to act aghast seems gauche and insincere. Both men were chastised for their involvement in the post-fight brawl, and Conor even seemed a bit abashed, for a little while.

The antagonism between the respective fans of Conor and Khabib fans also reveals how culturally disconnected certain world populations remain, despite the increase in social communications. Both men continue to swipe at each other using social media, for this is one feud that may have been fueled by the media but likely will continue as long as Conor or Khabib has the spotlight. For MMA always will be inextricably linked to the evolution of sports media and the long history of fighters who excel in self-aggrandizement.

# CONCLUSION

## The Future of Fighting Sports

In 2020, the novel coronavirus pandemic shut down nearly all professional sports competitions. Quarantines, travel restrictions, physical distancing, and the threat of illness severely limited athletes from training, let alone competing.

Despite lockdowns and health concerns, the UFC continued to hold events throughout the spring and summer even as Covid restrictions forced changes in locations, opponents, and regulations. The UFC's Covid-era events required pre-fight coronavirus testing, eliminated audiences, and met with difficulty as contract athletes declined to participate or were prohibited by governmental travel restrictions. The state of Florida allowed the UFC to host shows in Jacksonville, but in June 2020 the UFC announced that it would hold multiple events in July in Abu Dhabi in the United Arab Emirates, which Dana White renamed "Fight Island." Sports fans around the world were desperate for live events, and "Fight Island," which included four shows over the course of the month and featured a total of four title fights, was an interesting solution. Although "Fight Island" allowed the UFC to circumnavigate the restrictions placed on its business by hosting events with no fans, the shows were not without obstacles.

In early July, as people around the world hunkered down in the midst of the coronavirus pandemic, UFC welterweight champion Kamaru Usman of Nigeria learned that his forthcoming title defense against challenger Gilbert Burns had been canceled. Just days before the men were to battle in Abu Dhabi, Burns tested positive for Covid-19, removing him from the card and leaving the main event in jeopardy. From across the world, and with less than a week until the fight, Jorge Masvidal leaped at the opportunity to compete for the title. Usually contenders prepare for months, slowly and safely cutting weight and planning for a specific opponent. But Masvidal did not have months. Instead, he flew from Las Vegas to Abu Dhabi and cut nearly twenty pounds within a few days. It was a tough weight loss, and everyone, from his coaches to Dana White, breathed easier when Masvidal hit the scale at 170 pounds, grinning broadly at the relieved, albeit small, crowd. Although Masvidal would lose by a unanimous decision, he earned the respect of MMA fans everywhere when he agreed to the last-minute fight without hesitation.

Usman, Masvidal, and the rest of the UFC fighters who competed on "Fight Island" in the midst of a world pandemic risked a great deal when they traveled to Abu Dhabi. Only a few months earlier, UFC strawweight champion Zhang Weili moved from Thailand to Abu Dhabi to Las Vegas as borders shut down and quarantines went into effect around the world. She finally was able to return home after nearly three months of travel, competition, quarantine, and isolation. Some media pundits criticize modern fighters as pampered athletes who would not have been able to cut it in the "glory days" of fight sports. But 2020's coronavirus pandemic revealed the strength and perseverance of modern fighters, who had their training camps curtailed, competed in isolation in front of silent stadiums, experienced separation from family and loved ones, and risked contracting a potentially deadly virus. Tragically, UFC lightweight champion Khabib Nurmagomedov lost his beloved father to complications from coronavirus. At this writing, it is unclear when Khabib will return to the octagon, or when the rest of the world will return to some semblance of normality.

Usman and Masvidal may have fought in 2020 CE, but their eagerness to fight each other during a world crisis, without the typical twenty-first-century luxuries of time and preparation, reflects the history of the many fighters who came before them. Over the past seven thousand years, people have sought ways to test themselves, constructing various crucibles in boxing, wrestling, kickboxing, and interdisciplinary fighting sports. From boxing in ancient Greece and Mesopotamia, to African and European wrestling, to the warriors of Asia and the contenders in South, Central, and North America, fighting remains an integral part of the human experience. Fighting sports evolved during times of war and wealth, and when humans were at peace or experiencing atrocities. In the twentieth century, calls to sanitize and organize sports reached the fighting world, resulting in continuity in rules and regulation across place. The combined forces of globalization and communications technologies have diminished the distances between disparate communities, making us more connected than ever before. However, globalization also has threatened to erode the many indigenous fighting arts that have fought to withstand the powerful tides of capitalism and cultural homogenization.

MMA is inextricably linked to sports media and the corporations that sponsor events, promote athletes, and market convergent products such as video games and clothing lines. The UFC, as the largest international mixed martial arts venue, has flourished as a company and helped legitimize the sport around the world.

As we discussed in chapter 5, after conquering the United States, the UFC set out to invest in other international markets, which required a multitiered approach. To generate ticket sales and viewership in the local and international markets, the fights need to include both internationally recognized names and local superstars. The venue also has to reckon with local officials and ordinances that might preclude some standard business or exhibition practices. The UFC worked to corner the MMA markets in Europe, China, Japan, New Zealand, Australia, and Abu Dhabi, but the UFC could target numerous other audiences that in the future would not only increase its fan base, but potentially generate some of the best fighters in the world.

Western, Central, and South Asia, northern and sub-Saharan Africa, South and Central America, Eastern Europe, and northern Asia are all areas that have provided the sport with fantastic athletes, yet the UFC has yet to develop a devoted fan base or invest in many training facilities. Part of cultivating a strong roster of future MMA superstars is investing in places outside the standard training grounds in the United States, Brazil, and Thailand. For many current international UFC fighters, the only way to prepare for the top echelon of competition is to travel to the United States to train with a world-renowned team.

However, as the sport grows, and as more professional athletes retire to establish their own gyms and fight teams, the options for training camps have increased significantly. Many fighters no longer feel obligated to leave their home countries to train, although some still choose to do so, perhaps to isolate themselves from distractions. But as preeminent fighters remain in their home countries and cities, forming camps and fostering new teammates, the sport of MMA will benefit from the diversity and uniqueness of training camps around the world.

The Covid-19 travel restrictions made it even more imperative for fighters to have elite-level training in their home countries, but not every place has the capacity to train professional MMA fighters. It behooves the UFC and other major MMA venues such as ONE Championships and Combate Americas to invest in places outside their standard media market to nurture a fertile training environment for athletes and generate new audiences. Representation matters, and providing fans around the world with a diverse roster of athletes will help audiences recognize their own culture in MMA. Growing the sport of MMA requires corporate endowments that foster equitable training grounds around the world, especially in impoverished communities. But it also needs MMA enthusiasts, fighters, and fans to recognize the contributions that diverse cultures have made to the sport throughout history.

The development of MMA is deeply entwined with the history of cultures around the world. Although the most celebrated moments in the history of MMA have focused on famous people and major events, the real growth of the sport has taken place not in the octagon, but in fighting communities, large and small, that trained and tested the martial arts of their ancestors. When we look at the history of fighting sports, even today, when access to numerous sources and instant information is at our very fingertips, knowledge gaps remain, eager to be filled by the scholar in every martial arts enthusiast.

Although this book has attempted to trace the development of MMA throughout history, fighting arts and traditions still warrant exploration and scholarship. No time is better suited to seeking out the older martial artists in our various communities and learning their stories. For MMA to continue to thrive in the twenty-first century, fighters everywhere must appreciate the rich traditions of individual, indigenous arts practiced around the world, and the stories of the many fighters who stepped outside their sport's boundaries to test themselves and represent their cultural heritage. MMA is not just an assemblage of various techniques; it is an amalgamation of the many martial arts traditions inherited from fighters thousands of years ago.

# NOTES

## I. ANCIENT FIGHTING SPORTS

1. Homer, *The Iliad* (New York: Oxford University Press, 2014), book 23.
2. Michael B. Poliakoff, *Combat Sports in the Ancient World: Competition, Violence, and Culture* (London, UK: Yale University Press, 1987), 27.
3. Hugh M. Lee, "The Later Greek Boxing Glove and the 'Roman' Caestus: A Centennial Reevaluation of Juthner's 'Ueber Antike Turngerathe,'" *Nikephoros*, 10 (1997): 161–78.
4. Nigel B. Crowther, *Sport in Ancient Times* (Westport, CT: Praeger, 2007), 121.

## 2. PUTTING THE 'MARTIAL' IN MARTIAL ARTS

1. William J. Baker, *Sports in the Western World* (Champaign: University of Illinois Press, 1988), 37.
2. Sydney Anglo, "The Man Who Taught Leonardo Darts: Pietro Monte and His "Lost" Fencing Book," *Antiquaries Journal*, 69 (1989): 261–78.
3. Sydney Anglo, *The Martial Arts of Renaissance Europe* (New Haven, CT: Yale University Press, 2000), 109.
4. Anglo, *Martial Arts*, 188.
5. Anglo, *Martial Arts*, 188.
6. Anglo, *Martial Arts*, 188.
7. Anglo, *Martial Arts*, 192.
8. Anglo, *Martial Arts*, 193.

9. Anglo, *Martial Arts*, 193.

10. John Clements, "Masters of Defense," in *Martial Arts of the World: An Encyclopedia of History and Innovation*, vol. 1, edited by Thomas A. Green and Joseph R. Svinth (Santa Barbara, CA: ABC-CLIO, 2010), 319.

11. Henry Barnard, "English Pedagogy: Education, the School, and the Teacher," in *English Literature*, vol. 2 (Buffalo, WY: Creative Media Partners, 2019), 409.

12. Stanley E. Henning, "Chinese Boxing," in *Martial Arts of the World: An Encyclopedia of History and Innovation*, vol. 1, edited by Thomas A. Green and Joseph R. Svinth (Santa Barbara, CA: ABC-CLIO, 2010), 27.

## 3. COLONIZING MARTIAL ARTS

1. *London Journal*, June 23, 1722.

2. Pierce Egan, *Boxiana: Volume 1* (London: Printed by and for G. Smeeton, 1830), 300.

3. *Daily Post*, November 12, 1699–June 16, 1730.

4. Egan, *Boxiana*, 403.

5. Egan, *Boxiana*, 405.

6. Egan, *Boxiana*, 361.

7. Egan, *Boxiana*, 361.

8. Egan, *Boxiana*, 264.

9. Egan, *Boxiana*, 474.

10. Egan, *Boxiana*, 474.

11. "Slave Voyages, "Transactlantic Slave Trade Estimates—Portugal/Brazil," SlaveVoyages.com, https://www.slavevoyages.org/assessment/estimates (accessed July 2, 2020).

12. Thomas Jefferson, *Letters and Addresses of Thomas Jefferson* (National Jefferson Society, 1903), 45.

13. *Cincinnati Enquirer*, September 15, 1874–July 17, 1910.

14. *National Police Gazette*, March 1, 1884–March 30, 1895.

15. Frederick Douglass, *The Life and Times of Frederick Douglass: From 1817–1882* (London: Christian Age Office, 1882), 119.

16. Thomas J. Desch-Obi, *Fighting for Honor: The History of African Martial Art Traditions in the Atlantic World* (Columbia: University of South Carolina Press, 2008), 95.

17. Frederick Douglass, *Narrative of the Life of Frederick Douglass* (Clayton, DE: Prestwick House, 2004), 65.

## 4. FIGHTING AROUND THE WORLD

1. Allen Guttmann, *The Olympics: A History of the Modern Games* (Champaign: University of Illinois Press, 2002), 12.

2. Lee Wedlake, "Kenpo Karate," in *Martial Arts of the World: An Encyclopedia of History and Innovation*, edited by Thomas A. Green and Joseph R. Svinth (Santa Barbara, CA: ABC-CLIO, 2010), 51.

3. Thomas A. Green and Joseph R. Svinth, "Brazilian Jiu-Jitsu," in *Martial Arts of the World: An Encyclopedia of History and Innovation*, edited by Thomas A. Green and Joseph R. Svinth (Santa Barbara, CA: ABC-CLIO, 2010), 33–34.

4. "Champion Entertains Soldiers in So. Korea," *Las Vegas Sun*, June 28, 1976, 21.

5. "Award Stripped from Ali," *Lincoln Star*, June 28, 1976, 16.

6. "What if Inoki Actually Hurt Ali?," *Capital Journal*, June 24, 1976, 39.

## 5. GLOBALIZATION, MEDIA, AND MMA

1. David Plotz, "Fight Clubbed," *Slate*, November 17, 1993, https://slate.com/news-and-politics/1999/11/fight-clubbed.html (accessed January 3, 2020).

2. Cheryl Cooky, Michael Messner, and Michela Musto, "'It's Dude Time!': A Quarter Century of Excluding Women's Sports in Televised News and Highlight Shows," in *Communications and Sport*, 3.3 (June 2015): 266–67.

3. "Mixed Martial Arts Firm One Championship Raises $70 mln, But Cuts 20% of Staff," *Reuters*, June 15, 2020, https://www.reuters.com/article/one-championship-funding/corrected-mixed-martial-arts-firm-one-championship-raises-70-mln-but-cuts-20-of-staff-idUSL4N2DT0JQ (accessed June 16, 2020).

4. Josh Kosman, "UFC Negotiates with China in Hopes to Double Profits," *New York Post*, September 10, 2019, https://nypost.com/2019/09/10/ufc-negotiates-with-china-in-hopes-to-double-profits/ (accessed February 17, 2020).

# BIBLIOGRAPHY

Anglo, Sydney. "The Man Who Taught Leonardo Darts: Pietro Monte and His 'Lost' Fencing Book," *Antiquaries Journal*, 69 (1989): 261–78.

———. *The Martial Arts of Renaissance Europe*. New Haven, CT: Yale University Press, 2000.

Atyeo, Don. *Blood 'N' Guts: Violence in Sports*. New York: Paddington Press, 1979.

"Award Stripped from Ali." *Lincoln Star*, June 28, 1976, 16.

Aycock, Colleen, and Mark Scott, eds. *The First Black Boxing Champions: Essays on Fighters of the 1800s to the 1920s*. Jefferson, NC: McFarland, 2011.

Ayles, James. "Bellator Europe Chief David Green Targets Continued Progress after Encouraging Growth in 2019." *Forbes*, January 31, 2020, https://www.forbes.com/sites/jamesayles/2020/01/31/bellator-europe-chief-david-green-targets-continued-progress-after-encouraging-growth-in-2019/#52a1653a59a6 (accessed March 14, 2020).

Baker, William J. *Sports in the Western World*. Totowa, NJ: Rowman & Littlefield, 1982.

Baker, William J., and J. A. Mangan, eds. *Sport in Africa: Essays in Social History*. London: Africana, 1987.

Barnard, Henry. *English Pedagogy: Education, the School, and the Teacher in English Literature*, vol. 2. Buffalo, WY: Creative Media Partners, 2019, 409.

Barrabi, Thomas. "Who Owns the UFC?," *Fox Business*, February 27, 2020, https://www.foxbusiness.com/sports/ufc-owners-investors-endeavor-dana-white (accessed May 5, 2020).

Beekman, Scott. *Ringside: A History of Professional Wrestling in America*. Westport, CT: Praeger, 2006.

"Bellator Europe on Growing MMA and Rivalling UFC." *Sports Industry Group*, February 21, 2020, https://www.sportindustry.biz/features/bellator-europe-growing-mma-and-rivalling-ufc (accessed March 16, 2020).

Boddy, Kasia. *Boxing: A Cultural History*. London: Reaktion, 2008.

Bodner, Allen. *When Boxing Was a Jewish Sport*. Westport, CT: Praeger, 1997.

"Bokator Forever." *Black Belt Magazine*, July 25, 2019, https://blackbeltmag.com/bokator-forever (accessed February 3, 2020).

Borota, Sinisa. "ONE Championship Adds 14 New Athletes to Their Roster," *Asian Persuasion MMA*, June 4, 2020, https://apmma.net/one-championship-adds-14-new-athletes-to-the-roster/ (accessed June 24, 2020).

"Boxing." *Olympics*, https://www.olympic.org/boxing (accessed September 13, 2019).

Brasch, R. *How Did Sports Begin? A Look at the Origins of Man at Play*. New York: McKay, 1970.

"A Brief History of Wrestling." *United World Wrestling*, https://unitedworldwrestling.org/organisation/history-wrestling-uww (accessed October 10, 2019).

Broome, Richard. "Theatres of Power: Tent Boxing Circa 1910–1970," *Aboriginal History*, 20 (1996): 1–23 (accessed August 17, 2020), www.jstor.org/stable/24046127.

Cairus, Jose. "Nationalism, Immigration and Identity: The Gracies and the Making of Brazilian Jiu-Jitsu, 1934–1943," *Martial Arts Studies*, 9 (March 2000): 28–42.

Campbell, Charlie. "Meet the Chinese MMA Fighter Taking on the Grandmasters of Kung Fu," *Time*, November 8, 2018, https://time.com/5448811/mma-kung-fu-xu-xiaodong/ (accessed January 17, 2020).

Carroll, Rory. "Irish Government Contacts UAE over Crime Boss Role in Fury-Joshua Bout," *Guardian*, July 11, 2020, https://www.theguardian.com/sport/2020/jun/11/irish-government-contacts-uae-over-boss-role-in-fury-joshua-bout (accessed July 12, 2020).

"Champion Entertains Soldiers in So. Korea." *Las Vegas Sun*, June 28, 1976, 21.

Chiari, Mike. "Tito Ortiz Beats Alberto Del Rio Via Submission in Combate Americas Fight," *Bleacher Report*, December 7, 2019, https://bleacherreport.com/articles/2865244-tito-ortiz-beats-alberto-del-rio-via-submission-in-combate-americas-fight (accessed May 7, 2020).

Cochrane, Joe. "MMA's Fast, Furious and Bloody Rise in Asia," *Asia Times*, August 17, 2019, https://asiatimes.com/2019/08/mmas-fast-furious-and-bloody-rise-in-asia/ (accessed March 23, 2020).

Connolly, Matt. "Interview: UFC Co-Founder Campbell McLaren on New Ownership, Dana White and More Following $4B Sale," *Forbes*, July 23, 2016, https://www.forbes.com/sites/mattconnolly/2016/07/23/interview-ufc-co-founder-campbell-mclaren-on-new-ownership-dana-white-and-more-following-4b-sale/#59757ad48a67 (accessed January 11, 2020).

———. "ONE Championship Breaks Ground for MMA in Thailand with Historic Sellout Event," *Forbes*, May 28, 2016, https://www.forbes.com/sites/mattconnolly/2016/05/28/one-championship-breaks-ground-for-mma-in-thailand-with-historic-sellout-event/#6b2b5b1b39fc (accessed May 4, 2020).

Cooky, Cheryl, Michael Messner, and Michela Musto. "'It's Dude Time!': A Quarter Century of Excluding Women's Sports in Televised News and Highlight Shows," *Communications and Sport*, 3.3 (June 2015): 266–67.

Cornwell, Alexander, and Jacob Greaves. "UFC Looks to Grow Sport in Middle East with Abu Dhabi Deal," *Reuters*, September 5, 2019, https://www.reuters.com/article/us-mma-ufc-ufc242-interview/ufc-looks-to-grow-sport-in-middle-east-with-abu-dhabi-deal-idUSKCN1VQ1WD (accessed November 30, 2019).

Corry, Michael. "Kavanagh on the Struggles MMA Faces Compared to Other Irish Sports," *Pundit Arena*, February 20, 2020, https://punditarena.com/mma/mcorry/kavanagh-mma-sport-ireland/ (accessed March 5, 2020).

Coutinho, Reubyn. "'I Knew What I Had Signed up For'—Jorge Masvidal Reveals Details of Brutal Weight Cut before UFC 251," *Essentially Sports*, July 17, 2020, https://www.essentiallysports.com/ufc-news-i-knew-what-i-had-signed-up-for-jorge-masvidal-reveals-details-of-brutal-weight-cut-before-ufc-251-on-fight-island (accessed July 20, 2020).

Critchfield, Tristan. "M-1 Challenge Announced Partnership with UFC to Focus on Russian MMA Talent," *Sherdog*, July 18, 2018, https://www.sherdog.com/news/news/M1-Challenge-Announces-Partnership-with-UFC-to-Focus-on-Russian-MMA-Talent-139655 (accessed April 12, 2020).

Crowther, Nigel B. *Sport in Ancient Times.* Westport, CT: Praeger, 2007.

Davies, Richard O. *Sports in American Life: A History.* Malden, MA: Wiley-Blackwell, 2012.

Dawson, Alan. "Asia's $1 Billion Fight Firm Is Exporting Its 'Wholesome' Image to the US to Take on UFC, a Company It Says Taints MMA by Promoting 'Anger, Hatred, and Violence,'" *Business Insider*, October 9, 2019, https://www.businessinsider.com/one-ceo-chatri-sityodtong-says-ufc-butchers-mma-2019-10 (accessed May 4, 2020).

"The Day Conor McGregor Attacked the Bus: How Those Who Were There Remember It," *ESPN*, October 3, 2018, https://www.espn.com/mma/story/_/id/24885232/the-conor-mcgregor-bus-attack-words-were-there (accessed April 7, 2020).

Desch-Obi, Thomas J. *Fighting for Honor: The History of African Martial Art Traditions in the Atlantic World.* Columbia: University of South Carolina Press, 2008.

Draeger, Donn F., and Robert W. Smith. *Asian Fighting Arts.* Palo Alto, CA: Kodansha International, 1969.

Ellis, William. *Polynesian Researches, During a Residence of Nearly Eight Years in the Society and Sandwich Islands.* London: Fischer, Son & Jackson, 1831.

"Exclusive: How Bahrain Helped Make Khabib Nurmagomedov a Global UFC Star," *Arab Business*, August 28, 2019, https://www.arabianbusiness.com/sport/426693-exclusive-how-bahrain-helped-make-khabib-nurmagomedov-global-ufc-star (accessed May 8, 2020).

Fleischer, Nat. *The Heavyweight Championship: An Informal History of Heavyweight Boxing from 1719 to the Present Day.* New York: Putnam, 1949.

"The French Judo Federation Threatens with [Expulsion] Those Who Teach MMA," *L'Equipe*, February 20, 2015, https://www.lequipe.fr/Judo/Actualites/La-radiation-pour-les-profs-de-mma/537772?xtref=http%3A%2F%2Fm.facebook.com%2F (accessed December 12, 2019).

Glionna, John M. "'Who's Lookin' for a Fight?' On the Road with the Last Boxing Tent in Australia," *California Sunday Magazine*, May 31, 2018, https://story.californiasunday.com/australia-boxing (accessed April 22, 2020).

Goldman, Eddie. "African Warriors Fighting Championship," *Black Belt Magazine*, May 22, 2020, https://blackbeltmag.com/african-warriors-fighting-championship-2646041687 (accessed June 8, 2020).

Gorn, Elliott J. *A Brief History of American Sports.* New York: Hill & Wang, 1993.

———. *The Manly Art: Bare-Knuckle Prize Fighting in America.* Ithaca, NY: Cornell University Press, 1986.

Green, Thomas A., and Joseph R. Svinth, eds. *Martial Arts in the Modern World.* Westport, CT: Praeger, 2003.

———. *Martial Arts of the World: An Encyclopedia of History and Innovation*, 2 vols. Santa Barbara, CA: ABC-CLIO, 2010.

Gross, Josh. "Latin America, Like China Before It, Is Becoming an Untapped MMA Market," *Atlantic*, September 17, 2019, https://theathletic.com/1218986/2019/09/17/latin-amer ica-like-china-before-it-is-becoming-an-untapped-mma-market/ (accessed May 4, 2020).

Guillen Jr., Adam. "Dan Henderson Breaks Down Differences in Fighting for UFC and PRIDE FC," *MMA Mania*, April 2, 2017, https://www.mmamania.com/2017/4/2/15153916 /ufc-dan-henderson-breaks-down-differences-in-fighting-for-ufc-and-pride-mma (accessed October 11, 2019).

Guttmann, Allen. *The Olympics: A History of the Modern Games.* (London, UK: University of Illinois Press, 2002).

Harris, Talek, and Martin Abbugao. "One Championship Could Return to Ring Next Month: CEO," *Yahoo Sports*, June 15, 2020, https://sports.yahoo.com/asias-one-championship-cuts-staff-mma-shows-halted-045818959.html (accessed June 26, 2020).

Hewitt, Mark S. *Catch Wrestling: A Wild and Wooly Look at the Early Days of Pro Wrestling in America.* Boulder, CO: Paladin Press, 2005.

Hickok, Ralph. *The Encyclopedia of North American Sports History*, 2nd ed. New York: Facts on File, 2002.

Isenberg, Michael T. *John L. Sullivan and His America.* Urbana: University of Illinois Press, 1988.

Jennings, Leon. "Chatri Sityodtong Announced More Big Signings, More Big Plans," *Asian Persuasion MMA*, May 19, 2020, https://apmma.net/chatri-sityodtong-announces-more-big-signings-more-big-plans/ (accessed June 2, 2020).

———. "ONE Championships Announces Several New Partnerships," *Asian Persuasion MMA*, January 2, 2020, https://apmma.net/one-championship-announces-several-new-partnerships/ (accessed May 7, 2020).

Kimeria, Ciku. "How Senegalese Wrestling Became a Modern Martial Arts Sensation," *OZY*, April 16, 2018, https://www.ozy.com/the-new-and-the-next/how-senegalese-wrestling-became-a-modern-martial-arts-sensation/85790/ (accessed May 15, 2020).

Kimsong, Kay. "300 Participate in First Bokator Competition," *Cambodia Daily*, September 27, 2006, https://english.cambodiadaily.com/news/300-participate-in-first-bokator-competition-54950/ (accessed February 3, 2020).

King, Nolan. "Huge Senegalese Wrestler 'Reug Reug' Sends Opponent Airborne in Impressive Debut," *MMA Junkie*, December 16, 2019, https://mmajunkie.usatoday.com/2019/12/video-senegalese-heavyweight-oumar-kane-reug-reug-slams-opponent (accessed May 15, 2020).

Kosman, Josh. "UFC Negotiates with China in Hopes to Double Profits," *New York Post*, September 10, 2019, https://nypost.com/2019/09/10/ufc-negotiates-with-china-in-hopes-to-double-profits/ (accessed February 17, 2020).

Kyle, Donald G. *Sport and Spectacle in the Ancient World*. Malden, MA: Blackwell, 2007.

Leibs, Andrew. *Sports and Games of the Renaissance*. Westport, CT: Greenwood, 2004.

"Look Back at 50th Anniversary of First MMA Fight—'Judo' Gene LeBell vs. Milo Savage," *MMA Junkie*, December 2, 2013, https://mmajunkie.usatoday.com/2013/12/video-look-back-at-50th-anniversary-of-first-mma-fight-judo-gene-lebell-vs-milo-savage (accessed October 17, 2018).

"Lua: The Ancient Hawaiian Martial Art of Breaking and Dislocating," *Black Belt Magazine*, July 20, 2018, https://blackbeltmag.com/lua-the-ancient-hawaiian-martial-art-of-breaking-and-dislocating (accessed January 8, 2020).

Mahjouri, Shakiel. "Beneil Dariush Believes More Iranians Will Enter MMA: 'Everyone in Iran Has Wrestled,'" *Bloody Elbow*, March 8, 2019, https://www.bloodyelbow.com/2019/3/8/18254978/beneil-dariush-iran-iranians-ufc-wichita-mma-news-drew-dober-kelvin-gastelum-marvin-vettori (accessed May 21, 2020).

Mandelbaum, Michael. *The Meaning of Sports: Why Americans Watch Baseball, Football, and Basketball, and What They See When They Do*. New York: Public Affairs, 2004.

Mangan, J. A. *Europe, Sport, World: Shaping Global Societies*. Portland, OR: Frank Cass, 2001.

"Marc Ratner." *International Boxing Hall of Fame*, http://www.ibhof.com/pages/about/inductees/nonparticipant/ratner.html (accessed November 11, 2019).

McCarthy, Michael. "Battles Yield Winning 'Fighter,'" *USA Today*, May 10, 2005, https://usatoday30.usatoday.com/money/companies/management/2005-04-10-white-usat_x.htm (accessed May 2, 2020).

Mechikoff, Robert A. *A History and Philosophy of Sport and Physical Education: From Ancient Civilizations to the Modern World*, 3rd ed. Boston: McGraw-Hill, 2002.

Mee, Bob. *Bare Fists: The History of Bare-Knuckle Prize-Fighting*. Woodstock, NY: Overlook, 2001.

Meltzer, Dave. "Court Ruling Allows UFC Back on Television in Germany," *MMA Fighting*, January 9, 2015, https://www.mmafighting.com/2015/1/9/7521899/court-ruling-allows-ufc-back-on-television-in-germany (accessed December 13, 2019).

"Mixed Martial Arts Firm One Championship Raises $70 Mln, But Cuts 20% of Staff," *Reuters*, June 15, 2020, https://www.reuters.com/article/one-championship-funding/corrected-mixed-martial-arts-firm-one-championship-raises-70-mln-but-cuts-20-of-staff-idU SL4N2DT0JQ (accessed June 16, 2020).

Murphy, Phil. 'Combate Americas' $100,000 Copa Combate Aims to Establish Larger Role in MMA Universe," *ESPN*, November 10, 2017, https://www.espn.com/mma/story/_/id/21362993/combate-americas-copa-combate-100000-tournament-positioned-initiative-reach-new-fans (accessed May 7, 2020).

Ng, Philiana. "Mun2 Greenlights MMA Competition Series 'Combate Americas,'" *Hollywood Reporter*, December 18, 2013, https://www.hollywoodreporter.com/news/mun2-greenlights-mma-competition-series-666522 (accessed May 7, 2020).

"Olympic Games History," *International Boxing Association*, https://www.aiba.org/olympic-games/ (accessed September 13, 2019).

Pepe, Phil. "The Fight Hurt Nobody Except Fans Who Paid," *Hartford Courant*, June 27, 1976, C5.

Plotz, David. "Fight Clubbed," *Slate*, November 17, 1993, https://slate.com/news-and-politics/1999/11/fight-clubbed.html (accessed January 3, 2020).

Poliakoff, Michael. *Combat Sports in the Ancient World: Competition, Violence, and Culture*. New Haven, CT: Yale University Press, 1987.

Pope, S. W., and John Nauright, eds. *Routledge Companion to Sports History*. New York: Routledge, 2010.

Pujol-Mazzini, Anna. "A Modern Juggernaut with Traditional Roots: Inside Senegalese Wrestling," *National Geographic*, March 26, 2019, https://www.nationalgeographic.com/culture/2019/03/modern-juggernaut-traditional-roots-senegal-wrestling/#close (accessed October 20, 2019).

Rahim, Abdul. "Norway MMA Federation Achieves Government Recognition," *Olympic Sports*, April 7, 2019, http://theolympicssports.com/martial-arts/norway-mma-federation-achieves.html (accessed December 8, 2019).

Raimondi, Marc. "France to Recognize MMA as a Sport in Jan. 2020," *ESPN*, June 24, 2019, https://www.espn.com/mma/story/_/id/27048038/france-recognize-mma-sport-jan-2020 (accessed December 12, 2019).

Randall, Stuart. "The New Zealand Fighter Factory That Punches Well Above Its MMA Weight," *ESPN*, October 1, 2019, https://www.espn.com/ufc/story/_/id/27704537/the-new-zealand-fighter-factory-punches-well-mma-weight (accessed May 21, 2020).

"Rogan the Perfect, and Unlikely, Voice for UFC's Broadcasts," *Sports Illustrated*, April 21, 2012, https://www.si.com/mma/2012/04/21/joe-roganufc (accessed March 4, 2020).

"Royce Gracie Tests Positive for Steroids (Updated)," *MMAMania*, June 14, 2007, https://www.mmaweekly.com/royce-gracie-tests-positive-for-steroids-updated-2 (accessed March 6, 2020).

"Sanctions Force Iranian MMA Fighter to Quit UFC," *Iran Front Page*, November 2, 2019, https://ifpnews.com/sanctions-force-iranian-mma-fighter-to-quit-ufc (accessed March 24, 2020).

Sansone, David. *Greek Athletics and the Genesis of Sport*. Berkeley: University of California Press, 1988.

"Savate: From the Back Alleys of France to the Martial Arts World," *Black Belt Magazine*, May 19, 2014, https://blackbeltmag.com/savate-from-the-back-alleys-of-france-to-the-martial-arts-world (accessed May 13, 2018).

"SDG Indicators—Regional Groupings," *United Nations*, https://unstats.un.org/sdgs/indicators/regional-groups/ (accessed January 21, 2020).

Semaan, Jad. "Art of War: The Rise of MMA in China," *Bleacher Report*, August 8, 2008, https://bleacherreport.com/articles/45554-art-of-war-the-rise-of-mma-in-china (accessed January 26, 2020).

Shahar, Meir. *The Shaolin Monastery: History, Religion, and the Chinese Martial Arts*. Honolulu: University of Hawai'i Press, 2008.

Slowikowski, Synthia S. "Alexander the Great and Sport History: A Commentary on Scholarship," *Journal of Sport History* 16, no. 1 (1989): 70–78 (accessed August 17, 2020), www.jstor.org/stable/43609383.

Smith, Michael D. *Violence and Sport*. Toronto: Butterworths, 1983.

Solano, Alex. "MMA Pioneer Campbell McLaren Times 'Copa Combate' to Honor UFC 1," *Los Angeles Times*, November 10, 2017, https://www.latimes.com/sports/boxing/la-sp-mma-copa-combate-mclaren-20171110-story.html (accessed May 7, 2020).

Tabuena, Anton. "UFC Signs Chinese Stars Li Jingliang and Jumabieke Tuerxun," *Bloody Elbow*, January 26, 2014, https://www.bloodyelbow.com/2014/1/26/5346898/ufc-signs-chinese-stars-li-jingliang-jumabieke-tuerxun (accessed March 17, 2020).

Taylor, Tom. "African-Born Fighters Are Taking over MMA," *OZY*, January 19, 2020, https://www.ozy.com/around-the-world/africa-born-fighters-are-taking-over-mma/230490/ (accessed April 19, 2020).

Thrasher, Christopher. *Fight Sports and American Masculinity: Salvation in Violence from 1607 to the Present.* Jefferson, NC: McFarland, 2015.

"UFC Action Coming to SuperSport in 2019," *UFC* August 20, 2017, https://ru.ufc.com/news/ufc-action-coming-supersport-2019 (accessed May 23, 2018).

"UFC Statement Regarding the Regulation of MMA in France," *UFC*, February 10, 2020, https://www.ufc.com/news/ufc-statement-regarding-regulation-mma-france (accessed December 12, 2019).

"UFC to Hold Events on Abu Dhabi Island," *SuperSport*, June 9, 2020, https://supersport.com/ufc/ufc/news/200609_UFC_to_hold_events_on_Abu_Dhabi_island (accessed July 12, 2020).

von Duuglas-Ittu, Sylvie. "Kard Chuek for Women—What It Felt Like, What It Means," *8LimbsUs*, June 18, 2017, https://8limbsus.com/muay-thai-thailand/kard-chuek-women-felt-like-means (accessed October 10, 2019).

Voorhies, Barbara. *Prehistoric Games of North American Indians: Subarctic to Mesoamerica.* Salt Lake City: University of Utah Press, 2017.

Ward, William A. "Relations between Egypt and Mesopotamia from Prehistoric Times to the End of the Middle Kingdom," *Journal of the Economic and Social History of the Orient* 7, no. 1 (1964): 1–45 (accessed August 17, 2020).

"What if Inoki Actually Hurt Ali?" *Capital Journal*, June 24, 1976, 39.

Wiley, Mark V. *Arnis: History and Development of the Filipino Martial Arts.* Boston: Tuttle, 2001.

Wilkins, Sally. *Sports and Games of Medieval Cultures.* Westport, CT: Greenwood, 2002.

Wilson Jr., Leslie. "Bahrain Bids to Make Middle East an MMA and Boxing Global Powerhouse," *Gulf News*, May 21, 2020, https://gulfnews.com/sport/bahrain-bids-to-make-middle-east-an-mma-and-boxing-global-powerhouse-1.71616244 (accessed July 12, 2020).

Yeager, Robert C. *Seasons of Shame: The New Violence in Sports.* New York: McGraw-Hill, 1979.

Zidan, Karim. "Dagestani Dynasty: How Fighting Became the Nurmagomedov Family Business," *Bloody Elbow*, March 19, 2015, https://www.bloodyelbow.com/2015/3/19/8244663/ufc-khabib-abdulmanap-nurmegomedov-dagestan-dynasty-fighting-family-business-mountains-war-mma (accessed April 5, 2020).

———. "How Khabib's Dagestani Identity Dominated UFC 229 (Op-ed)," *Moscow Times*, October 11, 2018, https://www.themoscowtimes.com/2018/10/11/how-khabib-dagestani-identity-dominated-ufc-mcgregor-opinion-a63160 (accessed April 7, 2020).

Zirin, Dave. *A People's History of Sports in the United States: 250 Years of Politics, Protest, People, and Play.* New York: Norton, 2008.

# INDEX

# ABOUT THE AUTHOR

**L. A. Jennings** is a media studies professor specializing in cultural studies, gender studies, and history. She published her first book, *She's a Knockout! A History of Women in Fighting Sports*, with Rowman & Littlefield in 2013 and is the owner and head striking coach of Train.Fight.Win. MMA in Denver, Colorado. L. A. holds a doctorate in literary studies from the University of Denver and a BA and MA in English literature from Florida State University. She lives in Denver with her husband, Mike.